The Nathan Narrative
in 2 Samuel 7:1–17

The Nathan Narrative in 2 Samuel 7:1–17

A Traditio-historical Study

William W. Watty

WIPF & STOCK · Eugene, Oregon

THE NATHAN NARRATIVE IN 2 SAMUEL 7:1–17
A Traditio-historical Study

Copyright © 2016 William W. Watty. All rights reserved. Except for brief quotations in critical publications or reviews, no part of this book may be reproduced in any manner without prior written permission from the publisher. Write: Permissions, Wipf and Stock Publishers, 199 W. 8th Ave., Suite 3, Eugene, OR 97401.

Wipf & Stock
An Imprint of Wipf and Stock Publishers
199 W. 8th Ave., Suite 3
Eugene, OR 97401

www.wipfandstock.com

PAPERBACK ISBN: 978-1-4982-0000-4
HARDCOVER ISBN: 978-1-4982-8879-8
EBOOK ISBN: 978-1-4982-0001-1

Manufactured in the U.S.A.

To the memory of my Tutors at Union
Theological Seminary in Jamaica
(1955–1959)

The Reverend Herbert J. Cooke M.A. (Birmingham)
(Old Testament Language and Literature)

and

The Reverend David W.F. Jelleyman M.A. (Cantab)
(New Testament Language and Literature)

With a profound sense of gratitude and respect

CONTENTS

Preface | xi
List of Abbreviations | xiii

CHAPTER I

THE DAVID TRADITION IN THE HEBREW CANON—AN OVERVIEW | 1

David and the Nathan Narrative in the Law (Genesis–Deuteronomy) | 2
David and the Nathan Narrative in the Writings (Psalter–Chronicles) | 5
David and the Nathan Narrative in the Prophets (Joshua–Malachi) | 7
David and the Nathan Narrative in the Former Prophets (Joshua–Kings) | 9
David and the Nathan Narrative in Samuel | 11
David in the Nathan Narrative of 2 Samuel 7:1–17 | 15
Conclusion | 17

CHAPTER II

THE TRADITIO-HISTORICAL APPROACH | 18

The Traditio-historical Method Illustrated | 18
Gerhard von Rad | 18

CONTENTS

Martin Noth | 21
The Traditio-historical Method Examined | 22
Oral Transmission and Written Composition | 23
From Oral Transmission to Written Composition | 25
Traditio and Traditum | 28
The Strength and Weakness of the Traditio-historical Approach | 31
2 Samuel 7: 1-17 and the Traditio-historical Method | 34

CHAPTER III

THE ARGUMENT—2 SAMUEL 7:1-17 IN DEUTERONOMY-KINGS | 36

Martin Noth | 36
R. A. Carlson | 41
Dennis J. McCarthy | 43
Frank Moore Cross Jnr. | 43
Brian Peckham | 46
Antony F. Campbell | 48
Iain W. Provan | 53
P. Kyle McCarter Jr. | 56
Michael Avioz | 58
Other Deuteronomic Historical Studies | 61
Conclusion | 63

CHAPTER IV

2 SAMUEL 7:1-17 IN PRE-CANONICAL REDACTION | 67

The Deuteronomic Redaction (Exilic) | 69
2 Samuel 7:1-17 in the Deuteronomic Redaction (Exilic) | 73
The Deuteronomic Redaction (Josianic) | 76
2 Samuel 7:1-17 in the Deuteronomic Redaction (Josianic) | 80
The Deuteronomic Redaction (Hezekianic) | 82
2 Samuel 7:1-17 in the Deuteronomic Redaction (Hezekianic) | 93
Conclusion | 98

CONTENTS

CHAPTER V

2 SAMUEL 7:1-17—A LITERARY CRITICAL ANALYSIS | 101

The Problem of Unity in 2 Samuel 7:1-17 | 102
2 Samuel 7:1-17 and 2 Samuel 6 | 102
2 Samuel 7:1-17 and 7:18-29 | 103
2 Samuel 7:5-7 and 7:8-16 | 104
2 Samuel 7:8-11, 16 and 7:12-15 | 106
2 Samuel 7:8-9 and 7:10-11a | 107
2 Samuel 7:1-3 and 7:4-7 | 108
2 Samuel 7:1-17—A Commentary | 109
Conclusion | 124

CHAPTER VI

2 SAMUEL 7:1-17 IN ORAL TRANSMISSION—A FORM CRITICAL STUDY | 126

2 Samuel 7:1-17 as Prophecy | 128
2 Samuel 7:1-17 as Covenant | 131
2 Samuel 7:1-17 as *Hieros Logos* | 141
2 Samuel 7:1-17 as *Die Königsnovelle* | 150
Conclusion | 154

CHAPTER VII

2 SAMUEL VII: 1-17—THE EVOLUTION OF THE NARRATIVE—A SUMMARY | 159

2 Samuel 7:1-17 in the Period of the United Monarchy | 160
The Promise of a "House" (Dynasty) as Continuity | 160
The Promise of a "House" (Dynasty) as Tradition | 163
The Building of a "House" (Sanctuary) as Legitimization | 164
2 Samuel 7:1-17 in the Period of the Divided Monarchy | 167
The Response of the Monarchy to the Collapse of the Empire | 168
Monarchy and Cultic Reform | 169
The Deuteronomic Movement | 170
2 Samuel 7:1-17 in Period of the Single Monarchy | 172

CONTENTS

The *hieros logos* of the Hezekianic Reformed Temple | 174
The *hieros logos* of the Josianic Central Sanctuary | 176
2 Samuel 7:1–17 after the Fall of the Monarchy | 178

BIBLIOGRAPHY | 179

INDEX OF AUTHORS | 189

SCRIPTURE INDEX | 193

PREFACE

THIS STUDY IS A revision of the thesis of the same title that was submitted to the Department of Theology in the Faculty of Humanities and Education of the University of the West Indies and, following examination, was approved for the award of the PhD degree. The subject was chosen out of a concern that, whereas the traditio-historical approach seemed to be essential for an in-depth study of Old Testament literature, and especially so the Law and the Prophets, the concept seemed to be lacking in clarity; evidence of its contribution to the commentaries seemed scant; subject areas chosen for special study seemed to be wide-ranging and diffuse; and conclusions reached seemed somewhat obscure. I have therefore tried to be clear and consistent in the definition, to focus on a manageable area, and to be uninhibited in the application of the method with a view to reaching a clearer, deeper, and fuller understanding of 2 Samuel 7:1–17 and its place in the Joshua–Kings corpus.

Aspects of the study that might be of special interest are arguments for the importance of the canonical text for traditio-historical research and *vice versa*, and a case for one exilic redaction of the Joshua–Kings corpus prior to canonization of the prophets which accounted for the fall of the Davidic monarchy and two pre-exilic redactions—the first being a Hezekianic redaction of the book of the law.

A case has been presented for the pre-monarchy origins of the ark of the covenant based on its regular movements as a mobile sanctuary before the inauguration of the monarchy, which continued during the reign of

PREFACE

Saul (1 Sam 4–7:1; 14:18; 2 Sam 6–7), as well as the importance of the ark narrative as the *hieros logos* of a Davidic sanctuary and, much later, of the Temple as the Josianic central sanctuary. A question has also been raised concerning the interpretation of 2 Samuel 7:5 regarding whether or not it was originally a revelation that prevented David from initiating a temple building project on which he had set his heart. Alternative approaches to the concept of "tradition" and to the purpose and method of transmitting traditions have been suggested, and a reconsideration of the meaning of "covenant" and the practice of covenant-making, including the contrast between a "covenant of grant" and a "conditional covenant," has been urged.

The discovery of a document in the temple by the priest Hilkiah (2 Kgs 22:8) has been accepted as credible, except that the book of the law, begun in Northern Israel in the ninth century and completed in Jerusalem in the reigns of Hezekiah and Manasseh was, even from its inception, more than just a law code or the legal nucleus of Deuteronomy, but also included a history of the people of Israel from the Moses' leave-taking to the fall of northern kingdom and the deposition and deportation of Hoshea its king in 721 BCE.

I wish to express my gratitude to my supervisor, the Most Reverend Doctor John Holder, Archbishop of Barbados, for his wise and patient guidance during the preparation; and to the examiners, the Reverend Doctor Ian Rock, Principal of Codrington College, Barbados, and Doctor Stanley Walters, for their careful and diligent examination and their suggestions for improvement. Acknowledgements notwithstanding, I take responsibility for errors and other deficiencies that might appear in the chapters that follow.

William Watty

January 2015

ABBREVIATIONS

AB	Anchor Bible
BC	Before Christ
BCE	Before the Common Era
Bib	*Biblica*
BZAW	Beheifte zur Zeitschrift fur die alttestamentliche Wissenschaft
CBA	Catholic Biblical Association
CBQ	*Catholic Biblical Quarterly*
CBQMS	Catholic Biblical Quarterly Monograph Series
CahT	Cahiers Théologique
DLT	Darton, Longman and Todd
ELT	*Ephemerides Theologicae Lovanienses*
ExpTim	*Expository Times*
FRLANT	Forschungen zur Religion und Literatur des Alten und Neuen Testaments
HSM	Harvard Semitic Monographs
HUCA	*Hebrew Union College Annual*

ABBREVIATIONS

IDB	*The Interpreter's Dictionary of the Bible*
IDBSup	*The Interpreter's Dictionary of the Bible, Supplementary Volume*
IEJ	*Israel Exploration Journal*
JBL	*Journal of Biblical Literature*
JSOT	*Journal for the Study of the Old Testament*
JSOTSup	Journal for the Study of the Old Testament: Supplement
JSS	*Journal of Semitic Studies*
JTS	*Journal of Theological Studies*
LXX	The Septuagint Version of the Old Testament
MT	The Masoretic Text of the Hebrew Bible
RHPR	*Revue d'histoire et de philosophie religieuse*
SBL	Society of Biblical Literature
SBLDS	Society of Biblical Literature Dissertation Series
SBT	Studies in Biblical Theology
SCM	Student Christian Movement
SJT	*Scottish Journal of Theology*
SOTSMS	Society for Old Testament Studies Monograph Series
SPCK	Society for the Propagation of Christian Knowledge
TS	*Theological Studies*
VT	*Vetus Testamentum*
VTSup	Supplement to Vetus Testamentum
WZ	*Wissenschaftliche Zeitschrift*
ZAW	*Zeitschrift fur die alttestamentliche Wissenschaft*

CHAPTER I

THE DAVID TRADITION IN THE HEBREW CANON—AN OVERVIEW

Notwithstanding the wide variety and high quality of the studies, and the sustained level of the output, the questions have not all been answered nor has a consensus been reached on important issues pertaining to the Nathan narrative in 2 Samuel 7:1-17. Questions still unresolved include its authorship and composition, date and purpose, originality and genre, connections with and distinction within its literary setting, and its canonical status. Even so, its importance for the biblical tradition generally, and Samuel especially, has generally been recognized. Early hints of the narrative might be detected in Judges and 1 Samuel (Judg 17:6; 18:1; 19:1; 21:25; 1 Sam 2:2-10; 13:14; 15:28; 16:1-13a; 24:20; 25:28; 28:17), and echoes in 2 Samuel and Kings (2 Sam 23:1-7; 1 Kgs 11:36; 15:4; 2 Kgs 8:19), the Latter Prophets (Isa 9:2-7; 11:1-9; Jer 23:5; 30:9; Ezek 34:23-24; 37:24; Amos 9:11; Mic 5:2) and the Writings (Pss 78:68-72; 89:3-4, 20-37; 132:1, 10, 17-18; 1 Chr 17:1-14).

It would be useful, by way of introduction, to overview the canonical profile, since the inclusion of the canonical text on the traditio-historical agenda seems both plausible and practical. The canonical text is but the culmination of a growing and developing tradition. Therefore, to focus exclusively on the final product without reviewing the preliminary stages is to miss whatever distinctive quality there might be in the traditional material,

THE NATHAN NARRATIVE IN 2 SAMUEL 7:1-17

and to concentrate solely on the traditional material—its coalescence and growth in the pre-canonical stages—is to deprive the final product of its special significance. Either way, to detach the text from its pre-history is to risk overlooking the intricacies and complexities of its composition and essential qualities of its content that might not be immediately apparent.

The first complete copy of the Bible did not mysteriously appear, nor was its final shaping, as Brevard Childs has suggested, the automatic outcome of transmission of an earlier received form of the tradition, unchanged from its original setting.[1] There was no initial composition of the documents that predetermined the final shaping of the of the Old Testament text nor, on the other hand, was it wholly the outcome of an official approval conferred upon documents, previously unrelated, that were selected, assembled and arranged in a recognizable order. Moreover, canonization, far from being a formal *imprimatur*, involved basically the same systematic process of transmission. While, therefore, the canonical text marks the end of the evolving traditions, its special status need neither be compromised by, nor compromise, its contribution to an exploration of its origins and the history of its evolution, since it is the integrity and elucidation of the text that is the primary objective, and there, as nowhere else, the essential data for research have been preserved. Such considerations should both encourage and enhance a traditio-historical study of Old Testament literature.

DAVID AND THE NATHAN NARRATIVE IN THE LAW (GENESIS-DEUTERONOMY)

In the Law, otherwise designated "the Pentateuch," David's achievements, and especially the supremacy to which he raised Israel, were foreshadowed in covenant traditions of promises which God made to his ancestors regarding property in Canaan and innumerable descendants (Gen 12:1–3; 13:14–18; 15:1–18; 22:16–18; 26:24; 28:13–14; 35:11–12). While Ronald Clements has been able, by traditio-historical research, to retrace a Davidic covenant to a tradition of promises made to Abraham,[2] it is also evident that such traditions were reshaped in the course of their transmission. The nationalistic fervor that animated Noah's blessing of Shem (Gen 9:25–27) and Isaac's blessing of Jacob (Gen 27:1–29) reflected the Davidic and Israelite ascendancy over the Canaanite population in the one case, and

---

1. See Childs, *Introduction to the Old Testament*, 76.
2. See Clements, *Abraham and David*, 15–78.

domination of their Edomite neighbors in the other (cf. 2 Sam 8:13–14a; 1 Kgs 9:20–21; 11:15–16).

Although the Joseph narratives were originally intended to project Ephraim's superior status (Gen 37–50; cf. 37:5–11; 42–45; cf. Deut 33:13–17), the Davidic *tendenz* might also be discerned in the insinuation of Judah's seniority among his brethren (Gen 37:26; 44:14–31; cf. Matt 1:2). Also, the interruption of a Tamar episode (Gen 38:28–30) was, so Lansing Hicks has suggested, a staking of the ancestral claim of the tribe of Judah to which David belonged.³

Unlike the blessing of Moses, the blessing of Jacob showed a marked partiality that anticipated Judah's ascendancy, from whom a messianic ruler would come and around whom the tribes would unite (Gen 49:8-10; cp. Deut 33:7). Additionally, the Balaam vision of the rising of a star out of Jacob and the submission of the neighboring states reflected the exploits and conquests of David early in the tenth century BCE (Num 24:7–9, 17; cf. 2 Sam 8; 10–12).⁴

While such linkages are no more than suggestive, a clearer affinity is evident in the coincidence of phraseology:

ועשתי לך שם גדול (2 Sam 7:9; cf. Gen 12:2)

אשר יצא ממעיך (2 Sam 7:12; cf. Gen 15:4; 1 Kgs 8:19).

It is also noticeable that the latter references accentuate the importance of a biological heir for the fulfillment of promises which, being made against the recurring pattern of a barren spouse (Gen 11:30; 12:2; 18:9–15; 25:21; 30:1, 22; cf. 2 Sam 6:23), initiated a train of hazardous events through which the promises were brought to fruition (Gen 16; cf. 2 Sam 6:20–23; 11–12).

The Song of Moses at the Red Sea points to another aspect of the Nathan narrative, viz., the planting of Israel—YHWH's chosen people—in a place prepared for their inheritance; his establishment of a sanctuary; and, following his discomfiture of their foes, the inauguration of his eternal reign (Ex 15:13–18; cf. 2 Sam 6–7). Such sentiments coincide with pronouncements appearing in the narrative regarding the status and security of the people of Israel under the aegis of the Davidic regime (2 Sam 7:6–7, 10–11a, 23–24). It seems, therefore, that the exodus-conquest traditions that

3. See Hicks, "Perez," 729.

4. Albright, *Yahweh and Gods of Canaan*, 17, has however dated the oracle sometime between the Fall of Shiloh and the accession of Saul.

THE NATHAN NARRATIVE IN 2 SAMUEL 7:1-17

informed the Nathan narrative, though rooted in pre-monarchy traditions, became an important component for royal ritual in Judah and informed the composition of Deuteronomy–Kings (cf. Pss 78:52–72; 105:36-44; 136:10–24; cf. Deut 6:20–23; 26:8–9; Josh 24:6–13; 2 Sam 7:10-11a).

Monarchical rule was legitimized and regulated in Deuteronomic law. It required that the ruler be designated by YHWH and endorsed by the people (Deut 17:14–15; cf.1 Sam. 10:1–25; 11:15; 13:14; 15:28; 16:1–13; 2 Sam 5:1–5; 7:12–14; 1 Kgs 1:39–40; 8:1–6; 11:29–35; 12:20). Although hereditary succession was not, in principle, prohibited (cf. Deut 17:20), dynastic rule as proposed in the Nathan narrative was not envisaged; rather, sovereignty was affirmed in conditional terms of steady adherence to the Mosaic law (Deut 17:18–20; cp. 2 Sam 7:12–16) which, significantly, featured in the investiture of Solomon, David's immediate successor (1 Kgs 2:1–4; cf. 6:12; 8:25; 9:1–6).

In general, it might be noted that the composition of the Law was driven by three affirmations viz. that a people, at first few in number and enslaved, had become great and populous nation (Gen 12:1–5; Num 22: 1–4; Deut. 26:5), that once semi-nomadic and rootless, they had succeeded in gaining a secure foothold in Canaan (Gen 12:6–7; Deut 26:6–9; 2 Sam 7:10, 23–24) and that YHWH, their chosen God, had given them land in fulfillment of a promise he made to their ancestors (Exod 3:6–8; 19:5; 20:2–17; Deut 11:8–15; 28). They also show that the Law, albeit a self-contained canonical unit, gave Israel legal entitlement to the occupation of Canaan, and provided a basis for claims that were later made and institutions that were later established, such as the validity of prophetic witness (Num 11:29; 12:6–8; Deut 18:15–22); the appointment of a priesthood (Num 25:1–13; Deut 33:8–11); the establishment of a chosen sanctuary (Deut 12:10–11) and the legitimacy of a monarchy (Deut 17:15–20). On the other hand, differences between Genesis–Deuteronomy and Joshua–Kings are noticeable in such traditions as the miracle of the water-crossing (Josh 3:1–17; cf. Exod 14:14–28); the origin and meaning of the circumcision rite (Josh 5:5–9; cf. Gen 17:10–14; Exod 4:25–26); the inauguration and purpose of the paschal festival (Josh 5:11–12; cf. Exod 12:1–13); the locus of the Mosaic covenant (Josh 24:1–18; cf. Exod 19:4—20:17; Deut 5:2–3; 29:1); and the monarchy (Deut 17:15-20; cf. 2 Sam 7:8-29). Last but not least, the Law offered useful insights into the basis of Israel's tribal structure, which would become a critical factor not only for land distribution and settlement, but political stability and fragmentation (Gen 49:3–28; Deut 33:5–23; cf. Josh 13–21; 2 Sam 5:1–5; 2 Sam 19:9–15; 20:1–2; 1 Kgs 11: 26–38; 12:1–17).

DAVID AND THE NATHAN NARRATIVE IN THE WRITINGS (PSALTER-CHRONICLES)

The third category of the Hebrew canon, the Writings, otherwise designated *Hagiographa*, is bound at the one end by the Psalter and, at the other, by Chronicles. In both collections the figure of David is given a high profile. In the captions of the majority of the Psalms he is cited, if not as author, then certainly as the inspiration (Pss 2–41; 51–65; 68–72; 86; 101; 103–150). In conjunction with them are Psalms in which David is commemorated as progenitor of a royal lineage, his election is acclaimed and YHWH's promises to him are recalled (Pss 78:70–72; 89:3–4, 20–35; 132:10–11, and 17). In other Psalms of later Jewish interpretation, significant events in David's life were commemorated (Pss 3; 7; 18; 30; 34; 51; 52; 54; 56; 57; 59; 60; 63; 142) and two of the Psalms were quoted extensively in other literary contexts commemorating national milestones (Ps 18 in 2 Sam 22; Ps 105:1–15 in 1 Chr 16:23–33).[5]

With regard to the Nathan narrative, three psalms in particular seem to resonate. As in the narrative, so the concluding strophe of Psalm 78 recalls David's earlier pastoral occupation that prepared him for leadership (Ps 78: 70–72; cf. 2 Sam 7:8). The Psalm also connected Israel's settlement in the land with the blessing on the Davidic monarchy (Ps 78:65–72; cf. 2 Sam 7:8, 10–11a, 22–24).[6] Affinities with Psalm 89:1–4, 19–37 are so evident as to have suggested dependence. Both compositions recall a covenant in which YHWH pledged unswerving commitment to the monarchy (Ps 89:30–33; cf. 2 Sam. 7:14), and define the relationship between YHWH and the Davidic ruler in paternal-filial terms (Ps 89:26–27; cf. 2 Sam 7:14; Ps 2:7). While direct dependence in either direction is difficult to establish, the affinities suggest a common rootedness in earlier traditions that informed

---

5. For the various attempts at classification, e.g. along form-critical lines, see Gunkel, *Psalms*, 30–39; or in cultic categorizations, Mowinckel, *Psalms in Israel's Worship*; or, in the categorization of the Psalter headings, Snaith, *Hymns*, and Engnell, "Book of Psalms," 68–122; and for an exposition of the royal psalms, see also Eaton, *Kingship and Psalms*, 27–86.

6. For fuller discussion of the ideology, see Campbell, *Ark Narrative*, 213–27.

the royal ideology.⁷ While the connections between Psalm 132 and the ark narrative are closer (1 Sam 4:1—7:1; 2 Sam 6),⁸ linkages with the Nathan narrative may be discerned in the recollection of David's desire to build a sanctuary for YHWH (2 Sam 7:1-3; cf. Ps 132; 1-8), as well as the connection between YHWH's election of Zion as his abode and the legitimization of David's successors as rulers in Israel (2 Sam 6:1-17; cf. 7:5-7, 13a, 11-16; Ps 132:11-13, 17).

Whatever the dating of the Psalter as corpus, there can be little question that the majority of the Davidic psalms reflect a period when the throne of David was secure and occupied by legitimate successors. They also indicate that, far from being a *de novo* composition of a later period, the Nathan narrative (2 Sam 7:1-17) preserved traditions that reached back to the foundation of the Israelite monarchy in the eleventh century BCE.

The editors of the books of the Chronicles, also, were preoccupied with David's status as king of Israel and with the Judaean monarchy. For them, however, his significance lay primarily in his position in, and contribution to, the Jerusalem cultus, i.e., his conquest and occupation of the chosen city (1 Chr 11:4-8); his recovery of the ark of the covenant (1 Chr 11:13-14; 13:1-14); his initiatives and leading role in its installation (1 Chr 15-16); his appointment of its priesthood and his ordering of its worship (1 Chr 15:1-24; 16:4-6, 37-42); his acquisition of the chosen site (1 Chr 21:18-28; cf. 2 Chr 3:1); his plans and provisions for the building of a sanctuary (1 Chr 22:14-16); and his charge to Solomon and the leaders of Israel regarding its construction (1 Chr 22:6-19; 28:1—29:20). David's characterization in the Chronicles was essentially that of a religious leader from which unseemly features were excised and whose failure to build the temple was ascribed to ritual impurity (1 Chr 17:4; 28:3).

Written about the middle of the fourth century—almost two centuries and a half after the fall of the monarchy—David's religious devotion

---

7. For a discussion of dependence with respect to Psalm 89 and 2 Samuel 7, see Pfeiffer, *Introduction*, 371-72, and a comprehensive study by Mackenzie, "Dynastic Oracle," 187-218; but for a more acceptable view see Caquot, "La Prophétie de Nathan," 213-24. Caquot seems to be less preoccupied with the question of direct dependence or the quest for a common source than with the reiteration of ideological themes that indicate a common tradition. Ward, "Literary Form," 321-39, in a discussion of the relationship, has argued for an interpretation of Psalm 89 as a unified post-exilic composition.

8. For an exposition of the cultic background to Psalm 132 and the ark narrative (1 Sam 4:1—7:1; 2 Sam 6) see Bentzen, "Cultic Use," 37-53, and Porter, "Interpretation of 2 Samuel 6," 161-73. However, in neither study was the connection with 2 Samuel 7 included.

superseded political acumen or military prowess. For that reason, the Nathan narrative was reinterpreted less as a legitimization of the Davidic monarchy than as sacred legend authorizing the foundation of the Jerusalem temple (1 Chr 17:1–15). The Chronicles version was, therefore, not an exact transcript of 2 Samuel 7 (differences being due less to dependence on parallel *Vorlage* than to consistency of theological perspective).[9] The Chronicles show that the traditions of David lived on in Jewish lore beyond the fall of the monarchy and, by retracing his ancestry to Adam (1 Chr 1:1—2:15), established a genealogical basis for his legitimacy that also authorized the cultic institutions he introduced.

Included in the Writings is the book of Ruth, a narrative that alleged David's Moabite ancestry (Ruth 1:1–4; 2:2; 4:13, 17; cf. 1 Sam 22:3–4).[10] To the narrative, however, was appended a genealogy in which David was also recognized as the scion of a Bethlehem clan in direct descent from the patriarch Judah (Ruth 4:18–22; cf. Gen 38). Placed immediately before Βασιλειῶν in the Greek Bible (LXX), such connections made Ruth a fitting preface to the David epic (1 Kgdms 16:1—3 Kgdms 2:4).

DAVID AND THE NATHAN NARRATIVE IN THE PROPHETS (JOSHUA-MALACHI)

Whatever its significance for the Law and the Writings, it is the second collection, the Prophets, that became the canonical setting for the story of David (1 Sam 16:1—1 Kgs 2:4) and, with it, the Nathan narrative (2 Sam 7:1-17). An important consequence of the inclusion of Deuteronomy in the Law was an eclipse of the Sinai-Horeb covenant as the interpretative key to the Joshua–Kings collection, and therefore a closer affinity between the Joshua–Kings and the Isaiah–Malachi collections, and a sharpening of the significance of the Davidic tradition for the shaping of the Prophets; for it was in pronouncements made to, by and about David in Samuel-Kings that a messianic hope took shape in the writing Prophets (Isaiah–Malachi).

---

9. For a detailed literary-critical discussion of the differences between 2 Samuel 7 and 1 Chronicles 17, see van den Bussche, "The Text of the Prophecy of Nathan," 354–90.

10. The inclusion of Ruth with the Writings is witness to its non-Deuteronomic and non-prophetic character. Its special importance for the LXX is that it bridges the historical divide between the period of the Judges (Judg 21:25; Ruth 1:1–4), and the inauguration of an Israelite monarchy in the election of David (Ruth 4:17–22; 1 Sam 16:1–13a; 2 Sam 5:1–5).

THE NATHAN NARRATIVE IN 2 SAMUEL 7:1-17

A noticeable omission from Brevard Childs' *Introduction to the Old Testament* was an exposition of the Prophets as a canonical entity;[11] for, while the literary dissimilarities between Joshua–Kings and Isaiah–Malachi are evident, and the duplication of passages from 2 Kings into Isaiah and Jeremiah (2 Kgs 18:13—20:19 in Isa 36–39; 2 Kgs 24:18—25:30 in Jer 52) attests to their earlier independence, there must have also been a more compelling measure of compatibility between the two collections to validate their combination under the common prophetic rubric. While further exploration of the Former Prophets (Joshua–Kings) in this connection must be undertaken at a later stage, the canonical status of the Joshua-Kings corpus must raise questions for the applicability of Deuteronomistic presuppositions as the hermeneutical key.[12] Otherwise this will render the canonical composition either synonymous, superfluous, superficial, or misleading.[13] Such an exploration might also assist a distinction between the intrinsic prophetic contribution to the Joshua–Kings collection on the one hand, and the canonical designation on the other. It might also clarify the status of the Nathan narrative (2 Sam 7:1-17) in the Former Prophets, which hypotheses have seemed unable to deliver having overlooked the canonical factor.

References to David in the Latter Prophets (Isaiah–Malachi) as the promise of a hopeful future point to his special importance for the redactors (Is 55:3; Jer 30:9; 33:17; Ezek 34:24; 37:24; Hos 3:5; Amos 9:11). Though the historical monarchy did not, on the whole, meet with prophetic approbation (cf. 2 Sam 12:1-14; 1 Kgs 11:29-33; Isa 7:13; 39:4-7; Jer 22:1—23:5; 36:21-31; 37:17-19; 38:14-28; Ezek 17:12-18; 19:1-9; 21:25-27; 34:1-24; Hos 5:10; Amos 6:5; Mic 4:7), it appears that Isaiah (9:7; 7:13-25; 11:1-10), Jeremiah (23:5), Ezekiel (34:23-24; 37:15-25), Hosea (3:5), Amos (9:11-12) and Micah (5:2-5), in particular, based the hopes for a future recovery

---

11. Childs, *Introduction to the Old Testament*, 232-36; 308-10. Childs undertook a canonical exploration of the Joshua–Kings corpus and the Isaiah–Malachi collection, but separately.

12. "Deuteronomistic," as used in scholarly publications, will be referred to as "Deuteronomic" in this publication with the same meaning. The tendency to apply the "Deuteronomistic" designation to the Former Prophets, with or without the inclusion of Deuteronomy, suggests a reservation regarding the canonical perspective.

13. Driver, *Introduction*, 103, has adjudged the inclusion of the book of Joshua among the Former Prophets to be "artificial"—a superficial view that not only questions the canonical categorizations and Noth's hypothesis of a Deuteronomic History, but implies that a Hexateuch, rather than a Pentateuch, might have been a more viable option for the canonization of the Law.

on the appearance of a Davidic ruler. Such hopes may have sprung partly from the reputation of rulers of exceptional ability and devotion—such as Hezekiah (2 Kgs 18:3-5; cf. Jer 26:17-19) and Josiah (2 Kgs 22:2, 19; 23:25; cf. Jer 22:15-16; 26:17-19)—and particularly their commitment to the Mosaic law and the reformation of the Jerusalem cultus (2 Kgs 18:3-6, 22; 22:2; 23:3-25). More than likely, however, they resulted from the impact of ancient but enduring traditions concerning David and the future of his house, preserved in court annals, cultic festivals, and prophetic traditions (2 Sam 7:1-17; 1 Chron 17:1-16; Ps 89:1-4, 19-37),[14] which then became decisive for the formation of the Joshua–Malachi corpus. The recollection of the promises may have become a way of alleviating the doom predicted by the eighth and seventh century prophets which, having reached horrendous fulfillment in the downfall of the Hebrew kingdoms, fostered a renaissance of hope after the fall of the Babylonian Empire and the return of the Jewish exiles (Ezra 1:1-4; cf. Isa 40-55).

David and the Nathan Narrative in the Former Prophets (Joshua–Kings)

As historical narrative, Joshua–Kings, or the Former Prophets, may be interpreted at two levels. They are an account of the Israelite occupation of Canaan from the settlement of the tribes to the fall of the Southern Kingdom. Underlying the review are echoes of prophetic indictment of Israel's infidelity to YHWH in their persistent disregard for the Mosaic law and the Sinai-Horeb Covenant (2 Kgs 17:7-23; 21:2-16), of which the resulting catastrophes of their land loss and subjection to foreign rule were interpreted as punishment.

Included in that review was an evaluation of the Israelite monarchy, in which the character and performance of each ruler were summarily reported. The overall picture was not impressive. The history of monarchical rule in Israel was, for the most part, a history of decline. None of the rulers of the Northern Kingdom—or of Judah apart from Hezekiah and Josiah—was adjudged as wholly satisfactory. Highlighted in the account was a cultic

---

14. Court annals may have been represented by the ניר tradition found in 1 Kings 11:36, 1 Kings 15:4, and 2 Kings 8:19, annual cultic festivals in celebration of the enthronement as represented in the ark narrative in 2 Samuel 6 and Psalm 132, and may have included such prophetic pronouncements as appear in the Nathan oracle of 2 Samuel 7:1-17.

schism that was never healed (2 Kgs 17:21–23; cf. 1 Kgs 12:26–33),[15] as well as the rulers' indifference to, toleration of, and participation in cultic irregularities. These deficiencies resulted first in the fall of the Northern Kingdom in 721 BCE (2 Kgs 17:7–41; 18:11–12), and, aggravated by the apostasies of Manasseh and Amon, were also cited as the cause of the fall of the Southern Kingdom in 597 BCE (2 Kgs 17:19–20; 21:2–16; 23:26–27). It was, therefore, more than historical coincidence that the fall of the capital cities, Samaria and Jerusalem, the subjugation of the people, and the deposition and deportation of their rulers occurred in the same historical movement, viz., the rise and westward expansion of the neo-Mesopotamian kingdoms towards imperial domination (2 Kgs 17:1–6; 25:1–21).

Within the evaluation of the monarchy, the status of the Davidic monarchy was given special attention. The reason offered for its survival from overthrow in the rebellion of the northern tribes was a promise YHWH made to David of the allegiance of one of the tribes for the sake of Jerusalem, the city that YHWH had chosen. The connection with the Jerusalem sanctuary, therefore, invested a special religio-political significance in the Davidic monarchy. However, it meant that the fortunes of the Davidic monarchy and the city of Jerusalem were so entwined that the fall of the one presaged the end of the other. In the event, the liquidation of the monarchy was followed by the fall of Jerusalem, the extermination of its nobility, and the destruction of the temple (2 Kgs 24–25).

It seems, however, that neither the Deuteronomic provisions for an Israelite ruler (Deut 17:14–20), nor the "Jerusalem-connection" (1 Kgs 11:36; 15:4; 2 Kgs 8:19), exhausted royal ideology as was propounded in the Former Prophets. In the Nathan narrative was also preserved a witness to the security of the Davidic regime that was derived neither from its legitimization in the Mosaic law nor its connection with the religio-political status of Jerusalem (2 Sam 7:8–16).[16] It was not dependent on the fortunes of Jerusalem, nor conditioned by prohibitions and sanctions prescribed in the Sinai-Horeb covenant. Grounded in a dynastic covenant, David was

---

15. Up to the time of the Babylonian exile the re-unification of the two Kingdoms remained a dream still to be realized (cf. Is 11:13; Ezek 37:15–28).

16 The attempt to link the Nathan narrative to a royal ideology expounded in Kings, (viz., that the Jerusalem sanctuary was in the special care of the Davidic monarchy), explaining thereby the continuing allegiance of the tribe of Judah—a hypothesis that Cross, *Canaanite Myth*, 282, Nelson, *Double Redaction*, 105–12, and Provan, *Hezekiah and the Book of Kings*, 108 have espoused—seems to be, as shall be argued later, an over-simplification.

promised a kingship that was secured to his successors indefinitely (2 Sam 7:11b–12, 14–16). The Davidic monarchy was guaranteed a level of protection and support that set it apart from the other Israelite regimes (cf. 2 Sam 7:15). So irrevocable was the promise that, although misdemeanors in David's successors were envisaged, the penalties imposed would not extend to a forfeiture of the kingdom. Instead, the Davidic regime would endure far into the foreseeable future.

Prima facie, therefore, the promises in the Nathan narrative (2 Sam 7:11b–16) must raise questions for a historical account in which it featured prominently, which ended not merely with the overthrow and abolition, but also the humiliation and degradation of the monarchy (2 Kgs 25:27–30). The account shows Jehoiachin in Babylonian captivity; paroled after thirty-seven years of confinement; still kept under close surveillance as a political hostage; dependent on the favors of a foreign ruler for his daily rations; and, notwithstanding rehabilitation and improvement in personal appearance and status among his peers, being prevented from recovering his throne, dying in exile. Why a monumental composition in which the Nathan narrative (2 Sam 7:1–17) enjoyed such prominence should end in such glaring contradiction is a question that has not yet been satisfactorily answered.[17]

David and the Nathan Narrative in Samuel

The Samuel books have been devoted almost entirely to the story of David (1 Sam 16—1 Kgs 2). The refrain in the concluding chapters of Judges, in which were reported the socio-political and religious conditions of Israel in the pre-monarchy period (Judg 17:6; 18:1; 19:1; 21:25), anticipated the blessings that would attend the institution of a legitimate monarchy.[18] The

---

17. A basic redaction technique was the "re-framing" or "ring composition," which made the ending of the composition a critical clue to interpretation. This has been expounded by Ridout in "Prose Composition?" 36–37, and Willis in "Redaction Criticism," 83–85. On the other hand, Gray, *Kings*, 773, has cited primitive superstition as a probable explanation of the conclusion of the Former Prophets with the Jehoiachin pericope (2 Kgs 25:27–30).

18. "A legitimate monarchy," because the Abiezrite fiasco in which the reservations of Gideon (Judg 8:22–23), the diatribe of Jotham (Judg 9:7–20), and the ambition of Abimelech, who climbed to the throne through fratricide only to crash in shame and suicide at the Tower of Shechem (Judg 9), bespoke the dangers of a monarchy that derived from below in popular choice or personal ambition, rather than from above in divine election (1 Sam 16: 1–13a; 2 Sam 7:8).

early chapters of Samuel contain the following: the birth, novitiate, and call of the anointing prophet (1 Sam 1–3; 16:1–13); the long neglected ark of the covenant recovered later at David's initiative and installed on Mount Zion (a meritorious achievement that brought blessings upon his house [1 Sam 4:1—7:1; 2 Sam 6–7; cf. Ps 132]); the clamor for, misgivings about, and inauguration of a monarchy in the appointment of Saul as commander—נגיד—and his fall from favor that opened the way to David's accession (1 Sam 8–15; 2 Sam 5:1–5; 7:15). The David story fills the rest of Samuel. At the rejection of Saul, Samuel looked forward to "a man after YHWH's heart" (1 Sam 13:14), and one who was better than Saul (1 Sam 15:28; 28:16–17).

David's rise from pastoral obscurity to kingly rule and the founding of a ruling house became the dominant theme of the epic. It recalled the perils and vicissitudes he endured as a fugitive and outlaw (1 Sam 18–27), the indiscretions that tarnished and the tragedies that shadowed his reign (2 Sam 11–12), a rebellion led by his son Absalom that forced his flight from the capital and almost resulted in his overthrow (2 Sam 15–16),[19] and a revolt led by Sheba ben Bichri, a disillusioned Benjaminite (2 Sam 20:1–22). David's reign also experienced the harrowing effects of famine (2 Sam 21:1) and a deadly epidemic that swept away seventy thousand men (2 Sam 24:13–15). However, this epic also recorded military successes in the annexation of neighboring states and the creation of an empire that stretched from the entrance of Hamath to the Nile delta (2 Sam 5:17–26; 8; 10–11; 1 Kgs 8:65).

David's success bore witness to his election, protection, succor, and blessing by YHWH (2 Sam 4:9; 7:8–9; 2 Sam 22:1—23:7; cf. 1 Kgs 1:29). The story might, therefore, be read as the confession of faith in the legitimacy of the Davidic monarchy. In his exposition of Samuel, Brevard Childs called attention to the three oracular compositions, viz., the song of Hannah at the beginning (1 Sam 2:1b–10), the last words of David towards the end (2 Sam 23:1–7), and, about midway between, the Nathan narrative (2 Sam 7:1–17).[20] Taken together, they seemed to constitute the crux of the interpretation of the corpus. They rise out of the narrative like peaks, lifting the David epic above mere historical narrative to theological affir-

---

19. It would seem that the fortunes of the rebellion, the defeat of Absalom, and the victory of David's army depended less on military might or advantage in the field than on Absalom's rejection of the counsel of the renowned strategist, Ahitophel, in preference for the trickery of Hushai, the King's friend, whom David planted in Absalom's entourage precisely to mislead him (2 Sam 15:31–37; 16:20—17:14, 23).

20. See Childs, *Introduction*, 272–75.

mation. Hannah's song, composed ostensibly to commemorate the birth of Samuel, was essentially a hymn in expectation of a specially anointed king (1 Sam 2:10). In that confession, therefore, the tragedy about to unfold in the intervening reign was foreseen. Far from being the chosen one, Saul's kingship represented YHWH's reluctant concession to popular demand (1 Sam 8:7–19). On the other hand, the king to whom the song alluded (1 Sam 2:10) was David, elected by YHWH in sovereign freedom, long before he was officially endorsed by the people (1 Sam 16:1–13; cf. 2 Sam 2:4; 5:1–3). Thus, even while Saul reigned, David's suitability was already a popular theme (1 Sam 18:6–7; 21:11) and he was heralded, near and far, as the successor who was both eligible and worthy (1 Sam 24:20; cf. 13:14; 15:28; 25:28–31; 2 Sam 3:9–10; 5:1–3).

In the third composition (2 Sam 23:1–7), David, in prophetic mode, reflected on the character of his rule. He recalled a covenant God made with him, which envisaged an auspicious future for his house. Looking far ahead, he saw his regime secure against foes and evil doers. In spite of disaffection, secession, and attempts at usurpation, the house of David would remain sheltered and secured by an everlasting covenant—ברית עולם (2 Sam 23:5).

Situated between the song of Hannah (1 Sam 2:1b–10) and David's last words (2 Sam 23:1–7) was the Nathan narrative, which included a dynastic oracle (2 Sam 7:8–16). Similar in outlook, it not only affirmed David's election to greatness as YHWH's choice (vv. 8–9), but also registered YHWH's commitment to the ruling family (vv. 11b–16). This affirmation the song of Hannah anticipated, and from it David's swansong drew inspiration. The Nathan narrative (2 Sam 7:8–16) may therefore be viewed as a switch that turned Samuel and, by extension, the Former Prophets from historical narrative to a theological affirmation of the monarchy that was grounded in steadfast love—the divine חסד (2 Sam 7:15; cf. Isa 55:3)—provided the essential perspective for the Prophets, and established the David tradition in postexilic Judaism.

On closer examination, however, the Nathan narrative does not appear to fit comfortably into the story of David. It is awkwardly related to the succession narrative that followed (2 Sam 9–20: 1 Kgs 1–2),[21] in that notwithstanding the obvious linkage in Nathan's designation of the heir (2

---

21. The title, "Succession Narrative/Story," coined by Rost, *Succession to the Throne*, 65, has been challenged by a number of scholars including Flanagan, "Court History," 172–81; Delekat, "Bias and Theology," 26–38; and Ackroyd, "Succession Narrative (so-called)," 383–96.

Sam 7:12–13; cf. 12:24–25), and his critical role in securing for him the succession (2 Sam 12:24–25; cf. 1 Kgs 1:11–30), the narrative does not show anywhere that Nathan, Bathsheba, or David was aware of a revelation that had designated Solomon.

Also, the Nathan narrative raises questions for the ark narrative that preceded it (1 Sam 4:1–7:1; 2 Sam 6). While the opening verses of the Nathan narrative indicate a connection (2 Sam 6:1–20; 7:1–7; cf. Ps 132:18), the claim that YHWH had not dwelt in a house since the Exodus (2 Sam 7:6) is at variance with the account of the ark's movements, which shows that at Shiloh, and from its removal thence to its installation on Mount Zion, the ark had always been accommodated in substantial structures—except for the intervals when it was taken into battle (1 Sam 4:4–5)—or removed from house to house (1 Sam 3:3; 4:3; 5:2; 7:1; 2 Sam 6:10–11, 17).[22]

Last, but not least, the period described in the introduction to the narrative as one of " . . . rest from all his [the king's] enemies round about" (v.1b), was cited in Deuteronomic law as the propitious time for the building of the chosen sanctuary (Deut 12:10). However, not only did the military engagements abroad (2 Sam 8: 10–12) and the domestic crises reported in the chapters that followed (2 Sam 15–20) present a condition of persistent unrest and conflict, but the favorable conditions reported in the introductory verse seem to be contradicted later in the Nathan narrative (2 Sam 7:1, 10–11a; cf. 1 Kgs 5:15–17 [MT]).

Gerhard von Rad's exposition of "rest" (מנוחה) has, however, interpreted the promise in Deuteronomic usage as a tangible sociological condition that could be recognized and celebrated as a divine gift.[23] He has described it as the congenial state of a people who, having been long plagued by their enemies, and grown weary of wandering, had come into a secure inheritance. Such a definition must therefore raise a question concerning the thwarting of David's wish to build the chosen sanctuary when the conditions prescribed for such an undertaking existed (2 Sam 7:1; 1 Kgs 8:56; cf. Deut 12:9–10).[24]

The Nathan narrative is therefore paradoxically related to the historical perspective that informed Samuel in the sense that, although a

22. The identification of YHWH by the ark was so close symbolically that, by describing YHWH's movements, a reference to the ark was intended when 2 Sam 7:1–3 became the introduction to the narrative (2 Sam 7:6; cf. Num 10:35–36; 1 Sam 4:5–7).

23. See Von Rad, "There Remains Still a Rest," 95.

24. Carlson, *David, the Chosen King*, 102, has given verse 1b a cultic rather than sociological interpretation.

key-component, it appears to raise questions for its narrative setting that are both complex and far-reaching. In traditio-historical terms they point to unresolved issues of a late redaction which, while respecting the traditional material, varied from it in perspective, interpretation, and purpose.

David in the Nathan Narrative of 2 Samuel 7:1–17

The complex relationship between the Nathan narrative and the David epic in Samuel might be viewed as an extension of complexities that might be discovered in the narrative itself. A cursory reading might yield a semblance of unity and coherence. David's desire to build a house for YHWH, endorsed by the prophet Nathan, was disallowed on three grounds:

> It was incompatible with the history of YHWH as an itinerant deity (v. 6).
>
> It was presumptuous, since YHWH never expressed such a wish (v. 7).
>
> It pre-empted YHWH's plans for a house (v. 13a).

David, nevertheless, was reminded of YHWH's gracious acts towards him from his humble beginnings to his ascendancy (v. 8), and was promised still larger blessings of worldwide renown (v. 9), secure possession of the land by the people of Israel (vv. 10–11a), a kingdom that would endure beyond his allotted span (vv. 11b, 16), and a biological heir who would build the house (vv. 12–13).

Thus paraphrased, a semblance of unity might be allowed. Closer scrutiny will, however, reveal a more complex compositional structure. The narrative seems to have coordinated two basic themes, viz., a house (sanctuary) for YHWH (vv. 1–7, 13a) and a house (dynasty) for David (vv. 11b–16), which, brought together, vied for prominence. Whereas in the oracle proper (2 Sam 7:4–16) the building of a sanctuary is the dominant theme to which the promise of a regime is subsidiary, the inclusion of the prayer as a response to the oracle (vv. 18–29) makes the promise of a dynasty uppermost (vv. 11b–12, 15–16), and the building of a sanctuary an aside (vv. 1–7, 13–14).

So far as the sanctuary theme is concerned, the first two reasons for a prohibition, advanced in verses 5–7, should have excluded the third (v. 13a). Moreover verse 13a, although resuming the temple theme, appears, from the repetition in verses 12b and 13b, to be an intrusion. Also, the hiatus at verse 4 raises a question of continuity between verses 1–3 and 5–7.

So far as the dynastic theme in verses 8–29 is concerned, the repetition in the messenger formula (2 Sam 7:8; cf. v.5), but with an honorific title for YHWH,[25] introduces a change from the sanctuary theme (vv. 1–7) which, but for the intrusive verse 13a, would not have recurred. The rest of the chapter would then have been taken up entirely with a dynastic theme; and, on traditio-historical grounds, might more naturally have followed the ark narrative in 2 Samuel 6 (cf. Ps. 132:1–6, 11–12).[26]

There is also a literary-critical irregularity at verse 11b: "Moreover YHWH declares to you that a house YHWH will make for you." In the first place what was reported up to that point as a revelation from YHWH to the prophet Nathan for transmission to David, was changed abruptly to a revelation being communicated to David by the intermediary; and, from verse twelve and onwards, the narrative reverts to a revelation to the prophet for transmission to David. The awkwardness suggests an attempt at the resolution of a dilemma that may have arisen from the inclusion of a mediator for, significantly, the prayer of David that follows recalls a similar revelation as having been directly addressed to David, i.e. without an intermediary. "For you, YHWH SABAOTH, God of Israel, have revealed[27] to your servant saying 'A house I will build for you' " (v. 27). This raises a question of two identical revelations regarding the Davidic monarchy, given on separate occasions to different recipients, which seems to be answered in the oracle of David (2 Sam 23:5) where, also, David testifies to having been both the beneficiary of a promise and the immediate recipient of the revelation.

CONCLUSION

It is a subtle paradox of biblical scholarship that the larger the scope allowed to traditio-historical research, the more the literary-critical questions obtrude. Such a result need not, however, be disquieting. Gone is the period when literary-critical "problems" could be explained by editorial manipulation or scribal lapses. What they might more plausibly suggest

---

25. יהוה צבאות was an honorific title of YHWH as the deity commonly associated with the ark of the covenant as is evident in the expanded form in the ark narrative (cf. 2 Sam 6:2; 7:27; 1 Sam 4:4).

26. Simon, "The Prophecy of Nathan," 43, has, on the basis of the speech of Stephen (Acts 7:44–50) and a tradition he traced through Judaism, argued for an absolute prohibition of the Solomonic temple in the narrative.

27. Literally, "opened the ear of your servant to say."

is a special aptitude in traditionists for integrating traditions of diverse origins, forms and purposes, and reinterpreting them for further objectives. The more complex the literary-critical problems, therefore, the more they indicate the antiquity, complexity, and popularity of the traditional material that was preserved. It is this possibility that makes the Bible, and especially the Old Testament, incomparable as ancient literature both for the information it provides on the people who are the subject and the traditions they transmitted. Furthermore, being the production of people who were directly involved, and who valued the traditions for their contribution to self-understanding, they are invested with peculiar authenticity. In such analyses a dimension of depth is opened up in the literature of the Old Testament.

The Nathan narrative in 2 Samuel 7:1–17 is a fair example of the change of climate. Scathingly criticized in the last century by Robert Pfeiffer for its style, grammar, and diction,[28] it has more recently won the acclaim of Kenneth Craig as a gem of ancient rhetoric and a shining example of the subtleties of Hebrew prose.[29] The new appreciation is the result not only of a more sophisticated approach to narrative art in ancient literature generally, but also the discovery of depth in the literature of the Old Testament made possible through traditio-historical research, revealing with greater clarity the interests, concerns, and skills of the traditionists and redactors in reinterpreting traditional material for more meaningful and relevant composition.

28. See Pfeiffer, *Introduction*, 370–3.
29. See Craig, "Character(-ization) of God," 160–61.

CHAPTER II

THE TRADITIO-HISTORICAL APPROACH

THE TRADITIO-HISTORICAL APPROACH REPRESENTS one of the more significant developments in Old Testament research, which attracted wide attention in the later decades of the twentieth century. Tracing its earliest application to a systematic study to the 1930s, Douglas A. Knight cited two distinguished Old Testament scholars—Gerhard von Rad and Martin Noth—as pathfinders.[1] To them he gave credit for the fresh insights that emerged from their analyses and the originality of their methods and perception enabling them to break new ground in research and enable a clearer understanding of the issues that are at stake in Old Testament study and research.

THE TRADITIO-HISTORICAL METHOD ILLUSTRATED

GERHARD VON RAD

Gerhard von Rad's exploration stemmed from problems he encountered in his study of the Pentateuch (Genesis–Deuteronomy), from which he concluded that Pentateuchal criticism had reached a *stasis*.[2] The source-critics had done their work. The text had been shredded and re-configured according to their respective "sources," which were classified, labelled

---

1. See Knight, *Re-discovering Traditions of Israel,* 97.
2. See Von Rad, "The Form Critical Problem of the Hexateuch," 1–20.

THE TRADITIO-HISTORICAL APPROACH

and dated. He argued however that, in spite of its success, limitations in Wellhausen's hypothesis had also become apparent for, as long as the nature and evolution of the material that went into the production of the sources were irretrievable, the composition of the Pentateuch remained on the edge of a vast unknown.

In an attempt to resolve the mystery von Rad adopted a radically new line of approach. Applying form-critical methods proposed by Hermann Gunkel,[3] he selected certain passages, within and outside the Pentateuch, which seemed to offer clues as well to the faith that was confessed in early Israel as to their pre-history. They were Deuteronomy 26:5–9; 6:20–24; Joshua 24:2b–13; Exodus 15:1–18 and Psalm 136.[4] Though differing in length and style, and addressed to differing situations and at different times, they were all, in his view, of the same character and articulated virtually the same confession of and about the people of Israel. They recalled the hard and bitter bondage endured by the ancestors, who acknowledged that it was YHWH who brought them out of Egypt and gave them the land they possessed; and whereas evidence of stereotype may have been the result of a long process of alteration and adaptation, there could also be discerned an underlying tradition of faith of higher antiquity and regular usage.[5] More importantly, he recognized them as the common property of worshipping people long before they were taken over by literary elites. The *Sitz im Leben* was the cult.[6] They exuded the aura of festal celebration. They pulsated with the vitality of communal participation. Above all, they recalled occasions that were set apart for reflection on *Magnalia Dei*, momentous events, through which the people of Israel extolled YHWH as deliverer and protector, guide and provider. In such settings the ancient traditions were transmitted from one generation to another.

So far as the Pentateuch was concerned, von Rad reached two conclusions that seemed to him inescapable. In the first place, he concluded that the Sinai tradition must have been an independent tradition in the early stages of transmission, since it nowhere featured in the creedal formulations. He therefore suggested that it might have become integrated into the

---

3. See Gunkel, *Psalms* 1–4.

4. It is questionable whether the similarities are explicable by the pervasive Deuteronomic influence on a late redaction. The differences, notwithstanding the commonalities, point to origins that are more diverse than the explanation of a late redaction could give.

5. Ibid., 11.

6. Ibid., 5–12.

Heilsgeschichte as part of the considerable investment of a Yahwist editor in the composition of the Pentateuch.[7]

Secondly, he concluded from the structure of the credal statements that it was not merely possible, but plausible, to propose a Hexateuch rather than a Pentateuch, since in all the known examples, the occupation of the land as both promise and an achievement, and an integral component of the *Heilsgeschichte*, featured more prominently in the book of Joshua than in the Pentateuch.[8]

It was in his *magnum opus* on Old Testament Theology that the fruits of von Rad's research attained definitive exposition. There he expounded the vital distinction between "the history of Israel" and "Israel's history," insisting that the two presentations were not the same, nor did the objectives necessarily coincide. A history of Israel must have been the result of scientific investigation of events as they actually occurred, with a view to arriving at a "critically assured minimum."[9] "Israel's history" could hardly be defined in such terms. It was rather a celebration of the mighty acts of God.[10] It involved a correlation and coordination of originally independent traditions and, for a heightening of the dramatic effect, might have also included elements drawn from earlier sources that were mythological in character rather than historical. Such a "history" could hardly have been objective reporting but was rather extracts from popular ritual which offered insight into Israel's cultic celebrations, and what they chose to remember and why. It was anamnesis—an actualization in the present of momentous and epoch-making events of the past. It was for the insights into that practice of "remembering" that the literature of the Old Testament remained a valuable resource, and it was the exploration of the "theological maximum" of that practice that was the purpose of Old Testament study, for which a grasp of the traditions was a *conditio sine qua non*.[11]

---

7. Ibid., 13–26, 53–54.
8. Ibid., 74–78.
9. See von Rad, *Old Testament Theology 1*, 107–108.
10. See also Wright, *God Who Acts*, 53–86, 107–28, who offers a similar exposition, and "Cult and History," 3–20, in which he also notes some of the pitfalls.
11. See von Rad, *Old Testament Theology I*, 108–15.

THE TRADITIO-HISTORICAL APPROACH

MARTIN NOTH

In a monograph published during World War II, and translated into English in 1981, Martin Noth applied the traditio-historical method to the study of the Old Testament. It was a radical departure from earlier literary-critical methods and, in particular, attempts (then in vogue) to extend Wellhausen's Documentary Hypothesis beyond the Pentateuch, by tracing the J and E sources beyond Deuteronomy to as far as Kings.[12] On literary-critical grounds, Noth questioned the viability of a continuity from Genesis–Numbers to Deuteronomy–Kings. He also disputed the suggestion that Deuteronomy–Kings was a result of secondary editing of pre-Deuteronomic compositions, arguing instead for a single authorship in which traditional material of diverse origins were incorporated and arranged according to a pre-conceived plan.[13] It was in this sense that Noth considered his approach to be traditio-historical—a view from which Douglas Knight seems to have dissented, having restricted the traditio-historical definition to oral transmission.[14]

It was in his traditio-historical study of Genesis–Numbers that Noth's analysis more directly impinged upon, and closely complemented, von Rad's hypothesis of a Hexateuch (Genesis–Joshua). In his study on Old Testament theology, von Rad argued that Genesis–Joshua was a Hexateuch built up from ancient confessional formulae, and the derivation of a theological maximum from it was the proper theological study of Old Testament. However, Noth the historian was able to isolate antecedent units even from the most ancient of these confessional formulae,[15] discern the processes of convergence and coalescence that resulted in the making of the confessional formulae, and, having differentiated the ascertainable historical evidence from such processes, was able to present as the history of the emergence of Israel a critically assured minimum.[16]

Noth observed that not merely the Pentateuch as a whole or its constituent sources, but even the confessional formulae identified by von Rad, were in fact a secondary development, in that they proceeded from an "all

---

12. A useful summary of the history of such attempts has been offered by Eissfeldt, *Introduction*, 241–8.
13. See Noth, *Deuteronomistic History*, 10-11.
14. See Knight, *Rediscovering Traditions of Israel*, 27, 157–61
15. See Noth, *Pentateuchal Traditions*, 5.
16. This he achieved in his historical magnum opus, *History of Israel*.

Israel" premise.[17] They suggested that, from the earliest period of its emergence, "Israel" was an identifiable socio-historical entity—a people who were sprung from the same stock, whose ancestors had been inured to a semi-nomadic way of life, had groaned under, and were delivered from, the harsh conditions of Egyptian bondage, had covenanted with YHWH at Mt. Sinai, had been guided through the wilderness for a period of forty years and, still together, entered the land of Canaan, which they claimed as their common inheritance. Noth contended that, whatever the ideological mileage that might have been gained, it was an idealized version that could not be sustained as empirical history; but diverse themes, deriving from independent traditions, had been woven into a continuous narrative for the purpose of fostering unity and solidarity *after* various migrating groups, arriving from different directions, at different times and, for different reasons, settled in different parts of Canaan in different ways.[18] Therefore the enquiry into constituent units took the investigation beyond von Rad's analysis into a search for yet more basic material out which a Tetrateuch might have been composed.[19]

THE TRADITIO-HISTORICAL METHOD EXAMINED

The importance of the foregoing review is the insight it offers into the traditio-historical method. However, it must be noted that, notwithstanding their considerable prestige, Noth and von Rad did not monopolize the discussion, their studies did not exhaust the scope of the traditio-historical discussion, nor did their arguments and conclusions escape scholarly criticism. On the one hand, the radical dichotomy they proposed between a history of Israel and the Israelites' recital of their history was criticized by Ernest Wright as unduly polarizing, and needlessly reserved about the contribution of archaeological discoveries to a recovery of Israel's past.[20] On the other hand, the traditio-historical approach won enthusiastic support from Ivan Engnell who, in his advocacy of the decisive role of oral tradition in the making of the Old Testament, went further still to advocate an abandonment of the literary-critical method as anachronistic.[21] An exami-

   17. See Noth, *Pentateuchal Traditions*, 42–45, 47–51.
   18. See Noth, *History of Israel*, 58–81.
   19. See Noth, *Pentateuchal Traditions*, 198–213.
   20. See Wright, "Biblical Archaeology," 174.
   21. See Engnell, "Traditio-historical Research," 3–4.

THE TRADITIO-HISTORICAL APPROACH

nation of the traditio-historical method, and especially the issues that still await resolution, seems therefore to require, for a study such as this, both a setting of the parameters for definition and the suggestion of options on areas as yet unresolved.

ORAL TRANSMISSION AND WRITTEN COMPOSITION

Engnell's advocacy notwithstanding, the current focus of traditio-historical research seems to be on the literature, that is to say, its importance for the elucidation of the text. Indeed, G.W. Coats has defined it as a method of analyzing biblical literature in terms of the process by which it moved from stage to stage until it reached the final form.[22]

Thus defined, there seems to be little difference between the traditio-historical and redactio-critical methods; for although the processes of oral transmission phases might, conceivably, have been included in the "stages" referred to, because that possibility was not specifically addressed, nor was a differentiation between the stages of oral transmission and written composition directly discussed, it would seem that the "stages" implied written compositions. Such a limitation is, however, open to debate; for while it is evident that traditions, once orally transmitted would, in the course of time, have survived in written form and as a literary composition (and therefore it was mostly by way of the document or other inscription that oral traditions might be recovered), it still remains questionable to limit the importance of oral traditions to the purposes they have been made to serve in the written compositions in which they were finally incorporated, and to assume that traditions were built up and preserved in the oral stages over long eras of transmission merely for the purpose of providing material for written compositions for which they were not intended. No definition of the traditio-historical approach can be deemed adequate that undervalues traditions in the oral stages of transmission as ends in themselves, and quite apart from their contribution to, and status in, later compositions.

Walter Rast's reflections on the subject seem to concur with Coats' definition, especially in the analogies he has drawn from such ancient compositions as Homer's Odyssey and the Iliad, and the Gilgamesh epic. From them he argued that, while such literary works were not *de novo* compositions throughout, but incorporated even more ancient myths and sagas gathered from folk-lore that were built up over a span of centuries

22. See Coats, "Tradition Criticism," 912.

and transmitted orally, their importance as traditional material lay less in the traditions that they preserved than their status in, and contribution to, the compositions into which they were re-worked.[23]

Three responses, from the perspective of Old Testament literature, might be considered. In the first place its shaping in composition and sub-composition was, even as ancient literature, unique. It was not, at any point, designed to be epic, hagiography, or fiction, which could be embellished by imagination or improved by manipulation. It was, rather, a people's reflection on their past and their attempt to visualize a future. It was therefore not intended to be glamorous or star-studded. There was no attempt to cover the nakedness or hide the shame. Indeed, as *their* history, it was strange history. It was, for the most part, a confession of failure, and a record of reverses and disasters, humiliation and suffering. Its impact was less the result of literary skill than of events as they were recalled and interpreted, preserved and transmitted, before incorporation in literary compositions, and through further changes in the process of redaction.

In the second place, the motivations and objectives that prompted the literary compositions differed little from those that ensured the preservation of the traditions in the oral stages of transmission. They were, alike, existential. They represented an ongoing struggle for authentic existence in situations of crisis, and in an environment that was, for the most part, inhospitable, and even subversive. Therefore, underlying the modifications of the traditions in oral transmission, in the transition from oral transmission to literature, and in subsequent redaction, there was an underlying affinity and compatibility that wove the various traditions into one story and combined the several compositions in one history.

In the third place, and most important of all, because the Old Testament was a story about a people's faith covering many centuries, creativity was less operative in the writing stages of composition than in the settings and forms of oral transmission. It might conceivably be argued, as Roland deVaux has done, that in the predominantly oral periods, literacy and literature were not altogether unknown phenomena, nor were writings as scarce commodities as might be sometimes assumed.[24] Even so, the crucial matter is not so much about the general level of literacy or the availability or possibility of written literature, as it is about the appropriate vehicles for the transmission of the traditions underlying the composition of the

---

23. See Rast, *Tradition History*, 5–6.
24. See DeVaux, "Reflections on Pentateuchal Criticism," 35–6.

Old Testament. In a predominantly oral culture it was unlikely that such material for, and means of, transmission was written. Material culled from court records and similar sources listed by Eissfeldt,[25] whatever their importance for recording, documentation and later reference, could therefore have constituted no more than a negligible portion of the traditional material preserved in Old Testament literature. Therefore, to ignore or devalue the importance of oral transmission is to misconstrue the making of the Old Testament and, as a result, yield an inadequate analysis of its contents. It seems, therefore, that the traditio-historical approach will pay as much attention to the processes of oral transmission and to the changes occurring in transitions from the oral to the writing stages, as to redactions in the writing stages, each stage making a distinctive contribution to the discovery of Old Testament literature.

From Oral Transmission to Written Composition

This last observation brings into sharp focus an area of discussion that requires clarity and consistency. Notwithstanding his advocacy of the role of oral tradition and his call for an abandonment of the modern book view of the Old Testament as anachronistic, Engnell also pleaded for a complementary relationship between the oral tradition and the literature, contending that limiting the traditio-historical method to a theory of a hundred percent process of oral tradition was a caricature. He asserted that not only the smaller units, but even larger complexes must, in the oral stage, have reached forms so fixed that the writing required little that was new or revolutionary.[26]

Thus stated, the distinction between oral transmission and the written composition is so narrowed, and the boundaries are made so flexible, as to abate his scepticism of the literary-critical approach and his advocacy for the status of oral tradition. Knight, on the other hand, in defining a tradition, has identified, as a basic criterion, its capacity for adaptation and development, insisting that a tradition ceased to be such at the point of its entry into written composition when, removed from its normal setting in life, it lost its natural flexibility. He recognized, however, that even as

---

25. See Eissfeldt, *Introduction*, 18–32.
26. See Engnell, "Traditio-historical Research," 6–7.

written composition, to the extent that it conformed to the other criteria, it might also qualify as a tradition.[27]

When the two propositions, Engnell's and Knight's, are juxtaposed, they suggest that the difficulties raised by written compositions for the traditio-historical approach stem less from an inherent incompatibility than from the natural inclination to living situations of oral transmission as offering conditions more conducive to traditio-historical research. This, however, is hardly sufficient ground for choice or preference between oral and written forms of transmission of traditions, or for the claim for oral transmission as the only viable vehicle, implying that a tradition, having attained a written form or become incorporated into written composition, must necessarily have atrophied. It would seem a more fruitful approach to place oral transmission and written composition in a complementary relationship, as the two major stages of a *continuum* from the primary units of a tradition to the final shaping in written composition—an approach that is of special importance for the study of Old Testament literature, from which, chiefly, the oral stages can be recovered.[28]

This understanding of the traditio-historical process also raises the question of distinction and relationship between tradition-history and redaction-history. It is noteworthy that, in the study of New Testament literature, and especially the Gospels, such a distinction, in practice, does not arise precisely because the traditions were not arrested on becoming written literature but, in the continuing process of redaction, traditions about Jesus of Nazareth in the subsequent literature continued to grow. John Hayes and Carl Holloday have therefore urged that tradition criticism be not confined to an "oral period," but that traditions might be either written or oral, and that having persisted in oral transmission through several generations, they retained the character of traditions even when they came to be written, the only change being the manner of transmission. "Traditioning" might thus involve both oral and written traditions and therefore, in either case, tradition history is applicable to the study of biblical literature wherever indications of further growth and development are discovered.[29]

Because the growth of a tradition in the oral stages might also be described as a redaction process whereas, in practice, the terminology has been used in connection with written productions, it would also seem advisable,

---

27. See Knight, *Rediscovering Traditions of Israel*, 26–27.
28. That is the approach that will be adopted in this study.
29. See Hayes and Holloday, *Biblical Exegesis*, 94.

THE TRADITIO-HISTORICAL APPROACH

in the interest of clarity, to reserve "redaction" for the writing stages of transmission, and apply the traditio-historical definition to the entire process of the evolution of a tradition—the writing stages as well as the oral.

In complementing the two stages in the growth of a tradition—the oral and the written—the differences between the stages should not, however, be overlooked or minimized, nor should the complexities involved in the transitions be underestimated. Roger Lapointe has listed some of them in discussing the differences in the context of communication and linguistics.[30] He noted the inclination to relate the process of transmitting traditions more to situations of oral than of written communication.[31] He therefore cautioned against the tendency to a "logocentric prejudice" that tended to disfavour written composition against oral, to highlight identity and presence as the prerequisites for research, to require situational settings which are compatible with oral language but impracticable for texts, and to stress interaction between text and inter-text in oral language.[32]

In addition to Lapointe's insights some other aspects might be noted. Apart from dramatic productions, which are typically simulations, written accounts normally necessitate a narrative component, for purposes of elucidation and character differentiation, with a view to overcoming disadvantages of absence. This is superfluous for, and might be even disadvantageous to, oral intercourse in which there is an inherent anonymity and necessary reticence that must be overcome in the reporting, in order that the transmission, written or oral, might succeed. It is also unlikely that oral transmission could remain intact over an extended period, as is possible for the inscription or document. Furthermore, non-verbal factors intrinsic to oral communication such as pause, intonation, posture, grimace, and gesticulation which, though by their very nature defy transcription, require explication in the reporting.

In addition, therefore, to the reinterpretation and adaptation that remain the particular and primary concerns of the redactors, there are formidable factors that impinge upon the traditional material in oral communication, which may not have attained a written expression. While, however, Lapointe's description of the transition from oral to written language as a "qualitative jump" might be plausible in theory,[33] it might, in

30. See Lapointe, "Tradition and Language," 125–42.
31. Ibid., 127–29.
32. Ibid., 130.
33. Ibid., 133.

the majority of the actual cases, exaggerate the process which, as Engnell observed, may already have been evolving in oral literature, to such an extent that the modifications required for the earliest written forms are minimal. All of these considerations merely serve to underline the importance of, and the complications connected with, tradition-historical research, for the same factors that were involved in the transition from oral traditions to written compositions abide, and must also be taken into account, in a recovery of oral traditions from the written literature. On the other hand, when all the factors have been considered, the traditio-historical process makes possible a re-opening of questions that might have remained closed to literary-critical methods, but which required the further explorations, for which they were not adequately equipped.

Traditio and *Traditum*

In his definition of "tradition" Knight made a distinction between the process, which he labelled *traditio* and the material, which he labelled *traditum*.[34] There is, of necessity, an interplay in the application of the terminology, for not only is the material (*traditum*) both basic for, and the product of, the process (*traditio*); but while the process (*traditio*) is likely to maintain consistency, the material (*traditum*), impacted upon by factors inherent in the process (*traditio*), is always susceptible to change. For that reason the method of traditioning seems crucial for the determination of a tradition, of which Knight has listed the following characteristics.

1. It is received from others and transmitted further, especially from generation to generation.
2. It has both form and content. The history of a tradition can only be retraced as long as it remains "*formal greifbar.*"
3. It is the immediate property of a group or community.
4. It is "living," developing, malleable, and only relatively stable.
5. It is usually oral but can also be in written form.
6. It tends to be cumulative and agglomerative.[35]

---

34. See Knight, *Rediscovering Traditions of Israel*, 1, 20.
35. Ibid., 26.

THE TRADITIO-HISTORICAL APPROACH

Conceptually and ideally, little exception can be taken to the list proposed. However, as descriptive of the actual process, an important feature of *traditio* has been understated, since there is more to *traditio* than the receiving of *traditum* with a view to transmission. If, as Knight has observed above, a tradition is the immediate property of a group or community, and each generation finds tradition already as a part of its historical reality, i.e. of the situation in which the people must confront life, and if the power of a tradition is derived from its very presence,[36] then the notion of "receiving" *traditum* with a view to further transmission, as the *traditio*-priority, is likely to misconstrue both the nature of *traditum* and the purpose of *traditio*. Because tradition is already an integral part of, and not apart from, a people's *esse*, it is unlikely that it will have been received solely, or even primarily, with a view to posterity. Whatever else might be assumed for the process of traditioning, and however else tradition may be defined, the priority of the existential factor cannot be compromised. *Traditio*, at best, is a self-enhancing exercise of a community and, at very least, a coping mechanism. It is its contribution to a people's vitality that clothes tradition with acceptability, authority and social power. It is for that reason also that interpretation and appropriation are of the essence of *traditio*.

Writing on a quite different subject Professor Peter Ackroyd has thrown useful light on the derivation of *traditio*. Citing Professor David Daube's study of biblical law and its relation to Roman law, he has noted the latter's suggestion that *traditio* in Roman law involved the principle of taking over something that could not physically be transferred to the new owner.[37] In the light of such a definition, therefore, the "midwifery" role that Knight ascribed to *traditio* detracts from the ownership aspect inherent in the process, which establishes, as the primary and more immediate objective, the indispensable role of interpretation.

Such an understanding of *traditio* must also improve the understanding of *traditum*. Again, it is vital to distinguish between the idealism inherent in the definition and the reality. Not only has there been, in the conceptualizing of *traditio*, an inordinate interest in reception with a view to transmission, but in defining *traditum*, there has also been an inordinate preoccupation with the original *depositum*. In an essay on the subject, Walter Harrelson has placed special emphasis on the integrity of the "tradition" in a recognizable consistency notwithstanding the varying

---

36. See Knight, "Tradition and Theology," 1.
37. See Ackroyd, "Babylonian Exile," 340.

interpretations and the modifications that may have accrued from its application to changing conditions.[38] Following Josef Pieper, who also seems to have defined a tradition as that which was passed on as received, Harrelson has added that, in the transmission, the greatest care must have been taken to ensure that *traditum* was what was received and nothing else, and to hand on a tradition meant to hand it on intact. He argues that though traditions changed, were reformed and took on new shape and character in the course of transmission, that understanding of *traditio* should not misconstrue what traditionists understood their task to be, in that to the extent that they were passing down what had sufficient significance to be delivered whole to the next generation, to that extent it was to be delivered whole; and although the process of handing down might involve a measure of interpretation, the essential elements of the tradition, i.e. the *traditum*, must have also been recognizable.[39]

Harrelson goes on to expound the importance of distinguishing between the original "core tradition," as he called it, and the later modifications and embellishments; and also between a tradition and a theme or a set of motifs, arguing that traditioning is concerned with a discernible content that goes beyond the themes, embellishments or other amplifications that may have become attached. He therefore enquires into the possibility of reconstructing, however hypothetically, a "core tradition" beyond the themes and the motifs it may have attracted in the course of transmission.[40]

Here again, the idealism, typical of definitions, threatens to obscure, even misrepresent, the reality. The problem suggests that some attention might be usefully given to the differences between the concerns that motivated oral cultures whose traditions were under exploration, and the interests, assumptions and expectations driving that exploration in predominantly literate cultures. Whatever might be the interests and objectives of a later research, the traditionists (so-called), were probably less preoccupied with passing on *traditum* in pristine purity than with recognizing, through such techniques of interpretation as *traditum* invited and measures that *traditio* allowed what, for the time being, was "their tradition." Nor were such interpretations distinguishable as adjuncts to, glosses on, or modifications of, a carefully preserved and clearly demarcated "core" but were, *in toto*, the tradition as received, which then became *traditum* and, as such, capable

38. See Harrelson, "Emergence of Tradition," 15–17.
39. Ibid., 15–16.
40. Ibid., 18–24.

of further transmission. Indeed, it is debateable whether a "core" could be so immunized from interpretation as to necessitate or permit the distinction. It is unlikely that predominantly oral cultures were either preoccupied with, or fettered by, such questions. Integrated into *traditum*, accretions (so-called), became part of the tradition. Inseparably, they were transmitted and, similarly, they were appropriated as *traditum* for further transmission. It is only in that sense that a tradition could be cumulative and agglomerative and could, at the same time, achieve and retain the vitality that was imbued with social power. It may well engage the interest of later researchers, coming out of a different cultural milieu, which placed high premium on originality, accuracy, authenticity, and consistency, to investigate and isolate, for quite other purposes, evidence of reinterpretation to the end that an unimpaired and unalloyed "core" might emerge; but to assume that such concerns preoccupied the traditionists, or that it was a so-called "core" that they appropriated as "tradition," is to over-idealize, and thus misconstrue, ancient traditions as the process and product of transmission.

The theory raises the further question, viz., whether, in its origin, a tradition could have been so "core" as to be other than a particularly defining stage in the evolution of an earlier tradition or coalescence of traditions. A tradition, by definition, must have been connected in some way with antecedent traditions. Therefore, each *traditum*, however original, must have been a product of *traditio* and, as such, must have also been applicable to special revelations (so-called) which, being historically conditioned, could not have been unprecedented. The so-called "core" of a tradition might therefore be likened to the core of an onion; otherwise the traditio-historical process could be thrown into disarray if each stage of transmission was viewed as revelation and, by definition, a "core."

THE STRENGTH AND WEAKNESS OF THE TRADITIO-HISTORICAL APPROACH

The weakness of the traditio-historical approach is, paradoxically, the flipside of its strength. Its importance for Old Testament study is the dimension of depth it brings, and therefore the value of reaching beyond the analysis of text and its constituent sources to the more basic units of composition in the pre-literary stages of evolution. It thereby also affirms the Old Testament as the product of living, worshipping, pre-literate communities, who appropriated such traditions as they were able to access which, through reinterpretation in the process of transmission, gave new shape, vitality and meaning to their beliefs and practices, even as they were treasured as legacies of their ancestors. By the same token, it recognizes that the literature of the Old Testament originated not in a literary culture as compositions of scribes, who wrote *ex nihilo*, so to speak, or from experiences, with concerns and for purposes that might have been alien or indifferent to those about or for whom they wrote; but the writing stages, important though they undoubtedly were for preservation, authentication, and authorization, were in large measure the final stages and a faithful exercise, consistent with the longer process of growth and development of the traditions in oral transmission. Therefore, textual disparities, dissonances, and discrepancies that surface in the text from time to time, may have been due less to scribal lapses, interference or other deficiencies that beset literary productions, than to the normal and necessary process of integrating formerly unrelated traditions which, in the period of oral transmission, may not have considered posterity or anticipated holy scriptures. The traditio-historical approach, reaching back to the pre-literary stages, may therefore discover more about the text, and the people who were its subject, than was possible for other forms of literary criticism, and textual problems might reach resolution not only by invoking the rules of grammar and syntax or, still less, by pleading stylistic idiosyncrasies, but also by exploring and comparing thought-patterns recoverable from a common socio-cultural environment, contemporary with, and reflecting, the periods of oral transmission.

The traditio-historical approach also assists a more realistic and objective understanding of the emergence of the people of Israel, their beliefs, their way of life and their institutions, and an appreciation of both their continuity with, and identity among, the neighbouring peoples of the ancient Near East; and because language, beliefs, customs and institutions in Israel can be replicated in cultures outside of Israel, later ideological tendencies that informed the shaping of Old Testament literature can more easily be recognized as reflecting less an authentic account of Israel's evolution than later rationalizations and attempts at retrojection during the transitions from the oral to, and in, the writing stages.

It is therefore paradoxical feature of traditio-historical research of Old Testament literature, that although it invests heavily in the oral stages of transmission, its major resource for exploration is the text, in which oral traditions, originally independent, were both coordinated and superseded and, though not completely expunged may have become obscured

THE TRADITIO-HISTORICAL APPROACH

by reinterpretation. Traditio-historical research, beginning with the text, is therefore, of necessity, a disintegrative process that aims at recovery. It holds in abeyance claims to textual originality, unity, and purity. It breaks down in order to retrieve the oral material out of which sub-compositions, their constituent units evolved, how and why the coordination occurred, and the extent to which emerging compositions, at each stage, preserved or altered the traditional material. Where other approaches to Old Testament criticism may have taken for granted, and even defended, the unity of a composition, applauding the creative skill and originality of a literary genius, the traditio-historical task is to probe an amalgamation and so recover, restore and situate the components that existential realities beneath the text might emerge. It opens up, rather than plasters over, the cracks and fissures. It explores, rather than explains, the oddities and the dissonances; and, therefore, it is precisely the dominant figures, the unifying genres, and the over-arching themes that, invariably, are threatened in the research.

Last but not least, a major difficulty with respect to the traditio-historical method is the scarcity of the hard, independent, and corroborating evidence from which assured conclusions might be drawn. Since the oral phases of transmission are inaccessible, apart from the literature that is under scrutiny, conclusions reached can be only tentative which, corroborated by kindred evidence recoverable from the common environment, might reasonably be assumed for Israel. Such limitations notwithstanding, the major contribution of the traditio-historical method in the study of the literature of the Old Testament has been the insistence that, in spite of the positions that have prevailed in the text, the evidence that has been made available suggest that claims for the uniqueness of Israel and its institutions, customs, cultic practices, and beliefs can no longer be taken as self-evident, and therefore dogmatic positions on, and deriving from, the text, for convenient interpretation, or embarrassing features that might be ignored, avoided or rationalized by special pleading, can be clarified by recourse to traditio-historical research beyond the literary stages. Because the Old Testament literature is not only ancient literature but also, and more importantly, the repository of oral traditions coming from cultures of even higher antiquity wherein lay a people's faith, critical investigation might delve deeper into the history of Israel and its religion than the text of the Old Testament intended or expected, to find answers for baffling questions and bring closure to contradictions that must otherwise remain unresolved.

THE NATHAN NARRATIVE IN 2 SAMUEL 7:1-17

2 SAMUEL 7: 1-17 AND THE TRADITIO-HISTORICAL METHOD

When full measure has been taken of the factors involved in a traditio-historical study, it must seem somewhat adventurous to apply the method, at once and with consistency, to more than a limited portion of Old Testament literature. Earlier studies of extensive areas have tended to be diffuse and complicated, and to render the conclusions somewhat obscure. It is also unlikely that all of Old Testament literature is amenable to traditio-historical research. A more realistic approach, therefore, would seem to be a concentration of the study of key passages of limited scope, self-contained, and structurally well rounded, but with ramifications that are nevertheless wide-ranging and far-reaching. Complexities that surface, whether they are intrinsic to the passage or arise from its inclusion in a larger corpus, would indicate traditions that were of enduring importance for the people of Israel in the periods of oral transmission and of redaction in the writing stages. For such an investigation the Nathan narrative (2 Sam. 7:1-17) would seem to be ideally suited.

Its reappearance in the Psalter (Ps 89:19-37) and the Chronicles (1 Chr 17:1-16) bears witness to traditions that did not atrophy on reaching the writing stage but, through the creative interaction between scripture and the persistence of the oral transmission, continued to grow. Whether or not the variations can be thus explained, the basic issue is that were traditions to have atrophied in written literature, parallel versions should be similar, and where deviations obtruded, they should be marginal, minimal and agreeable. It might therefore be concluded that the end of a tradition in Old Testament literature lay less in its appearance as literature than in its canonical finality, and that regardless of subsequent interpretations in later redactions.

Finally, it might be important to note that the objective of the traditio-historical approach is not an alteration of the text with a view to improvement, but its elucidation by as thorough and extensive an exploration of its evolution as possible. Other methods of biblical criticism are taken a stage further. As textual criticism has recognized that the canonical text was not the only text, but that the existence of other ancient variants and alternative versions might throw light on the difficulties that appear in the received text; and as source criticism has shown that neither the text nor the penultimate composition was the original shaping, but sub-compositions might be discerned from closer analyses of the text; and as literary criticism has shown that correct interpretations have rarely been self-evident, and that exegetical difficulties have not always been a problem of language, whether

THE TRADITIO-HISTORICAL APPROACH

the original, in precise translation or in the vernacular, so the traditio-historical method is a salutary reminder that the literature of the Old Testament originated in a culture of illiteracy, and at no stage did the traditions evolve in a historical vacuum, or remain impervious to the impact of social, cultural, or political influences, that it represents neither, on the one hand, the result of automatic transmissions of received material nor, on the other hand, the success of conscientious, dispassionate, and heroic attempts at passing on traditions exactly as received. No: *traditio*, throughout, was a dynamic and creative process involving, at every stage, a hermeneutic imperative which, though historically conditioned, remained consistent with *traditum* and, in its survival, preserved vitality; and it was the freedom that enabled, and the integrity that governed, such a creative undertaking that preserved the traditions of Ancient Israel in the literature of the Old Testament. It therefore remains a salutary consideration that, as the transmission processes in oral communication and written composition entailed reinterpretation at every stage, even so, in the continuing, post-canonical *traditio*, whether in translation, exposition, exhortation, proclamation, or application, whether written or oral, whether in public discourse or private study, the hermeneutical imperative will ensure the perpetuation of the traditions in a revitalization of the Word, provided that neither the interpretations that have prevailed in canon of Old Testament literature, nor the further attempts at reinterpretation, are misconstrued as traditions that were preserved in, or have been restored to, pristine condition.

CHAPTER III

THE ARGUMENT—2 SAMUEL 7:1–17 IN DEUTERONOMY–KINGS

THE EXPOSITION OF THE traditio-historical approach attempted in the preceding chapter invites an exploration of 2 Samuel 7:1–17 at two, probably three, levels: first, as the component of a larger composition that was the outcome of successive stages of redaction, in the course of which it constantly underwent reinterpretation; second, as the repository of diverse traditions of varying genres, which were coordinated and preserved in various settings of oral transmission before attaining narrative coherence in a larger composition.; and a third possibility is of a literary composition, not markedly dissimilar in structure or content from the present narrative, which represented an advanced stage of oral transmission or, as the case might be, a written composition prior to incorporation in a larger literary corpus.

MARTIN NOTH

That such an exploration of Deuteronomy–Kings corpus could not reasonably have avoided a study of the place of 2 Samuel 7:1–17 in it, nor a study of 2 Samuel 7:1–17 have omitted its place in the stages towards canonization, might be taken as axiomatic. For that reason, its place in the Former Prophets, as outlined in the introductory chapter, must raise questions of

2 SAMUEL 7:1–17 IN DEUTERONOMY–KINGS

Martin Noth's hypothesis of a "Deuteronomistic History."[1] Stopping short of an exploration of its canonical status, the hypothesis reduced the interpretative capacity of the corpus and limited the significance of its narrative components. Here, as well as in his later traditio-historical study of the Pentateuch, Noth appears to have given the canonical imperative short shrift.[2] He apparently overlooked the hermeneutical consequences of including categories designated as "Tetrateuch" and "Deuteronomistic History" in the glossary of Old Testament studies and the implications they carried for established categorizations, viz., the Law and the Prophets.

A canonical perspective seems, however, to be unavoidable inasmuch as the final shape of the text, as a literary product, is indicative not of a status arbitrarily conferred, but the completion of a systematic process of transmission. Significantly, Brevard Childs has noted that, by investing the final form of the text with normative status, the canonical approach has encountered its strongest opposition from advocates for traditio-historical criticism for whom depth dimension was defended as the exegetical priority.[3]

The opposition not altogether one-sided seems, however, to be undesirable, unnecessary and unrealistic. Traditio-historical research cannot reasonably avoid the final form of the text, as the only available repository for the traditions and resource for the research, and therefore to settle for a preliminary stage, however promising the prospects or impressive the results, is to run the risk of overlooking the possibility of further stages of evolution, and of a misdirection of the study. Similarly, it is mistaken so to remove the final form of the text into normative isolation as to detach it from the processes that brought it into being. Whatever the advantages, the opposition does not assist an understanding of the history of the biblical traditions, the formation of a canon or the interpretation of the text. The two foci—the canonical and the traditio-historical—are not incompatible but complementary.

Furthermore, it is the earlier canonization of the Prophets that gives 2 Samuel 7:1–17 a traditio-historical edge over the parallel versions that have appeared in other literary settings—the Chronicles (1 Chr 17:1–15) and the Psalter (Ps 89:3–4, 19–37). This highlights an important distinction

---

1. Martin Noth, *The Deuteronomistic History*.

2. Confirmation of this view may be had from Noth's essay, "Re-presentation of Old Testament," 76.

3. See Childs, *Introduction*, 75.

between a still evolving tradition and a tradition that has attained canonical finality. Whereas in the former it is the later changes, and not the earliest forms, that become definitive of a growing tradition, in the latter case the tradition, having attained finality, and recognized as such, must relegate later evidence of *traditio*, if independent by comparison (as in the case of Psalm 89), to an alternative and parallel *traditio*, and if dependent (as in the case of 1 Chronicles 17:1-15), to *midrash*.[4]

Therefore, if it is the canonical status of the text that is decisive for interpretation, and not a preferred stage preceding canonization, the invoking of a "Deuteronomistic History" as if definitive for the interpretation of the Joshua–Kings corpus and, by implication, for a pericope such as 2 Samuel 7:1-17, is a debatable procedure, since both the pre-canonical designation, however insightful, must appear, on the further investigation, to be arbitrary, and its hermeneutical potential inadequate.

A further issue arising from the foregoing observation is the importance of exploring the further developments between a "Deuteronomistic history" (so-called) and the Prophets, i.e. Joshua–Malachi, wherein the *pericope* in 2 Samuel 7:1-17 was finally preserved and, correspondingly, the developments between the same "Deuteronomistic History" (so-called) and the Law i.e. the Pentateuch in which Deuteronomy, the point of departure for the "Deuteronomistic History," was finally located. It therefore should not be assumed that Noth's designation of a "Deuteronomistic History" and the post-canonical the Former Prophets were interchangeable designations, or that the Law, was ever conceived of as "Tetrateuch" without Deuteronomy, or as "Hexateuch" that included Joshua. The distinctions have become the more important in view of the studies proceeding from Noth's hypothesis that have rendered the status of 2 Samuel 7:1-17 in a "Deuteronomistic History" extraordinarily problematic.[5] Noth proposed that the Joshua–Kings corpus was a homogeneous composition, written by a single author in the period of the Babylonian domination. He had assembled a variety of traditional material out of which was composed a historical review of Israel's sojourn in the land of Canaan in order to ex-

---

4. For further discussion of the significance of the Chronicler as evidence of an evolving Old Testament tradition, including his aims, techniques, and results, see Ackroyd, "Chronicler as Exegete," 16–32.

5. Whereas much has been written on both 2 Samuel 7:1-17 and Deuteronomy–Kings separately, not as much has been forthcoming on the place of 2 Samuel 7:1-17 in the composition of Joshua–Kings, or the implications of the composition of Joshua–Kings for the shaping of 2 Samuel 1–17.

plain the catastrophes that had over taken the Hebrew Kingdoms, resulting in political annihilation, mass dislocation and, social degradation.[6] He interpreted these events as YHWH's righteous judgment upon the people of Israel for persistent breaches of covenant law, in spite of repeated warnings by the prophets. Their expulsion from the land and its occupation by aliens confirmed YHWH's rejection of his people, leaving them under a cloud of irrevocable doom.[7]

A striking feature of the composition, Noth noted, was a sequence of orations that punctuated the historical review at significant junctures (Josh 23; Judg 2:11-23; 1 Sam 12; 1 Kgs 8; 2 Kgs 17:7-41). Whether the spokesperson was a notable figure in the composition or the narrator/redactor in a summation and commentary, the passages were all of a similar character and served a similar purpose. The past was reviewed, the future scanned, and, in that perspective, the people were called to recommitment to YHWH in fidelity to the Sinai-Horeb covenant and the observance of the Mosaic law.[8] In that perspective Deuteronomy might have been included as archetypal. Spoken by Moses on the eve of entry into the Promised Land, a history of unfaithfulness in the wilderness was recalled (Deut 1:1-5; 20-46; 9:6-29; 11:5-6; 32:15-28), temptations to apostasy in the new land were envisaged (Deut. 4:25-26; 6:10-17; 7:1-6; 8; 18:9-14), and in that context the people were called to covenant-renewal (Deut 29) and a more conscientious observance of the Mosaic law (Deut 30:11-20).

Noth's study, though hailed as a significant breakthrough, was not received without criticism. Even as von Rad, endorsed the "Deuteronomistic" designation, and commended Noth for having closed a gap in the study of the Old Testament,[9] he recognized some of its more obvious limitations, especially its failure to take full measure of the treatment of David and the Davidic monarchy in Samuel-Kings in which David was commemorated as an object of divine favor and model of kingly rule for his successors.[10]

Von Rad, for his part, was able to extrapolate from the Joshua-Kings corpus a prophecy-and-fulfillment schema which demonstrated the vitality of the word of God once spoken, and its power to attain fulfillment in

---

6. See Noth, *Pentateuchal Traditions*, 4-11.
7. See Noth, *Deuteronomistic History*, 98-99.
8. Ibid., 5-6.
9. See von Rad, *Studies in Deuteronomy*, 74.
10. Ibid., 84-88.

THE NATHAN NARRATIVE IN 2 SAMUEL 7:1-17

history (Josh 21:45; 23:14; 1 Kgs 8:56; 2 Kgs 10:10; cf. Deut 32:46–47).[11] Heading the schema was YHWH's promise to establish David's family as a ruling house indefinitely and raise up a son and heir who would build a sanctuary for YHWH (2 Sam 7:12–13). One part of the prophecy was fulfilled in the accession of Solomon and his construction of the temple at Jerusalem (1 Kgs 8:20); but the other part was frustrated by the overthrow of the monarchy in the sixth century BCE. However, von Rad interpreted the Jehoiachin pericope (2 Kgs 25:27–30) as a possible pointer to fulfillment.[12] Contrary to Noth's negative evaluation, he saw in Jehoiachin's release and rehabilitation a glimmer of the hope adumbrated in the Nathan narrative (2 Sam 7:11b–16), concerning which he argued that it exhibited a traditional element which, though un-Deuteronomic, reflected a cycle of messianic conceptions.[13]

Although 2 Samuel 7 seemed formally to meet the criteria Noth applied for the identification of the orations, its exclusion from his sequence of orations is understandable. Its optimism did not harmonize with the exilic dating he proposed. Noth also questioned its Deuteronomic character. He viewed the disapproval of a sanctuary (vv. 5–7) and the high valuation placed on the Davidic monarchy (vv. 11b–16) as incompatible with the Deuteronomic spirit. He adopted, instead, Rost's analysis in which verses 1–7, 11b, 16, 18–21, and 25–29 were reckoned to have been an original text, to which the other verses in 8–17, were added to create the pre-Deuteronomic text.[14] The Deuteronomists then made two additions—the insertion of verse 13a, in which the designation of a builder altered the prohibition (vv. 1–7) to an injunction for a postponement, and verses 22–24, drawn from the pre-Deuteronomic text.

Noth's reasons for his exclusion of 2 Samuel 7 from the sequence of orations provoke two responses. Firstly, without verse 13a, which by Noth's own reckoning was a Deuteronomic addition to a pre-existent text,[15] a *prima facie* interpretation of verses 1–7 (MT) as anti-temple does not exist. Secondly, the alteration of a pre-Deuteronomic text, by the insertion of a verse seems inexplicable unless it was already amenable to Deuteronomic

---

11. Ibid., 78–81.
12. Ibid., 90–91.
13. Ibid., 86.
14. See Noth, *Deuteronomistic History*, 55.
15. Ibid., 55.

interpretation. Both considerations should therefore have argued for, rather than against, a Deuteronomic pedigree for 2 Samuel 7:1–17.

This also raises the more general criticism of Noth's analysis, viz., the omission of a discussion on the narrative potential of what he reckoned to be the traditional material. Much as such a discussion might have impaired his case for a single authorship, it is not possible to evaluate the narrative potential of material assembled for the composition of Joshua–Kings as incoherent, or to credit its compositional profile wholly to a Deuteronomic composition. In particular, it is difficult to dispute the narrative character and content of the David epic in Samuel, relatively free though it might be of Deuteronomic ideology, idioms, nuances, and clichés. In sum, the hypothesis of a single author and the attempt at presenting a monochrome portraiture of Joshua–Kings, by avoiding compositions in it that were incompatible, seems to have been a somewhat arbitrary procedure that rendered the place of a prominent composition like 2 Samuel 7 unmanageable. Also Hans Walter Wolff, commenting on Noth's hypothesis, wondered why an Israelite of the sixth century B.C. would have reached for his pen if all he intended was an explanation of the end of Israel's history as the righteous judgment of God.[16]

R.A.CARLSON

An early attempt at presenting 2 Samuel 7 as a component of the Deuteronomy–Kings corpus, following Noth's important study, was a monograph by R.A. Carlson. The author's ability to identify linkages between Samuel and the books in the Deuteronomic corpus preceding Samuel, viz., Judges, Joshua and Deuteronomy, must be reckoned as its chief merit for, in so doing, he went some way in answering von Rad's denial of the Deuteronomic character of Samuel-books and Noth's exclusion of 2 Samuel 7 as "un-Deuteronomic."

Carlson was able to highlight in 2 Samuel 7 theological emphases adumbrated in Deuteronomy that were also critical for the interpretation of Joshua and Judges. Most significant among them was the theme of "rest"—מנוחה—promised by YHWH (Deut 3:20; 12:9–10; 25:17–19), which was fulfilled initially in the settlement of the tribes under the leadership of Joshua (Josh 22:1–2; 23:1; cf. Deut 2:30—3:20), decisively in David's victories over the enemies of Israel (2 Sam 7:1; cf. 1 Sam 30:1–20; 2 Sam

---

16. See Wolff, "Kerygma of Deuteronomic Historical Word," 85.

THE NATHAN NARRATIVE IN 2 SAMUEL 7:1-17

5:17–25; 8:12; cf. Deut 25:17–19), and finally and symbolically in Solomon's building of the temple in Jerusalem (1 Kgs 5:16–19 (MT); 8:16–21; cf. Deut 12:9–10).[17] Allied to the theme of "rest"—מנוחה—were contrasting motifs, "sat/wandered"—ישב/התהלך—, "house/tent"—בית/אהל—that highlighted the "election"—בחר—ideology and marked the Davidic-Solomonic period as the high point of the Israelite occupation, crowned by the building of a "house" for YHWH (2 Sam 7:1–7, 13a; cf. Deut 12: 10-11; 1 Sam 17:54; 26:19; 2 Sam 5:6–11; 6:17; 1 Kgs 6–8).[18]

Above all, he observed in the theme of "blessing and cursing" a prominent feature of Deuteronomy and the Deuteronomic orations (Deut 11:1–32; 28–30, 32:1–43; Josh 23; Judg 2:11–23; 1 Sam 12), which also characterized the Samuel account of David's career as an early period of "blessing" marked by good fortune, success and a steady rise to greatness (1 Sam 16—2 Sam 9), followed by a period of "curse" which was marked by a dysfunctional and deeply troubled family, racked with internal dissension, which deteriorated to a popular revolt that forced David to flee the capital and submit to the rage and insults of disenchanted subjects (2 Sam 13–20). The cause of these reverses was David's infringement of the Deuteronomic law, which provoked prophetic indictment (2 Sam 11–12 cf. Deut 5:17–18, 21; 22:22). In all these particulars, Carlson was able to discern the Deuteronomic influence in the Samuel account of David's career and especially in 2 Samuel 7:1–17, the introductory dialogue of which he interpreted as the realization of the Deuteronomic expectation of the defeat of Israel's immediate enemies and the appointed time for the building of the chosen sanctuary (2 Sam 7:1–3; cf. Deut 12:10–11; 25:19).[19]

Notwithstanding Carlson's adroitness in identifying the linkages, it is not clear from his approach that the case for 2 Samuel 7 as a Deuteronomic composition, and an integral component of a Deuteronomy–Kings corpus, has been made, since he omitted from the examination of the narrative a discussion on the merits of the non-Deuteronomic features; nor is a plethora of characteristic idioms and clichés, by themselves, decisive, unless a Deuteronomic monopoly on, or claim to, the vocabulary can be established.[20] It might, however, be noted that the Deuteronomic character

---

17. See Carlson, *David, the Chosen King*, 101–4.

18. Ibid., 99–100.

19. Ibid., 106.

20. Short of the demonstration of a Deuteronomic redaction of the Psalter, themes cited by Carlson might be found in Old Testament literature outside the Deuteronomic

of 2 Samuel 7 was not the sole or primary purpose of the study, which was an exploration of the whole of the David epic in Samuel. Its limitations with respect to a comprehensive analysis of 2 Samuel 7 might therefore be more readily appreciated.

DENNIS J. MCCARTHY

Dennis McCarthy's essay on 2 Samuel 7, may be viewed as partly complementary to, and partly a corrective of, Carlson's analysis, in the sense that its purpose was to establish the chapter as, structurally, an integral component of Deuteronomy–Kings. Following the lead of Noth in the identification of a sequence of orations he, unlike Noth, included 2 Samuel 7 in his sequence, by devising a more elaborate schema.[21] However, not only was his basis for selection of the orations largely subjective[22] and, as Nelson has noted, incorrect in certain particulars[23] but, more importantly, in his schema, Deuteronomy was virtually marginalized in the sense that it proved to be as viable without Deuteronomy as with it.[24] A curious dilemma has thus been presented by the place of the Nathan narrative (2 Sam 7:1-17) as part of a Deuteronomic composition, in the sense that, whereas an insistence of the importance of Deuteronomy for the shaping of the Former Prophets has tended to render the place of 2 Samuel 7 problematic, the attempt to entrench 2 Samuel 7 structurally, as an integral component of a Deuteronomic History has tended to a marginalization of Deuteronomy.

FRANK MOORE CROSS JR.

The Old Testament scholar, post-Noth, whose contribution to an elucidation of Samuel–Kings has been the most influential is Frank Moore Cross

---

corpus or its sphere of influence, e.g., Pss 1, 77, 78, 80, 95, 103, 105–107, 114, 135–136.

21. See McCarthy, "II Samuel 7," 137.

22. Such a schema, it would appear, required a literary-critical analysis, (eschewed by McCarthy, ibid., 131), for the establishing of the relationship of each passage selected to the rest of the corpus.

23. See Nelson, *Double Redaction*, 105–6.

24. McCarthy's only reference to Deuteronomy in the schema was Deuteronomy 31, which referred to the conquest (not the distribution) of the land. Furthermore, Moses did not command the conquest, but promised that YHWH would give the land to them. The choice of Deuteronomy 31 suggests that nothing more apposite was available in Deuteronomy for support of the schema he proposed.

Jr., who proposed a double rather than a single redaction, viz., a preexilic or Josianic redaction and an updating and revision, following the overthrow of the Davidic monarchy and the fall of the Southern Kingdom, i.e., an exilic redaction.[25]

Cross identified a first edition of the "Deuteronomistic History" which he labeled "Dtr1."[26] Written from the perspective of legitimacy, two contrasting themes were set forth, viz., the sin of Jeroboam ben Nebat, whose failure to emulate the faithfulness of David, was compounded by the crime in his establishment of a counter cultus, with idolatrous rites at Bethel and Dan, in schismatic alienation from the temple cultus at Jerusalem, and which persisted throughout the regimes that followed him;[27] and, in contradistinction, the grace resting on the Judaean monarchy because of YHWH's commitment to David, his faithful servant, and to Jerusalem, his chosen city.[28]

The second theme was climaxed in the Josianic reformation, which Cross interpreted as an attempt at the restoration of the Davidic kingdom by an abolition of the counter-cultus established at Bethel by Jeroboam and a centralization of the cult in Jerusalem according to the ancient law of the sanctuary (Deut. 12:9–14).[29] Such hopes were dashed by the tragic death of Josiah at Megiddo in 609 BCE and the deportation of Jehoahaz, the chosen successor. With the appointment of Eliakim by Pharaoh Necho as the vassal-ruler, a reaction set in (2 Kgs 23:29–35), the ideological fervor for a reformation waned, the apostasies revived and the decline reached its nadir in the Chaldean invasion and occupation of 597 BCE. It was this Deuteronomistic history that was overwritten by an exilic editor (Dtr2), in the light of the catastrophes, to produce a document for the edification of the exiles.[30]

The impact of Cross's analysis might be measured by the number of studies for which it has provided the essential perspective. While reference might still have been made to Noth's seminal work, it was no longer possible to discuss it without placing Cross's modifications alongside and noting the differences. Indeed, Richard Nelson, concluding an elaborate study that confirmed for him the validity of Cross's analysis, asserted that, whatever

25. See Cross, *Canaanite Myth*, 285–89.
26. Ibid., 278–85.
27. Ibid., 279–81.
28. Ibid., 281–85.
29. Ibid., 283–84.
30. Ibid., 285–89.

course future studies on the Deuteronomistic history might take, a double redaction would prevail as the best explanation of all the data.[31]

Cross' analysis appears, however, to have raised about as many questions as it has attempted to answer:

1. Having dissented from Noth's analysis, Cross attached the designation "Deuteronomistic" to the Josianic redaction (his Dtr1),[32] without addressing its essentially Deuteronomistic character and the relationship of its main projection, viz., the ideology of the Davidic monarchy, to the designation.

2. As Noth seems to have avoided the significance of narrative compositions in the traditional material, so Cross seems to have omitted a discussion of the compositional potential of the traditional material that went into the making of his Dtr1 and their implications for the redaction.[33]

3. In accentuating the ideological contrasts between the Davidic monarchy and the regimes of the Northern Kingdom in Kings, Cross may have underestimated the evidence for commonality and its implications for a Deuteronomic redaction.[34]

4. Cross's analyses of 2 Samuel 7 and the royal ideologies in Kings, having been undertaken separately, may have resulted in an over-interpretation of what might have appeared to be affinity. The case for the removal of the Manasseh pericope to an exilic retrojection is unconvincing, there being little ground save its negative contribution to the attempt at the presentation of a consistently favorable portraiture of the Davidic monarchy in an original redaction, his Dtr1.[35]

---

31. See Nelson, *Double Redaction*, 128.

32. See Cross, *Canaanite Myth*, 278.

33. This observation is strengthened by the spate of more recent critical studies relating to preexilic compositions (Kings) that have been proposed as pre-Josianic, some of which are to be given passing comment later in this chapter.

34. There was, for example, the promise to Jeroboam, the arch-secessionist, of a "house" as sure as David's (1 Kgs 11:38), which needed to be an unconditional promise such as was preserved in the Nathan narrative (2 Sam 7:11-16). Furthermore, doing/not doing right in YHWH's sight seems to have been based on a Deuteronomic, rather than a Davidic, standard, applicable to all rulers, David included (cf. Deut 12:8; 17:20; 1 Kgs.11:38; 15:5, 11).

35. It is difficult to interpret the total annihilation envisaged in 2 Kings 21:12-14, even if exaggeration, as *vaticinium ex eventu* (cf. 2 Kgs 25:25-26). More than likely, it

5. No study or discussion on Samuel–Kings can be deemed satisfactory, which has left unresolved the over-arching tension between the guarantees enshrined in 2 Samuel 7:11b–16 and the extinction of the monarchy in the death-report on Jehoiachin at the conclusion (2 Kgs 25:27–30).

BRIAN PECKHAM

An unusual approach to the composition of Deuteronomy–Kings is that of Brian Peckham. Its peculiar merit is that it is the first attempt, since the eclipse of the Documentary hypothesis, at including the sources of the Pentateuch other than Deuteronomy in a study of the composition of the Former Prophets. He reckoned Noth's basic mistake to be his devaluation of the other Pentateuchal sources, viz., J, E, and P, as fragmentary and discontinuous.[36] He argued for J, however, as a narrative of six episodes, to which Dtr1 (of Cross's definition) was attached as a sequel.[37] This was to become the basic source of Dtr2. It was then re-written by P, following which E was added. Thus presented, a linkage was forged between Noth's Tetrateuch, i.e., Genesis–Numbers and the Deuteronomy–Kings.[38] It also explained the presence of Pentateuchal sources, other than Deuteronomy, in the Joshua–Kings corpus, and offered alternative suggestions for the redactional stages leading to the formation of both the Pentateuch and the Former Prophets.

It is strange, however, that an analysis that gave promise of a significant departure should have omitted, from all of the redactional stages in the composition of Joshua–Kings, an evaluation of the place and significance of 2 Samuel 7, and of 2 Kgs 25:27–30) as the conclusion. Although he affirmed that Dtr1 wrote the history of Israel from the perspective of Judah and David,[39] his citing of Hezekiah's reign as the conclusion, as though self-evident, seems to have allowed the discussion of the compositional char-

---

reflects the contemporary mood of apprehension and despair following the death of Josiah, the deportation of Jehoahaz, his approved successor, and the rapid decline of the regime, represented by Jehoiakim, a pathetic vassal-ruler, squeezed between Pharaoh Necho, his overlord for the time being, and Nebuchadnezzar the neo-Babylonian emperor on his westward march towards Egypt *via* Judah.

36. See Peckham, *Composition of Deuteronomistic History*, 3.
37. Ibid., 3–7.
38. Ibid., 1–2.
39. Ibid., 8.

2 SAMUEL 7:1–17 IN DEUTERONOMY–KINGS

acter of J+Dtr1 to avoid the significance of both 2 Samuel 7 and 2 Kings 25:27–30, and of either of them for the other.

A further problem may have been due to an over-reliance on assumptions that fell short of demonstration. If, as he suggested, Dtr1 was a sequel to J,[40] how integral was the connection? What precisely were the connection and the contribution of J to Dtr1 and why were they so weak and so minimal as to have permitted the observation that Dtr1 narrated a history "from the last days of Moses?" Surely, as sequel, the earlier and substantive portion of the history, i.e., the J component in Genesis–Numbers should have had such an impact on the whole composition as to have indicated, even in outline, the compositional connection and continuity of Dtr1 with J that linked the period of Moses with the reign of Josiah. A similar observation might be made of the Dtr2 history, which Peckham evaluated as " . . . a comprehensive and systematic revision of the sources."[41] In that case, with a knowledge of, and considering the nature, context and purpose of Dtr2, it is difficult to understand how certain portions of Genesis–Numbers, e.g. the Balaam oracles (Num 22–24) or of Deuteronomy–Kings, e.g., the Song of Hannah (1 Sam 2:1–10) or David's Last Words (2 Sam 23:1–7), survived such a revision so obviously.

Nor did his analysis answer the questions raised by the Jehoiachin pericope as the conclusion of the historical work. Peckham's study has therefore fallen under the same stricture that Wolff leveled against Noth's analysis, and by implication Cross'. In attempting to relate the other Pentateuchal sources to Deuteronomy–Kings, Peckham's exploration was commendable;[42] but it appears that his commitment to the perspective of a "Deuteronomistic History," as expounded by Cross, proved to be an obstacle that he was not able to surmount.

---

40. Ibid., 7.

41. Ibid., 21.

42. Such an analysis has not been attempted since the eclipse by Martin Noth's hypothesis in *Uberlieferungsgeschichtliche Studien I* in 1943, of the application of the Documentary Hypothesis to Joshua–Kings, by which time Karl Budde had undertaken a method of dividing the pre-Deuteronomic content of Joshua–Kings between J and E in a way that had already stirred considerable interest. See Eissfeldt, *Introduction*. 244.

THE NATHAN NARRATIVE IN 2 SAMUEL 7:1-17

ANTONY F. CAMPBELL

Another study bearing directly on the place of 2 Samuel 7 in the redactional history of Joshua–Kings is that of Antony Campbell, who claims to have discovered a pre-Deuteronomic source that he labeled a "Prophetic Record,"[43] and in which was traced a history of prophetic activity in Israel from the anointing of the first two kings of Israel (1 Sam 10:1; 16:1–13) to the anointing of Jehu as king of Israel (2 Kgs 9:1—10:28).[44]

In it he identified narrative complexes such as the story of David's rise (1 Sam 16—2 Sam. 5),[45] the Nathan narrative (2 Sam.7),[46] the succession narrative (2 Sam 11–20: 1 Kgs 1–2)[47] and other narratives in Kings, which traced the causes, course and consequences of the withdrawal of the Northern tribes from allegiance to the Davidic monarchy (1 Kgs 3–12), the increasing activity, mounting tempo and the differentiation in the prophetic movement (1 Kgs 13–16; 22), and the tensions between the YHWH prophets and successive regimes of the Northern Kingdom (1 Kgs 17–19; 21), which finally escalated in the military revolt under the leadership of Jehu, and by instigation of the prophet Elisha, which resulted in a liquidation of the Omri-dynasty and the gruesome obliteration of Tyrian Baalism (2 Kgs 9–10).[48]

The basic validity of Campbell's investigation will be readily conceded. The prophetic characterization of Joshua–Kings has been recognized from as early as the formation of the Hebrew canon when that collection was combined with the prophetic collection that followed, viz., Isaiah–Malachi, and was designated the Prophets. Artur Weiser offered an explanation of the canonical designation in the common belief the authors were prophets.[49] Whereas von Rad extrapolated a prophecy-fulfillment schema in Joshua–Kings,[50] Ernest Nicholson has argued that the redactors of the Deuteronomic History were prophets.[51]

---

43. See Campbell, *Of Prophets and Kings*, 1.
44. Ibid., 17–41.
45. Ibid., 70–71.
46. Ibid., 72–81.
47. Ibid., 82–84.
48. Ibid., 85–101.
49. See Weiser, *Introduction to Old Testament*, 145.
50. See Von Rad, *Studies in Deuteronomy*, 78–81.
51. See Nicholson, *Deuteronomy and Tradition*, 113–16.

2 SAMUEL 7:1–17 IN DEUTERONOMY–KINGS

Furthermore, the historical emergence of a prophetic movement and a monarchy in Israel concurrently was hardly a coincidence. Both institutions evolved from a pattern of charismatic leadership represented by the Judges, of which their divergence might be viewed as a bifurcation.[52] Consequently prophet and king continued in a symbiotic relationship of tension and dependence. As monarchical power consolidated in absolutism, so the prophets either shrank to subservience, service and compliance or reacted in opposition.[53] In that sense, the history of the monarchy, especially in the Northern Kingdom, will not be adequately represented unless the witness of the prophetic movement is included, nor will the prophetic movement in Israel be properly understood without some evaluation of the nature and extent of their political involvement.

It seems, however, that in attempting a comprehensive characterization, Campbell may have been less than precise in defining the extent and limits of the prophetic involvement in the passages so identified. He seems to have claimed for prophetic authorship or redaction narratives in which a prophet happened to be included, overlooking the possibility, noted by Steven McKenzie, that writers, other than prophets, could as easily have written about prophets as prophets could about other persons.[54]

Consequently, a further limitation on Campbell's hypothesis is a noticeable unevenness of prophetic contribution in the narratives so identified. Samuel, the first prophet, seems to have filled a prominent and probably indispensable role in the inauguration of the monarchy in Israel—the appointment and rejection of Saul (1 Sam 8–15; 28) and the designation of David (1 Sam 16:1–13a)—and, towards the end, it was the prophetic pronouncement of Elijah that legitimized, and the anointing of Elisha that precipitated, the Jehu-revolution (1 Kgs 17–18; 19; 21–22; 2 Kgs 9–10). To a lesser extent a similar case might be made for the involvement of Ahijah of Shiloh in the encouragement of the secession and the appointment and, afterwards the overthrow of Jeroboam ben Nebat and elevation of Baasha (1 Kgs 11:26–38; 14:7–11, 14–16), and for the prophet, Jehu ben Hanani, in the removal of Baasha (1 Kgs 16:1–4). Still less can the claim be made,

---

52. Bentzen, in *King and Messiah*, 44–45, points to the Sumerian LU GAL, the first man whose office combined the functions of king, prophet and priest. The combination is apparent in the leadership of Moses who was prophet (Num 12:5–8; Deut 18:15–22), priest (Exod 2:1–10) and leader and judge (Exod 18:13–26). Samuel, also combined the offices of prophet (1 Sam 3, 9–10), judge (1 Sam 7:15–17), and priest (1 Sam 13:6–13).

53. Nathan exemplified both tendencies (2 Sam. 7:1–3; 12:1–7).

54. See McKenzie, *Trouble with Kings*, 14.

THE NATHAN NARRATIVE IN 2 SAMUEL 7:1-17

as Campbell has attempted, for the Story of David's Rise (1 Sam 16–2 Sam 5) from which Samuel, having anointed him as Saul's replacement, retired without the naming of a successor (1 Sam 16:1–13; 19:18–22; 25:1).

With respect to Campbell's analysis and interpretation of 2 Samuel 7:1–17,[55] it is only fair to observe that the uniqueness and complexity of the pericope must render hazardous any attempt at a precise categorization. Unlike other prophetic narratives, the prophet in 2 Samuel 7:1–17, ironically, is distinguished for his reticence. His only reported utterance (v. 3)—an ambiguous acquiescence—was repudiated in the ensuing revelation (vv. 4–7, 13), throughout which he remained the passive recipient, and the communication of which was omitted, except for a later editorial note (v. 17; cp. 2 Kgs 9:1–10).[56] Therefore, to label such an account as prophetic, because one of the leading characters happened to be so identified, seems to be an over-stretching of the definition.

The larger complex of the succession narrative (2 Sam 9–20; 1 Kgs 1–2) also presents a difficulty for the prophetic characterization of Nathan. Generally, his role appears to be that of a court-functionary, who was committed to protecting the interests of a preferred heir-apparent (2 Sam 7:12–13; cf. 12:24–25; 1 Kgs 1:11–25). Typically, the YHWH prophet was less involved in political in-fighting, than in fomenting regime-change as the situations seemed to warrant (1 Sam 15:28; 16:1–3; 1 Kgs 11:29–39; 14:5–11; 15:1–4; 19:16; 21:19–24; 2 Kgs 9:1–13). Apart, therefore, from Nathan's confrontation with David in the matter of Uriah, the Hittite (2 Sam 12:1–15; cf. 1 Kgs 15:4)—in which, significantly, his prophetic office was not identified—the narratives about Nathan, including the narrative in 2 Samuel 7:1-17 depict more strikingly a political activist involved in a succession-struggle[57] than the detachment that normally distinguished the YHWH prophets.

Campbell also entered a claim that the promise to David of lasting rule was made by the prophet Nathan (2 Sam. 7:11b, 16), thus qualifying the narrative for inclusion in the "Prophetic Record."[58] Such an interpretation is, however, by no means self-evident. On examination, the gravamen

---

55. See Campbell, *Of Prophets and Kings*, 73–81.

56. Generally and typically the content of the revelation is given in the narrative not at the point of reception but of delivery. In the Nathan narrative (2 Sam 7:17) it is the redactor who has certified the delivery.

57. Ishida, "Solomon's Succession," 177, portrayed Nathan in similar terms, describing him as the ideologue of Solomon's party.

58. See Campbell, *Of Prophets and Kings*, 79.

of verses 5–7 seems, in part, to be a discrepancy between Nathan's personal acquiescence (v. 3) and the will of YHWH, communicated to him (vv. 4–16), which virtually vetoed the plan as a Davidic initiative.[59] It is a similar distinction that underlies the textual problems that bristle at verse 11b, where the identity of the benefactor seemed to be so crucial that the prophet was distanced from the promise, the messenger from the message and the benefactor's name, YHWH, should be repeated.[60]

Campbell also endorsed the hypothesis that 2 Samuel 7:6–7a was an added statement in explanation of a prohibition, interrogatively couched, which was implied in verses 2 Samuel 7:5, 7b.[61] Such an argument is questionable for the following reasons:

1. It is not an unusual feature of Hebrew rhetoric that, in the course of altercation, interrogatives should precede, enclose or follow explanatory or supporting statements not, however, interrogatively couched (cf. Gen 31:26–30, 36–42; Judg 17:23–24; 2 Sam 3:33–34; 19:11–13; Job 38:4–18; Is. 40:12–25; Amos 3:3–8).[62]

2. If, indeed, the statement, though explanatory in intent, was rhetorically disruptive, the disruption might have been overcome by an explanation also interrogatively couched, and thereby improve the rhetorical effect (cf. Num 11:11–13a). This suggests that the explanatory statement may have represented the traditional material rather than a later insertion.

3. It is also significant that the verses, which Campbell deemed to be an insertion, were precisely those that elucidated the import of the response in verses 5 and 7, and whose removal would make the

---

59. Notice especially the rhetoric of repetition of the imperative לך, first in Nathan's diplomatic encouragement of the king (v. 3), and later in YHWH's repudiation of the plan (v. 5).

60. Had the narrative maintained its logical course in reported speech, and freed from the need to clarify the identity of the giver, verse 11b might have read ". . .. I will make (build) you a house" (cf. v. 27)—a reading that would then have misidentified the prophet as the giver.

61. Ibid., 75.

62. But see Campbell, *Ark Narrative* 213–9, an earlier study, in which he interpreted the narrative, in its earlier setting, as marking a "revolution of the epochs" in the rejection of the old Israel of the Judges, signified by the abandonment of the Shiloh sanctuary, and the celebration of the new Israel of Davidic monarchical rule, in the election of Jerusalem as the new cult center. In such a case, the reference to the "judges" (2 Sam. 7:7) should, logically, be irrelevant.

reference to the "judges" in verse 7 serve as an explanation, and, as a consequence, leave the interpretation of verses 5 and 7b open to either a prohibition or commission. Far from being disruptive, therefore, verses 6–7a seems to have been decisive for interpretation.

Last, but not least, Campbell's hypothesis has raised the broader question of the boundaries. The dichotomy he inferred from the composition of the Deuteronomy–Kings corpus, between the prophetic word, as promoted in the prophetic record, and the Deuteronomic law, as expounded in the Deuteronomic history,[63] raises a question as to whether it can be supported by the evidence, or their combination be satisfactorily accounted for in the Josianic redaction, as Campbell seems to suggest. In Deuteronomic law may be found clear definitions of such Israelite institutions as kingship (Deut 17:14–20) and equally clear criteria for an authentication of prophecies (Deut 13:1–5; 18:15–22), both of which influenced the shaping of a Deuteronomic corpus, but were not limited to the "Prophetic Record" as identified by Campbell. On the other hand, while there is, throughout the corpus references to the Mosaic law they are, apart from the Book of Deuteronomy, more a general insistence on its preeminence and its determinative role for the people of Israel than specific prescriptions for specific situations.

Also, Walther Zimmerli has noted the commitment of the eighth century prophets to the Mosaic law, and the influence of the Sinai-Horeb covenant tradition on the activities of the earlier prophets mentioned in the Joshua–Kings corpus.[64] Whether the suggestion of a connection of the prophetic movement in Israel with the Mosaic tradition was of Deuteronomic origin or a Deuteronomic adoption of an already existing tradition, in neither case can the differentiation that Campbell attempted be sustained. Furthermore, it might be noted that neither the sequence of prophetic orations as identified by Noth, nor the prophecy-fulfillment schema as extrapolated by von Rad, was confined within the boundaries of the prophetic record delineated by Campbell, viz., the birth of Samuel (1 Sam 1–3; 9), and the Jehu-revolution (1 Kgs 19:15–17; 2 Kgs 10:28). The question raised by Campbell's investigation, therefore, is whether, from the evidence he gathered, combined with the earlier suggestions of Noth and von Rad, a more plausible case might have been made for a Deuteronomic composition within

---

63. Ibid., 112.
64. See Zimmerli, *Law and Prophets*, 62–65.

2 SAMUEL 7:1–17 IN DEUTERONOMY–KINGS

a Josianic redaction, which was more extensively Mosaic and consistently prophetic than the Document he identified.

IAIN W. PROVAN

In a penetrating analysis of the composition of the latter part of the Former Prophets, i.e., the Samuel–Kings corpus, Iain Provan has called attention to the following areas:

The במות theme
  The David theme with sub-themes of:
  David as a comparative figure
  David as a promissory figure

Because it is the David theme that bears more directly on a study of 2 Samuel 7, it is in that connection primarily that his contribution will be assessed;[65] and because the two sub-themes, as presented, appear to corroborate the conclusions he reached with respect to the composition, some attention will first be given to his defense of the conclusions he reached on David as a comparative figure.

Provan argued that, in the regnal formulae introducing the reigns in the earlier portions of Kings, and culminating in the account of the reign of Hezekiah, there were references to David's faithfulness as critical for the stability of the rule of his successors and which, thereafter, diminished towards the ending of the corpus. This, combined with other pointers, such as the death of Sennacherib in 681 BCE, and referred to in the account of Hezekiah's reign, suggested to him a dual redaction, viz., a preexilic edition and a later exilic redaction that resulted from the downfall of the monarchy.

Provan also cited a number of passages in Kings to show how YHWH's promise of sustained rule for the monarchy was conditional on the ruler's faithful adherence to the Mosaic law (1 Kgs 2:4; 8:25; 9:4–5).[66] However, alongside the conditional promises were other passages in which promises of sustained rule were predicated on YHWH's special regard for David to the end that dominion—ניר—might be preserved in Jerusalem for the monarchy (1 Kgs 11:36; 15:4–5; 2 Kgs 8:19),[67] as well as YHWH's protec-

---

65. See Provan, *Hezekiah and Books of Kings*, 94–98, 100–113, 117–31.
66. Ibid., 100–108.
67. Ibid., 94–98.

tion of Jerusalem for David's sake (2 Kgs 19:34; 20:6)[68]. The latter group passages also suggested a preexilic edition, inasmuch as it also reflected a period when the monarchy was thought to be relatively secure. This was followed by a later exilic redaction, with promises of a conditional nature that were designed to explain the fall of the monarchy.

Three issues arise from the evidence presented by Provan for the delineation of the character of David in Kings as a comparative figure.

There is nothing in the account of David's reign, or in later reflection, to authenticate his faithfulness in terms that could be cited as a basis for comparison.

The paucity and formulaic inconsistency of the references, and especially those introducing the reigns from Jehoshaphat to Ahaz, suggest that such a comparison might not have been the intention.

Throughout Kings, doing "right" (or "evil") in YHWH's sight referred more consistently to Deuteronomic stipulations (cf. Deut 12:8-9, 28; 31:29; Judg 2:11-13; 3:7, 12; 4:1; 6:1; 10:6; 13:1; 17:6; 21:25) than to exemplary features that may have distinguished David's rule. This suggests that such tendencies to an idealization of David, far from being basic to an early redaction, were more likely later insertions for another purpose.

A pertinent issue arising from the classification of the references pointing to David as a promissory figure is which, if any, of the references derived from, or was in any way connected with, the promises made in the Nathan narrative (2 Sam 7:11b-16). In the one group of references in which David appears as a promissory figure, it is implied in the case of Abijah's infidelity (1 Kgs 15:4-5) and stated in reflecting on Jehoram's apostasy (2 Kgs 8:19) that YHWH took no action against the king because he had promised ניר, dominion, to David.[69] In the other group promises of continuing rule were conditional upon the obedience of Solomon and his successors (1 Kgs 2:4; 8:25; 9:4-5).[70]

In his discussion of the relationship of the passages to 2 Samuel 7:1-17, Provan dissented from Richard Nelson's claim that the phrase כסא־ישראל —"the throne of Israel"—in the conditional passages (1 Kgs 2:2-4; 8:25; 9:4-5) pertained exclusively to the throne of the Northern Kingdom, implying that the conditional promises applied to Davidic rule over Northern Israel only, and therefore the punishment threatened in

---

68. Ibid., 117.
69. Ibid., 94.
70. Ibid., 106-111.

2 SAMUEL 7:1–17 IN DEUTERONOMY-KINGS

the Nathan narrative (2 Sam 7:14), alluded specifically to the secession,[71] though the promise made in the Nathan narrative was not recorded elsewhere in the Deuteronomic History.[72]

Notwithstanding his dissent, Provan took note of a possible connection between the promise in 2 Samuel 7:13b, and one of the conditional passages, viz., 1 Kings 9:4–9, in the recurrence of a phrase, כסא ממלכתו—the throne of his kingdom—(v. 5a), which also featured in the Deuteronomic law concerning kingship (Deut 17:18), but nowhere else in Deuteronomic literature, and which, in his judgment, suggested a reinterpretation, in 1 Kings 9:4–5, of the promise concerning the seed of David in 2 Samuel 7:12-13, hence the common phrase; but which, unlike the promise to Solomon in 1 Kings 9:4–9, was of an unconditional nature that would not be threatened by misdemeanors in David's successors.[73]

Even so, such an explanation does not suffice, since it is unlikely that the mere recurrence of a phrase could, without the corroborating evidence, have been the result of an attempt at a reinterpretation of what was explicitly and directly contradictory. Indeed, the recurrence, insufficient of itself to outweigh the contrast that prevailed, might more plausibly be explained as a coincidence of the phraseology. On the other hand, a connection might be entertained, as probability, that 2 Samuel 7:13a, being a gloss,[74] may have derailed the thrust of a pre-existent text, of which the phrase ממלכותך כסא in verse 13b was a relic which, being also in close ideological affinity with 1 Kings 9:5a and Deuteronomy 17:18, was also consistent with a common conditional promise corresponding with 1 Kings 2:4; 6:12, 8:25 (cf. Ps 132:12), and therefore pointed to a more extensive composition with a more consistently conditional ideology.

In the meantime, it might also be more a feasible approach to accept that none of the promissory passages cited, whether conditional or unconditional, was derived from, or connected with, the promises as they were preserved in 2 Samuel 7:1–17. Clearly, the conditional promises identified above, are disqualified. However, the absence from 2 Samuel 7:1–17 of a reference to dominion—ניר—in Jerusalem, or of the prospects of a tribe maintaining allegiance to the Davidic monarchy, against the secession, must

71. Ibid., 107–108.
72. Ibid., 107–109.
73. Ibid., 108–109.
74. This view has been established on other grounds, e.g. the repetition of 12b in 13b.

also compromise claims made for the second group; for not only is there no hint, in the promises in 2 Samuel 7:11b–16, of a special significance of Jerusalem for the Davidic monarchy but the very logic of the promises must have precluded the prospect of a secession and, therefore, the necessity for the allegiance of a remnant tribe or for ניר in Jerusalem.

P. KYLE MCCARTER JR.

In his commentaries on Samuel, P. Kyle McCarter has given extensive treatment of the composition of the Nathan narrative (2 Sam 7:1–17), whose importance for the making of the Deuteronomic History he unambiguously affirmed for, from his study, he was able to identify the typical Deuteronomic emphases and catch-phrases. At the same time he recognized that the *pericope* was not wholly a Deuteronomic creation, for he was able to extract from it two antecedent layers.[75] The thrust of the earliest layer, as he saw it, agreeable though it was to Deuteronomic theology, also featured in royal notices and building inscriptions throughout the ancient Near East,[76] which mirrored the ideological connection between the king's provision of, and attentiveness to, the sanctuaries of the patron deity, and the deity's blessing of the regime with lasting rule. That layer he traced in verses 1a, 2–3, 11b–12 and 13b–15a. Because David had signified his intention to build a suitable accommodation for the ark, YHWH promised to build him a house by blessing him with descendants who would rule far into the future.

A second layer, which he identified in 2 Samuel 7:5b–7, seemed to reverse the thrust of the first layer.[77] It repudiated the proposal for a sanctuary since it had not been requested, and confirmed YHWH's preference for the more primitive tent shrine, which represented more aptly the traditions of early Israel. In altercation-mode David's proposal for a sanctuary was rejected. The emphatic repetition of the two personal pronouns, "you"— אתה— and "me"—לי— (2 Sam 7:5) suggested, furthermore, that the grievance had less to do with fabric (2 Sam 7:1–2, 6–7) than with David's presumption in hoping to be YHWH's benefactor. David may not build a house (sanctuary) for YHWH but YHWH would build a house (dynasty) for David. With the inclusion of 2 Samuel 7:8–9 McCarter recognized a

---

75. See McCarter, *2 Samuel*, 220–21.
76. Ibid., 224–5.
77. Ibid., 226–8.

pre-Deuteronomic layer that defined kingship as a divine gift which, mediated through a prophet, could likewise be taken away.[78]

McCarter also recognized in a third layer, an attempt at harmonization, which introduced the building of the temple as within the divine will.[79] Accordingly, David was commended for having conceived the plan. It was good that it was in his heart (1 Kgs 8:18–19); and since YHWH had not addressed any Israelite leader on the subject (2 Sam 7:7), David should not be unduly perturbed by his inability to implement the plan. The time had not yet come. The people had not yet attained their "rest." They were still surrounded by enemies whom David must subdue in order to secure the "place" (מקום) for a sanctuary. David therefore had a preliminary task that was of a military nature, which was to create the conditions conducive to the building of the sanctuary (2 Sam 7:10–11a)—a project that his successor, would be able to undertake (2 Sam 7:13).

The chief merit of McCarter's analysis is not only in his identification of the layers, but his locating in each of them the two dominant themes, viz., the building of a sanctuary and the establishment of a regime. What he omitted, however, was a summary of the transmission processes and their historical settings in which the layers coalesced in a single narrative. It is therefore also unlikely that his analysis has met the contradictions that have survived in the text and, in particular, the connection between 2 Samuel 7:1–3 and 2 Samuel 7:4–11 which, within the terms of his analysis, remains problematic. In the first layer the king—מלך—(2 Sam 7:1) appears to be David—עבדי דוד—(2 Sam 7:5, 8) whose pious intention, though frustrated, YHWH commended (cf. 1 Kgs 8:17–19). However, in the second layer the king, still David, was reproved for wishing to make YHWH a gift that was not requested and, in the third layer, it would appear that the king designated to undertake the project was Solomon (2 Sam 7:1–2, 13a; cf. 1 Kgs 5:16–19 MT).

Who, then, was the unnamed king in 2 Samuel 7:1–3? If he was David, the argument supporting the third layer is in contradiction, since David would have been commissioned to subdue enemies (vv. 10–11a) who had already been subdued (cf. 2 Sam 7:1); and if Solomon, the reproof of the second or prophetic layer seems inappropriate, since it would appear that the father was reproved for presuming to make an offering (2 Sam 7:5–7) that was acceptable in his son (2 Sam 7:13). Furthermore, the reproof,

78. Ibid., 229–30.
79. Ibid., 231.

addressed to David, without the introductory verses (2 Sam 7:1–3), could not *prima facie* be sustained.

Secondly, to suggest that David should not have been unduly perturbed by a prohibition against his building of a sanctuary for YHWH, because no such request had been made of the judges (2 Sam 7:7), is to misconstrue David's status in that segment of the narrative, in which he is explicitly addressed not as a "judge"—שפט— but as YHWH's servant —עבדי— (cf. 2 Sam 7:5, 7). That was precisely the point at issue, viz., the passing of the era of the judges in which "every man did what was right in his own eyes" (Deut 12:8–11; cf. Judg 17:6; 21:25), and the inauguration of a new era of monarchical rule, which David represented, and therefore the building of a sanctuary should have been approved rather than forbidden.

McCarter's study is therefore another example of the limitations of the literary-critical method for the solution of problems that obtrude in this and similar Old Testament narratives which, though presented as written literature, reflect an earlier and more complex history of oral traditions which have not only be preserved in, but have so impacted, the literature that without an exploration of the pre-literary stages of transmission, literary-critical methods, however innovative or skillfully applied, will not suffice for a resolution of all the textual difficulties nor yield fullest and clearest interpretation that is possible. In this particular case, the major question raised in the narrative is the implication for kingship, of the king, having been disallowed the coveted task of building a sanctuary for the patron deity, is nevertheless recognized, legitimized and endorsed as divinely chosen, and promised a secure regime, as if he had not only been so authorized to build the sanctuary, but had succeeded in the task. The answer to such a question is not available through literary-critical methods.

MICHAEL AVIOZ

A more recent study of 2 Samuel 7, though undertaken within the more limited compositional setting of Samuel, is Michael Avioz's monograph in which he explored its thematic connections with Samuel, and echoes of it in Kings. An important aspect of the study is its apparent alignment with the latest trends in Joshua–Kings studies, and especially the shift of focus away from the perspectives that guided the analysis of Martin Noth; for although Avioz affirmed that his approach was "tightly related to the

2 SAMUEL 7:1-17 IN DEUTERONOMY-KINGS

so-called Deuteronomistic History hypothesis,"[80] a caveat in his explicit reminder of its hypothetical status as well as his disengagement from the redactio-critical method, might be taken as serving notice of an "adieu."

Therefore, without undertaking an exhaustive evaluation, the focus will be on those aspects of his presentation that appear to be germane. A noticeable omission is a structural analysis of the Samuel corpus, similar to D.J. McCarthy's attempt with respect to a Deuteronomic History, in order to determine the place of 2 Samuel 7 in the composition of the David epic (1 Sam 16—2 Sam. 23); for while earlier hints of the narrative in the history of David's rise (1 Sam 2:10; 13:13–14; 15:28–29; 20:14–15; 24:20–21; 25:28; 28:17–19), and echoes of it in David's last words (2 Samuel 23:1–7) and beyond the Samuel corpus are instructive, a coincidence of vocabulary and a repetition of themes will hardly suffice for the interpretative task, since it is the suitability and purpose of 2 Samuel 7 for the larger narrative complex that is the basic issue; for, as was noted in the introductory chapter, the place of the narrative in Samuel seems, even from an overview, to be at once both prominent and problematic. Therefore, having retreated from a hypothetical Deuteronomistic History to a more limited and, presumably, secure compass, the significance of 2 Samuel 7 for the David story should have been more compelling.

The omission of a structural analysis raises the deeper question regarding current tendency, in studies relating to Joshua–Kings, to limit the investigation to pre-selected segments, arbitrarily delimited, as a more viable approach.[81] For whatever the viability of the Prophets as a canonical entity, the reasons for the sub-divisions in the Joshua–Kings corpus, or the appropriateness of the captions, it is unlikely that the contents of the Isaiah–Malachi, or more so the Joshua–Kings collections, were canonized scroll by scroll, and the segmentation with captions was so arbitrary, that evidence of narrative continuity between the adjacent scrolls or of a progression throughout was coincidental; and therefore a collective designation could shed no light on the contents and *vice versa*. In fact, any study of the Samuel corpus, or any other pre-selected portion, that has not been tested by its connectedness with the whole corpus, is unlikely to yield a satisfactory result, regardless of the themes that might overflow outwards

---

80. See Avioz, *Nathan's Oracle*, 9.

81. Two of them, Provan, *Hezekiah and Books of Kings*, and Campbell, *Of Prophets and Kings*, have already been mentioned, and will again be cited in the chapter following. Other studies, which do not as closely impinge upon 2 Samuel 7 will be briefly noted in the next section.

or inwards, or of any other insightful discoveries that might accrue. Furthermore, elusive as the "Deuteronomists" might well be,[82] and debatable as the terminology has doubtless become, there is a continuous, coherent, and consistent historical narrative from Moses' leave-taking at Moab (Deut 1–34) to the last days of Jehoiachin's captivity in Babylon (2 Kgs 25:27–30) that is above dispute. It is therefore unlikely that the study of any part of the Joshua–Kings corpus will in any way be compromised by a grasp of its meaning for the corpus as a whole, or *vice versa*.

Avioz has also made some preliminary observations that are important for the exposition of 2 Samuel 7 which, compared with evidence from ancient Near Eastern sources suggested that a king was not entitled to build a temple for his god without having first been divinely commissioned.[83] From ancient Near Eastern sources he also understood that the building of a temple guaranteed the establishment of the regime.[84] Those two claims appeared to him to be basic for interpretation of 2 Samuel 7. If, however, David's observation in verses 1–3 was evidence of a violation as verses 5–7 seem to suggest, the evidence of a transgression should have been more pronounced and the terms of the disqualification made more explicit[85]. That is to say, it is hardly sufficient to deduce an offence from a passing observation by alleging what David may have implied, but neither expressed nor pursued towards implementation and was *prima facie* open to another interpretation. The strictest interpretation of 2 Samuel 7:1–3 is an observation, made in private by David, who compared his dwelling, cedar-built, with the cloth tent in which the ark was placed. That is insufficient evidence of transgression; for, even if criticism was implied, it might equally have been, in self-criticism, a confession of negligence (cp. Deut 8:12–14; Hag 1:4).

Also, Avioz's explanation of the promise to David of a sure house and enduring rule, notwithstanding his failure to build a house for YHWH his God, is unclear.[86] His argument suggests, however, that unlike the extra-biblical evidence, David and his successors attained blessing of an everlasting dynasty even though he did not complete the building of a house for

---

82. See Avioz, *Nathan's Oracle* 3, 9–10.
83. Ibid., 16.
84. Ibid., 33.
85. As was done in Chronicles, cf., 1 Chronicles 17:4; 22:8; 28:3.
86. Ibid., 18–19, 33–35.

his God.[87] In that case the ancient Near Eastern parallels he invoked seem less relevant than was expected. However, if the patterns that prevailed in ancient Near Eastern custom were at all applicable, then a case for acquiescence rather than altercation and commission rather than veto might be claimed for verses 5–7, with the consequence of endorsement and authorization rather than disqualification.

Avioz's study is another indication that, whatever the feasibility of a "Deuteronomistic" hypothesis, an in-depth traditio-historical exploration, including a reasonably extensive redactio-critical compass, is essential for the elucidation of 2 Samuel 7. From whatever direction the investigation is undertaken, the literature of the Old Testament must be recognized as the result of a long and complex process of transmission that preceded the writing stage, and a resolution of the complications that arise from the text requires an exploration of that process. Whoever were the persons who assembled the material, and whatever the names that might be assigned, it is a more viable approach, in the long run, to recognize the product as the culmination of traditions that grew and changed as sub-compositions with even more primary units were utilized for purposes other than those for which they were originally intended. A project, deemed to be desirable but not undertaken (2 Sam 7:1–7), explained as excusable postponement (2 Sam 7:13; 1 Kgs 5:17–19 MT), later rationalized as ritual disqualification (cf. 1 Chr 17:4; 22:8) and therefore interpreted as peremptory prohibition (2 Bas 7:5 LXX) was ultimately vindicated in initial disavowal (Acts 7:43–49).[88]

OTHER DEUTERONOMIC HISTORICAL STUDIES

It is perhaps appropriate, at this point, to refer to some other studies of the Deuteronomy–Kings composition that have attempted to take Cross' analysis further but which, because they have been confined to the Kings corpus, do not bear directly on this study. Through close analysis of regnal formulae and a comparative study of the reigns in Kings, they have attempted to confront the redactional problems. The result is not only a confirmation of later redactions, Josianic or exilic, but also the isolation of pre-Josianic compositional material. Helga Weippert focused on an evaluation of the

---

87. Ibid., 33–35.

88. See Simon, "The Prophecy of Nathan," 43, who has argued from Stephen's oration that David never planned or considered the building of a temple, but desired only a tabernacle.

regnal formulae in Kings to the extent of claiming different authorship in the differing expressions of the same valuation.[89] Her over-precise analysis seems to assume for authors/redactors a commitment to particular forms of reporting royal notices, which were not susceptible to deviation or modification even when the circumstances required it. The result was an excessive differentiation that was modified by Andre Lemaire, who, modification notwithstanding, shared Weippert's basic approach and reached similar conclusions.[90] Baruch Halpern and David Vanderhooft, having cast a wider net, more finely meshed, examined in minute detail, additional items of the regnal formulae, such as obituary notices, the Queen Mothers and source citations, to discover what they indicated about date and authorship.[91] It is particularly instructive to note that, whatever the point of departure, or the criteria that were applied, the studies all seemed to converge on or about the reign of Hezekiah as the most likely date for a preexilic redaction. Although an exhaustive examination of the more recent studies, apart from Iain Provan's, Antony Campbell's, and Michael Avioz's, falls outside the scope of this study, four observations seem to be germane.

The first observation concerns methodology. Underlying the analyses is an assumption that deviations, wherever discovered or however occasioned, pointed to differences in authorship and/or redaction—a conclusion that is by no means foregone. Here Ivan Engnell's caution against the anachronism in the modern European approach which, though originally intended for his advocacy of the relevance of oral tradition, is apposite in its caution against the assumption that ancient authors/redactors were driven by the same passion for accuracy and consistency as their modern counterparts.[92] It is unlikely that the Old Testament traditionists or redactors so strictly adhered to rules of precision and consistency that the only conclusion to be drawn from deviations was different authorship. It is also unlikely that formulae employed were as inflexible as the studies seem to suggest, or that authors/redactors intentionally devised specific forms for their own purposes, to the extent that divergences meant a change in authorship. It is just as likely that changes in the style and form of the reporting were due less to changes in authorship as to the nature and content of the report

---

89. See Weippert, "Deuteronomistic Judgments of the Kings," 301–39.

90. See Lemaire, "Towards the history of the Redaction of the Books of Kings," 221–36.

91. See Halpern, Baruch and David Vanderhooft, "Editions of Kings," 179–244.

92. See Engnell, "Traditio-historical Research," 3, 98.

which then determined the "form." Indeed, the expectation of consistency in formulae, which influenced the analyses, seems unrealistic for an ancient language of limited vocabulary that required flexibility and adaptability.

Secondly, the mechanisms involved in the redaction process would seem to make the possibility of a multiplicity of redactions each of separate authorship, which a plethora of deviations implies, somewhat remote. Such conclusions assume the availability of the modern facilities for re-writing, over-writing, insertions, deletions, corrections and the like.

A third and more pertinent observation concerns the lack of synthesis not only of the studies but of their implications for composition of the corpus in its entirety. A basic premise for a Deuteronomic history must be that a continuous narrative composition, beginning with Moses and ending with the Babylonian captivity, preceded the book divisions;[93] therefore, to concentrate on one portion of the corpus, large or small, without reference to the rest of the composition, while agreeable with the limited objectives of source criticism, seems inadequate as an approach for redaction criticism and, for that reason, must render tentative the conclusions reached since the discovery of a particular redaction may have preserved evidence of sub-compositions, which must have been in a narrative relationship of continuity with the larger composition. Without such delineation the composition could hardly have qualified as a redaction.[94]

This leads to the fourth observation to which Wolff's structure is once more applicable. There is clearly a hermeneutical problem that becomes increasingly insistent the more the sub-compositions are discovered. It hardly suffices to focus on the similarities or variations in style, vocabulary, phraseology, and the like, since for each sub-composition there must also have been a purpose that can be demonstrated.

CONCLUSION

The review, so far undertaken, has shown that the Noth hypothesis and the various attempts at modification or refinement have raised difficulties for 2 Samuel 7:1–17 and vice versa, so intractable as to advise a re-examination of the methodology. To begin, the designation "Deuteronomistic History"

---

93. It might not be inapposite to observe that a nomenclature-appeal, which appeared to legitimize the exclusion of the Samuel books would not have been possible for the Greek Bible (LXX) where there are four, and not two, books of Kings.

94. For a more judicious approach, see Ackroyd, "Kings," 517.

must raise questions for a composition of such scope and complexity as the Joshua–Kings corpus, since it is by no means obvious that the perspectives of Deuteronomy monopolized the composition or prevailed throughout. Therefore, however suggestive the linkages, or impressive the results of such a hypothesis, it appears that the method applied was less than systematic, making the conclusions inevitably questionable. An immediate consequence of such a method was, as has been shown, its inability to accommodate significant portions of the composition, which were then marginalized for reasons that have been proved in the review to be inadequate and even arbitrary, a notable case being 2 Samuel 7:1–17.

Secondly, it would seem that later post-Cross studies, while purporting to be attempts at redaction-criticism, were reminiscent of source criticism, i.e. attempts at the recovery of earlier literary units from the final composition. Thus, when Nelson entitled his monograph "The Double Redaction of the Deuteronomistic History," it was nowhere shown in what sense, and to what extent, either of the redactions was "Deuteronomistic." When Cross labeled a "Josianic" redaction Dtr1,[95] or Provan suggested that the original books of Kings may have been, in part, the attempt of a nationalist and proto-Dtr group in the court of Josiah to justify their position,[96] the essentially Deuteronomic character and content of that collection seems not to have been discussed. Merely to isolate a sub-composition on the basis of common rhetoric, reporting-style, terminology, phraseology, ideology, theme, and the like, and to accentuate those features as paramount without also addressing the more basic questions of whence and wherefore the composition first came into being or the purpose of its incorporation into the larger complex, seems less suggestive of a redactio-critical than a source-critical method; and the identification of such sub-units does not by itself, promote an understanding of the final composition.[97]

Thirdly, it is of some importance to recognize in the canonization process more than a formal endorsement of the penultimate stage in the redaction process but was itself an interpretative exercise, differing from the preceding stages only in intensity, and that because of the finality constraint. Canonization was not only a certification of certain documents as the Law or the Prophets, but was also the input of an interpretative prerogative that

---

95. See Cross, *Canaanite Myth*, 270.

96. See Provan, *Hezekiah and Books of Kings*, 155.

97. Friedman, "From Egypt to Egypt," 167, has made a useful distinction between source- and redaction-criticism, and discusses their relationship.

contributed decisively to the qualification. In traditio-historical terms the canon, by virtue of its hermeneutical prerogative, superseded *traditum* to become the tradition. It stands to reason, therefore, that the canonization of the Prophets marked that stage in the redaction process when its earlier Deuteronomic character, though still discernible, was superseded in a definition of the Joshua–Kings corpus which, combined with the Isaiah–Malachi collection, was not merely designated but was positively recognized and validated as prophecy; and to neglect or avoid that reality is to run the risk of an inadequate result.[98]

The canonical factor is therefore the starting point for a traditio-historical study of the Old Testament. As Brevard Childs has noted, it cannot be dismissed as either intolerable or irrelevant to recognize that, whatever their interpretative capacity, labels such as "Tetrateuch" and "Hexateuch" were not canonical designations but, rather, the Law that did not end at Numbers but with Deuteronomy,[99] and that a "Deuteronomistic History" was not a canonical categorization, but rather the Prophets from which Deuteronomy was omitted, and in which Joshua–Kings and Isaiah–Malachi were conjoined. While, therefore, the study of the Old Testament is not exhausted by the canonical shaping, its relevance is surely indispensable, since to proceed regardless is to risk omitting crucial stages in the making of the Old Testament.

Fourthly, Deuteronomic historical studies cannot reasonably avoid an exploration of the process whereby Deuteronomy became a part of the Law. If, as is apparent, and as the title "Deuteronomistic History" implies, Deuteronomy was, at an earlier stage, integrally connected with Joshua–Kings,[100] there must have also been, at some point, a recognizable affinity between Genesis–Numbers and Deuteronomy–Kings, which not merely facilitated a literary transfer, but rendered the transfer theologically plausi-

---

98. A striking example is Mayes, *Story of Israel*, in which chapter headings appear to recognize the canonical arrangement of the Former Prophets, with the exclusion of Ruth, but, nevertheless, assuming a Deuteronomistic rather than a canonical identity of the scrolls in the inclusion of Deuteronomy and the exclusion of the Isaiah–Malachi collection. Fretheim, *Deuteronomic History*, notwithstanding the book-title, likewise arranged his chapter-divisions on a quasi-Hebraic canonical pattern in the omission of Ruth but excluding also the Isaiah–Malachi component.

99. Childs, *Introduction to the Old Testament*, 232–33.

100. For a study of the unitary nature of the composition of Deuteronomy–Joshua see Wenham, "Deuteronomic Theology in Joshua," 140–48. Also, in the account of the conquest and settlement of the tribes on both sides of the Jordan under Moses and Joshua as a joint operation, is evidence of a unified composition.

ble.[101] Therefore, by assuming a Deuteronomic History as the interpretative key to the Joshua–Kings corpus, without also addressing the issues relating to canonicity and the separation of Deuteronomy, Noth's hypothesis, and the studies proceeding from it, seem to be methodologically flawed, in that while the Deuteronomic input is not in dispute, the Joshua–Kings corpus by itself, and still less as part of the Prophets, was no longer as definitively "Deuteronomistic" as the arguments set forth in Noth's hypothesis sought to assert or the designation he proposed appeared to dictate.

---

101. It is precisely such a trend, proceeding from the Documentary Hypothesis proposed by Julius Wellhausen, which was aborted by the disjunction in Noth's hypotheses of a Deuteronomistic History (Deuteronomy–Kings) and a Tetrateuch (Genesis–Numbers). For a historical review of the change (even before recognition was given to the relevance of the canonical factor), cf., Eissfeldt, *Introduction*, 242–48.

CHAPTER IV

2 SAMUEL 7:1–17 IN PRE-CANONICAL REDACTION

AMONG THE FEATURES THAT distinguish the Hebrew Bible from the Septuagint (LXX) are the selection, arrangement, and perspectives of the books following the Pentateuch (Genesis–Deuteronomy). Whereas, in the Septuagint they have been so arranged as to give an account of the Hebrew people from the conquest of Canaan to the Maccabean revolt, in the Hebrew Bible, the Joshua–Kings corpus and the Isaiah–Malachi collection immediately following form a distinct canonical category, viz., the Prophets, from which the intervening books as listed in the Septuagint, i.e. from the Chronicles to the Song of Songs, also Ruth, Lamentations and Daniel, have been accommodated in a third canonical category, viz., the Writings. Another observable difference is in the captions. The first two of the four books in Septuagint entitled "Of the Kings" appear in the Hebrew Bible as "Samuel"—a difference that carries enormous implications for interpretation.[1]

The juxtaposition of the Joshua–Kings and Isaiah–Malachi collections in the Hebrew Bible seems, therefore, to have been designed to project a particular perspective, however obscured it may be by differences in presentation. Prophecy in the Prophets referred not merely to the rise of a prophetic

---

1. See Dines, "Septuagint," 622, has called attention to the important fact that LXX was not merely translation but also interpretation in the process.

movement in Israel, or the role of prophets as leaders of thought and action, or a prophecy-fulfillment schema or oracular compositions independently compiled and inserted into, or connected by, narratives. None of these features could have sufficed for the canonical definition, since the prophecies, having been fulfilled in the downfall of the Hebrew Kingdoms, would have ceased as such to be prophetic, but remained as historical and other forms of literary reflection on prophetic activity in Israel from the settlement in Canaan to the returning of the Jewish exiles.

It was precisely an unfulfilled prophecy such as was preserved in the Nathan narrative (2 Sam 7:11b–16; cf. 2 Kgs 25:1–7, 27–30) that maintained for the Joshua–Kings corpus its prophetic character (cf. Deut 18:21–22), and made possible a continuity with the Isaiah–Malachi collection. One indication of such an intention is the duplication of a passage (Isa 39 // 2 Kgs 20: 12–21), in which an oracle of doom, pronounced on the descendants of Hezekiah was fulfilled in and after the overthrow of the Judaean monarchy (2 Kgs 21:23; 23:29, 33, 35; 24:12–15; 25:6–7, 27–30). Therefore, Jehoiachin's long incarceration and death in captivity (2 Kgs 25:27–30 // Jer 52:31–34), represented the outcome of two prophecies reported in the same corpus—one fulfilled and the other unfulfilled.[2] However, prefacing the Isaiah prophecies of a coming Davidic deliverer (Isa 6:1—9:7; 11:1–9), the Jeremiah oracles of the resurrection of a Davidic descendant (Jer 22:24–30; 23:5–6), and Ezekiel's vision of the coming of a Davidic prince and shepherd (Ezek 34:22–31; 37:24), the Jehoiachin pericope (2 Kgs 25:27–30) and, by extension, the history of the Davidic monarchy, made possible a messianic reinterpretation of oracles in the Latter Prophets.

Similarly, the prophecy of doom in the Isaiah collection (Isa 39 // 2 Kgs 20:12–21), awakened by the Assyrian incursions (Isa 36–37 // 2 Kgs 18:9—19:37), was enclosed by and taken up into, salvation oracles that envisioned not only the end of the captivity and the return of the exiles (Isa 35; 40–55) but also a reconfirmation and democratization of the promises to David in an everlasting covenant (Isa 55:3–5; cf. 2 Sam 7:10–11a 16; Isa 61:8–9). Thus, from promises to David found in the Nathan narrative (2 Sam 7:11–16; cf. 2 Sam. 23:1–5), through the fall of the House of David (2 Kgs 24:18—25:7; 25:27–30), and a reinterpretation of the messianic oracles

---

2. The Jehoiachin pericope (2 Kgs 25:27–30) as fulfillment of the Isaiah-prophecy (2 Kgs 20:16–18; cf. Isa 39:3–8), which may have been primary in an Exilic redaction, became a non-fulfillment of the Nathan-prophecy (2 Sam 7:11b, 16), in its re-application for the canonization of the Prophets, in that it immediately precedes the proclamation of the end of captivity (Isa 40:1–11; cf. Jer 52:31–34).

2 SAMUEL 7:1-17 IN PRE-CANONICAL REDACTION

in the canonical Prophets (Isa 6:11–13; 7:13-25; 9:1–7; 11:1–9; Amos 9:11), it seems that continuity was forged for the raising of hopes of national recovery in the coming of a Davidic messiah.

Also, to the extent that the oracles of doom in the writing Prophets were fulfilled in the subjugation of the people of Israel to foreign domination, to that extent the essentially prophetic character was exhausted. However, in salvation oracles regarding a future for Israel, in Isaiah (40–66), Jeremiah (23:5; 30–35), Ezekiel (34:23–24, 37:15–28), Hosea (3:5; cf. 14:2–8), Amos (9:11–14), and Micah (5:1–3), hopes, rooted in promises preserved in the Nathan narrative (2 Sam 7:10–11a), reestablished the prophetic character of the writing Prophets and justified the naming of the Hebrew collection of Joshua–Malachi as the Prophets.

The arrangement in the Greek Bible (LXX) suggests a somewhat different perspective. The de-emphasizing of the prophetic character of the Joshua–Kings collection, apparent not only in the Βασιλείων captions or the intrusion of demonstrably non-prophetic literature within and between the Joshua–Kings and Isaiah–Malachi collections,[3] but also in the skillful emendation of certain key-texts, including the Nathan narrative (2 Kgdms 7:11b (LXX); cp. 2 Sam 7:11b (MT)), carried far-reaching consequences for interpretation. With the prophetic emphasis thus eroded, the Joshua–Esther literature became, in part, a history of the Jewish people from the Conquest of Canaan to the period of Persian overlordship. Also, Kings (Βασιλείων) preceding Appendices (Παραλειπόμενων), prefaced by a genealogy from Adam to the descendants of Meri-baal (1 *Par* 8:34–40; cf. 2 Sam 9), tracing biological descent from the origin of humankind to the returned exiles, suggests the abandonment of a prophetic perspective for a projection of the Babylonian captivity as the end of historical Israel as a political entity and its re-emergence of an ancient Hebrew religious community.[4]

---

3. Within the Joshua–Kings collection is Ruth and the Isaiah–Malachi are Lamentations and Daniel, and between the two collections are Chronicles, Ezra,, Nehemiah, Esther, Job, Psalms, Proverbs, Ecclesiastes, and Song of Songs.

4. Significantly the LXX rendering of 2 Βασιλείων 7:11b, ὅτι οἰκονοίκοδομήσεις αὐτῷ (" . . . that you [David] shall build a house for him [YHWH]"), subverted the dynastic promise and oriented the narrative to a temple theme.

THE NATHAN NARRATIVE IN 2 SAMUEL 7:1-17

THE DEUTERONOMIC REDACTION (EXILIC)

It therefore seems that, sometime between the fall of the Davidic monarchy and the canonization of the Prophets, guarantees enshrined in the dynastic oracle of 2 Samuel 7:1–17 provoked a profound ideological crisis in the Jewish community, and the more so after the death of Jehoiachin (2 Kgs 25:27–30). In spite of the promises in the Nathan oracle (2 Sam 7:11b–16), and the more than four centuries of unbroken rule,[5] the monarchy, following the death of Josiah, rapidly unraveled to an ignominious end, marked by capitulation, execution, deportation, subjugation, and a prolonged incarceration (2 Kgs 23:31—25:30).[6] Such a tragic turn of events must have stirred anxious questions, especially when all hope for a restoration of the monarchy dissipated.[7] Although Otto Eissfeldt has argued that Psalm 89 was composed when the Davidic monarchy was still in existence,[8] its high conception of the monarchy offers clues to the traumatic impact of the death of Jehoiachin on the Jewish royalists under the Babylonian occupation (Ps. 89: 19–51; cf. Jer 28:1–4). It seems that it was to address such a crisis that a Davidic epic was re-visited.

Indications of that intention might be discerned by a comparison with the laconic, almost indifferent, reporting style in the account of the fall of Jerusalem.[9] The widespread destruction of the city, including the sacking of the temple and the execution or deportation of its leading citizens, was reported dispassionately, without dirge, imprecation or theological reflection (cp. Lam 1–4; Ps 137). There was no evidence of somber introspection (cp. 2 Kgs 17:7–18). The implications of the catastrophe for the inviolability of Zion as YHWH's dwelling place by which Jerusalem was protected, and

---

5. The only break was the Athaliah interregnum of six years, following a massacre of the princes, which was ended by a counter coup instigated and led by the Jerusalem priesthood.

6. Between the deportation of Jehoiachin in 597 BCE and the date of the accession of Evil-Merodach, a period of not less than thirty-seven years of imprisonment has been estimated.

7. A nationalist party remaining in Palestine envisaged not only a brief period of captivity but the release of Jehoiachin and the restoration of the monarchy following the imminent end to Babylon domination (cf. Jer 28:1–4).

8. See Eissfeldt, "Promises of Grace," 201–2.

9. The absence of a theological reflection on the destruction suggests that the exilic editor was not a prophet, a priest, or the Deuteronomist (cp. Jer 7:1–15; Lam 1–5).

2 SAMUEL 7:1-17 IN PRE-CANONICAL REDACTION

which had fuelled the euphoria following the lifting of the Assyrian siege (2 Kgs 19:20-34; cf. Pss 46, 48, 125), were passed over in silence.[10]

The abolition of the monarchy provoked a quite different reaction. The consistently negative evaluation in the summary reporting of the reigns of Josiah's successors is fair indication of the change of mood, of perspective and therefore of authorship, in which the cause of the rapidly deteriorating trend was located less in the failings of individual rulers than in a more deeply seated and chronic disorder. Whereas the kings of Judah up to Josiah had been evaluated on the basis of personal merit, so to speak, and some more favorably than others, Josiah's successors—three sons and a grandson—were all adjudged evildoers in YHWH's sight as were their predecessor(s) (2 Kgs 23:32, 37; 24:9, 19),[11] no consideration having been given to mitigating factors such as the brevity of the reign, the pressures of foreign overlordship, social instability, moral perplexity, and cultic derangement in a period of deepening crisis. It seems, furthermore, that their predecessors, including the pious Josiah of the latest redaction (2 Kgs 22:2; 23:25), were all brought under the common condemnation as "evildoers in YHWH's sight" (2 Kgs 23:32, 37; 24:9, 19).

The shift of perspective is indicative of an exilic redaction, whose objective was an explanation of the fall of the Israelite monarchy. Whereas David had been venerated for his unstinting and exemplary devotion (2 Sam 6:1-19; 1 Kgs 3:6; 6:12; 8:24-25; 9:4-5; 11:4, 39; 15:3-5a, 11; 2 Kgs 18:3; 22:2), a eulogy appended to an evaluation of Abijah, included a jarring note that cited the matter of Uriah the Hittite (1 Kgs 15:5b) which, being a gloss as John Gray opined,[12] seems to be a late insertion that called attention to a matter of grave consequence. Retrospectively, it called into question the earlier eulogies to David. Prospectively, it presaged failure in the monarchy, and climaxed in the indiscriminate indictment of the last rulers, by uncovering an ancient wrong (2 Kgs 23:31—24:30). Specifically, the matter of Uriah the Hittite resurrected an odious episode that tarnished the reputation of the ancestor. It was the pin that punctured the Davidic epic.

It would therefore appear that, in the death throes of the monarchy (2 Kgs 25:7-26), the importance of "dynasty" surfaced in Jewish thought.

---

10. The tradition seems to have been the basis of the interpretation, by the residents, of the lifting of the siege in 701. So suggests Clements, *Isaiah and Deliverance* 72-89.

11. The most likely explanation for the Zedekiah exception was his seniority in relation to his nephew, Jehoiachin, his immediate predecessor (2 Kgs 25:17, 19), which therefore nullifies an argument for a deviation from the pattern.

12. See Gray, *Kings*, 348.

THE NATHAN NARRATIVE IN 2 SAMUEL 7:1-17

The progenitor long deceased attained, as Aage Bentzen has explained, the status of "Patriarch"—the First Man, the prototype, who embodied the essence and determined the fate of the lineage.[13] His successors were perceived as having partaken of his character, even as they inherited the name. Each was, so to speak, a Davidide in whom the spirit of the ancestor continued actively to reside. Therefore, as a crucial aspect in the evaluation of a ruler was the extent to which he "walked in the way of (n) his ancestor," so the destiny of the ruling "house" was determined by the moral baggage that was bequeathed and his successors inherited.

The rapid dissolution of the monarchy coupled with the growing dynastic consciousness (cf. Ps 89) resulted, therefore, in a special interest in David, which might account for his virtual monopolization of the Samuel corpus (1 Sam 16–2 Sam 23). Whatever the pre-history of the David epic, there could have been little purpose in concentrating such an elaborate reflection on one figure—a feature unexampled in Hebrew literature—apart from the light it shed on the decline and fall the monarchy. It might also explain the strange addendum to the Abijah evaluation (1 Kgs 15:5). In sum, the crux of the David story in Samuel was the matter of Uriah the Hittite (2 Sam 11–12), since no other purpose could have been served by including, and any political reason might have sufficed for suppressing, an episode that so defaced the legend except that, upon reflection, it held the vital clue to the adversities that hounded the monarchy while it ruled, as well as to the swiftness of its decline and the completeness of the fall (2 Kgs 21:23; 23:29–30, 33; 24:12–13 25:6-7, 27–30).

In the redactio-critical perspective, the preface to the prophet Nathan's formal indictment must therefore be read, less as a summation of the divine leading in David's meteoric rise (2 Sam 12:7–12; cf. 1 Sam 16–2 Sam 5; 7:8–9), than as the typical prophetic accentuation of the moral contrast between the extraordinary favors that were bestowed upon the beneficiary and the gravity of the offence in which he was implicated, and therefore justification for the sentence that was about to be passed. It explained not only the upheavals in the later years of David's reign but also the misfortunes and reversals that continuously afflicted the lineage to the latest posterity, which were attributable not to the failings of particular rulers, or the horrendous adversities that proved in the end to be insurmountable, but to a single act of infamy that caused the prophet to pronounce the curse, "Now,

---

13. See Bentzen, *King and Messiah*, 45–46.

2 SAMUEL 7:1-17 IN PRE-CANONICAL REDACTION

therefore, a sword shall not be turned away from your house for all time . . ." (2 Sam 12:10).[14]

2 SAMUEL 7:1-17 IN THE DEUTERONOMIC REDACTION (EXILIC)

More critical than the questions relating to the chronological situating of 2 Samuel 7:1-17, is its significance for the reassessment of the Davidic monarchy in an exilic redaction.[15] 2 Samuel 7, minus verses 1b, 12b–13a, has been interpreted by Ridout as a preface to chapters that follow which, in endorsement of Rost's interpretation, he designated a succession narrative (2 Sam 9–20; 1 Kgs 1–2)[16]—an account of the circuitous and hazardous course by which Solomon attained to the co-regency and later, the succession. However, apart from the fact that there were royal princes who were neither in contention for the throne nor casualties of the in-fighting (2 Sam 5:12–15; 1 Kgs 1:9; cp. Judg 9:5; 2 Kgs 11:1), a major flaw in Ridout's interpretation is that, for a narrative that was built around his designation and entitlement, Solomon's passivity throughout the unfolding drama, as well as its reticence on the oracle of Nathan, suggests that his accession was due less to a prophecy by which he was designated (2 Sam 7:12–13) than to the well orchestrated maneuvers that succeeded (1 Kgs 1:5–21).

There must, therefore, have been a clearer and firmer connection between the Nathan narrative in 2 Samuel 7:1–17 and the larger David epic in 1 Samuel 16–2 Samuel 23 in that, having marked the zenith of David's ascendancy, the Nathan narrative was also the fitting prologue to the matter of Uriah the Hittite (2 Sam 11–12), significant linkages being the location, viz., the king's "house" (2 Sam 7:1–2; cf. 11:1b–2), Nathan (2 Sam 7:2–4, 17; cf. 12:1, 7, 13, 15, 23), and the promise of an heir that was fulfilled in his birth, and later, his accession (2 Sam 7:12–15; cf. 12:1, 24–25; 1 Kgs 1:46, 48). It was by revelation to the prophet, Nathan, that David's accession and

---

14. עד־עולם (2 Sam 12:10) recalls the promise in the earlier narrative (2 Sam 7:16).

15. Ackroyd, 2 *Samuel*, 73–74, and Mauchline, *Samuel*, 228, have noted a chronological misplacement of the account of David's wars in 2 Samuel 8. Ackroyd has, however, commented that the redactor was concerned more with "significant order" than mere chronology.

16. Cf. Ridout, *Prose Composition*, 175. However, Rost, *Succession to the Throne*, 35–36, does not seem to support Ridout's view of that close attachment of 2 Samuel 7 as a prologue to the succession narrative.

rule were legitimized (2 Sam 7:8–9, 17),[17] the status of his family as the ruling house was confirmed (2 Sam 7:11b, 16), and his son, Solomon, was designated as his successor and the builder of the temple (2 Sam. 7:12–14; cf. 1 Kgs 8:18–20). What Carlson in his exposition of the Nathan narrative interpreted as the climax of the account of "David under blessing,"[18] was described in the narrative as "rest from all the enemies roundabout" (2 Sam 7:1b; cf. Deut 12:10; 25:19; Josh 23:1). However, it also foreshadowed the matter of Uriah the Hittite (1 Kgs 15:5; cf. 2 Sam 11–12) in that, having so generously provided against precisely such an eventuality (2 Sam 12:7–8), the offence was the more aggravating. It was to a pinnacle that David was raised, and it was from that pinnacle he fell—a fall that was the more tragic because of the safeguards that had been provided. The matter of Uriah the Hittite must have loomed large in an exilic reflection on the fall of the monarchy because the offence touched the raw nerve of the Davidic ideology. The offender was more than נגיד—leader—(2 Sam 7:5, 8; cf. 1 Sam 10:1;1 3:14; 1 Kgs 14:7; 16:2) or שפט—judge (2 Sam 7:7), but עבד־יהוה—YHWH's chosen servant—a distinction he shared only with Moses (2 Sam 7:8–9, 19–21, 25–29; Ps 89:3, 20–37; cf. Josh 1:2).

Allegorized in parable, the enormity of the offence was measured by the marriages David had contracted and the extramarital sexual partners he could legitimately recruit (2 Sam 12:1–8). While still a outlaw and fugitive, and already wedded to Ahinoam of Jezreel (1 Sam 25:43), David married Abigail, a Carmelitess and a widow recently bereaved (1 Sam 25:39–43; 27:3). After Saul's death, he reclaimed Michal, Saul's daughter who, in the period of his estrangement from Saul, had been remarried and whose spouse was still alive (1 Sam 25:44; 2 Sam 3:13–16). Other marriages were contracted when he reigned in Hebron—Maacah the Geshurite princess, Haggith, Abital and Eglah (2 Sam 3:2–5) and, on taking up residence in Jerusalem, he married yet more wives and further increased his harem (2 Sam 5:13; cf. 6:22), before the fateful evening when, from the roof of his palace, he saw the wife of the Hittite (2 Sam 11:2–27).

The detailed exposé of David's conjugal relationships was a corroboration of Nathan's indictment (2 Sam 12:8). YHWH's favors in that regard had been extraordinarily liberal in that David was generously provisioned

---

17. The reaction of Meri-baal to the Absalom revolt (2 Sam 16: 1–4) and the violent invectives hurled by Shimei, a relative of Saul, at Bahurim during David's flight (2 Sam 16:5–8), suggest that there were pockets of disaffection in the realm that viewed David as a usurper.

18. See Carlson, *David, the Chosen King*, 97–128.

2 SAMUEL 7:1-17 IN PRE-CANONICAL REDACTION

against the hazards besetting the human condition that ". . . it is not good for the man to be alone . . . " (Gen 2:18). There was also, however, the limit to his prerogative. It stopped at the door of the neighbor (Deut 5:18, 21; 22:22; cf. Exod 20:14, 17), whose wife was untouchable, even by the king, not merely because the Mosaic law forbade it, but because her status represented the "unconditional don't," recognized both outside and within Israel (cf. Gen 12:11-19; 26:7-11; 39:6-9).[19] For the Israelite ruler, such an infringement was tantamount to a flagrant abuse of power which, compounded by his ordering of the murder the wronged husband, and his marriage to the widow in her pregnancy to conceal the misdeed, made it the more reprehensible. The matter of Uriah the Hittite was, therefore, much more than a reckless and squalid escapade that miscarried. It was a crime that exposed the culprit as a social menace and, in a ruler, a ruthless tyrant. King or commoner, he deserved to die (2 Sam 12:5, 13-14; cf. Gen 2:16-18; Lev 20:10).

Whether or not the editor was conversant with the precedents, the parallels are unmistakable. Especially instructive are perspectives that might have been drawn from the Creation-narratives (Gen 2:16—3:24). Benedikt Otzen has interpreted the "tree of the knowledge of good and evil" as symbolic of the ambiguities of sexual capability (Gen 2:17; 3:3, 11–13).[20] The expected death-sentence did not take immediate effect but was commuted, as Wolff has noted, to banishment (Gen 2:16-17; 3:3, 23-24; cf. 2 Kgs 23:33-34; 24:12; 25:27-30).[21] Driven out of Eden, YHWH did not withhold steadfast love (cf. 2 Sam 7:15), but preserved the dignity of the transgressors by clothing them (Gen 3:21; cf. 2 Kgs 25:29). Though exiled, provision was made for sustenance (Gen 3:17-19; 2 Kgs 25:29-30), and they were able to reproduce (Gen 3:16; 4:1; 2 Kgs 25:30; cf. 24:12-14). A viable existence was therefore possible in the state of banishment; but death in exile was the irrevocable end (Gen 3:24; cf. 2 Kgs 25: 28-30; Jer 22:24-30).

---

19. Gentile horror at incurring such an offense, even in innocence (Gen 12:10-18; 20:1-18; 26:1-11), might have served as precedents, which aggravated the heinousness in an Israelite. Joseph's unhesitating and unambiguous rejection of the advances of Potiphar's wife (Gen 39:5-9) might also have served a similar purpose. It is also noticeable that, in the listing of the abuses that might stem from the royal prerogative, grown despotic and oppressive, the only member of the subject's household who was beyond the reach of the ruler's grasp was his wife (1 Sam 8:11-17).

20. See Otzen et al., *Myths in the Old Testament*, 49–50.

21. See Wolff, *Anthropology of the Old Testament*, 83–84.

THE NATHAN NARRATIVE IN 2 SAMUEL 7:1-17

Therefore, 2 Samuel 7:1–17 contributed significantly to an exilic redaction. Interfacing with the Jehoiachin pericope (2 Kgs 25:27–30), it expounded the fall of the monarchy as the inexorable outworking of a grave offence and confirmed, with precision, the Deuteronomic theology of retribution. Consequent on David's transgression, YHWH withdrew the promises enshrined in the Nathan oracle (2 Sam 7:10–16).[22] The Davidic monarchy, destined initially to rule indefinitely, came to share the fate of all failed regimes that rose out of obscurity, shone for a season and returned to obscurity. In spite of the pledge that YHWH would not take חסד away from David's heir as he had from Saul (2 Sam 7:15), just as the last official sight of Saul's dynasty was Meri-baal seated at the table of David, his Israelite sovereign (2 Sam 9:1–13), so the last official sight of the Davidic dynasty was Jehoiachin, seated at the table of Evil-Merodach, his Babylonian suzerain (2 Kgs 25:30).[23]

THE DEUTERONOMIC REDACTION (JOSIANIC)

A careful perusal will dispute that the Former Prophets could have been, as Martin Noth claimed, of wholly exilic composition.[24] Neither the dynastic promises enshrined in the Nathan narrative (2 Sam 7:11b–16), nor the optimism that inspired the last words of David (2 Sam 23:1–7) nor the original thrust of the David epic (1 Sam 16:1–2 Sam 4; 9:1—11:1; 12:26–31; 13:1—23:7),[25] integral as they were to the story of David, could have enhanced a redaction whose major preoccupation was the unraveling, downfall and

---

22. The suggestion that YHWH was incapable of a change of mind, whatever the inducement or the provocation is not supported in either the Law or the Prophets (cf. Gen 18:20–33; Exod 32:9–14; Deut 9:7–29; 1 Sam 2:27–34; Jer 11:11–14; Amos 7:1–4).

23. See Schipper, "Significant Resonances," 521–29, who proposed that the correspondence between 2 Samuel 9 and 2 Kings 25:27–30, was the significant feature of the redaction, but his attempt at making a parallel between Meri-baal's physical deformity with Jehoiachin's captivity is strained and unconvincing.

24. See Noth, *Deuteronomistic History*, 12.

25. Various interpretations have been canvassed with respect to the original purpose of the composition of 2 Samuel 9–20, 1 Kings 1–2, viz., Rost, *Succession to the Throne*, 67–70, and Whybray, *Succession Narrative*, 50–55, as justification of the succession of Solomon, Delekat, "Bias and Theology," 26–36, as diatribe against Solomon's legitimacy, Flanagan, "Court History," 172–81, as extracts from Court Annals of the latter phase of David's reign that were assembled in support of the Solomonic succession. Ackroyd, "Succession Narrative (so-called)," 383–96, has raised questions regarding the stability of the narrative's boundaries and therefore its feasibility as a self-contained document.

2 SAMUEL 7:1-17 IN PRE-CANONICAL REDACTION

abolition of the Judaean monarchy in 586 BCE. It must therefore have been earlier, in the aftermath of Josiah's tragic death in 609 BCE, but while the hope of a recovery lingered, that a review of Israel's occupation of Palestine was prepared in the light of the reforms that were implemented as a legacy of his reign.[26]

It highlighted a nation-wide movement of religious reform following the recovery of a scroll that was immediately recognized as the book of the law—ספר־התורה (2 Kgs 22:8; 23:1–20). As was noted in the preceding chapter, studies later than the analysis of Frank M. Cross have identified sub-compositions of a historical nature in the Samuel–Kings corpus, which were of preexilic dating but were incorporated, not so much in a Josianic as an exilic redaction.[27]

Evidence for a preexilic, Josianic redaction might, however, be claimed in the projection of the uniquely favored status of the Davidic monarchy above the other Israelite regimes and of the Jerusalem temple as the only legitimate sanctuary for Israel. The secession of the northern tribes, the cultic schism it engendered and the irregularities that resulted, were therefore denounced as apostasy (1 Kgs 13), and it was to the persistence of such a derangement of the divine purpose that the downfall of the Northern Kingdom was attributed (2 Kgs 17:20–23; cf. 1 Kgs 15:34; 18:19, 26; 2 Kgs 3:2–3; 2 Kgs 10:29, 31; 13:2; 11; 14:24; 15:9, 18, 24, 28). It was therefore the hope of the Josianic redactors that, notwithstanding the later aberrations of the Manasseh-Amon regime (2 Kgs 21:3–9, 19–22), and the unexpected demise of Josiah (2 Kgs 23: 29–30), the people of Israel, having assented to the reforms, and by their re-commitment to the Sinai-Horeb covenant and the Mosaic law, might regain divine favor or, failing, might be better prepared for the impending visitations (2 Kgs 22:16–17; 23:1–3; cf. Deut 31:9–12; Jer 7:1–15).

Structurally, a preexilic Josianic redaction might be discovered in the highlighting of three significant periods of Israel's history, in each of which the priority of a legitimate central sanctuary was uppermost. The first was the Moses-Joshua period of "Conquest" (Deut 3:1:28; Josh 1:1–15; 21:43—22:10;

---

26. 1 Kings 8:46–48, envisaging captivity and deportation to distant destination but not a destruction of the temple, suggests that a Josianic edition, which included Solomon's prayer of dedication, should be dated before 586 BCE. Even after the capitulation of Jehoiachin, there was an expectation among the fervent royalists of a brief captivity (Jer 28:1–4).

27. An exploration of the possibility of a pre-Josianic, as well as a Josianic, redaction will presently be undertaken.

Judg 2:7),[28] in which the stipulations for such a chosen sanctuary enjoyed the highest priority in the Mosaic law, including a ban on all other cult centers and on alien cultic practices (Deut 12:2–14; cf. Josh 22). However, because the Baal cults continued to flourish in the Canaanite environment, influencing Israelites to do evil in YHWH's sight, the breaches in the Mosaic law brought disasters and reverses on them (Judg 2:11–23).The second period was the Davidic–Solomonic period of "rest" (Deut 12:10–11; cf. 2 Sam 7:1b; 1 Kgs 5:18 [MT]),[29] in which the chosen site for the sanctuary was procured (2 Sam 6: 17; 7:10–11a; 24:18; I Kgs 8:1–11; cf. 1 Chr 21:24–22:1), its construction was commissioned and, upon completion, it was dedicated (2 Sam 7:5–7, 13a; 1 Kgs 6–8). However, notwithstanding the dedication, Solomon went on to build "high places" in Jerusalem for the benefit of his foreign wives (1 Kgs 3:1-2; 11:4–8), and following the secession, Jeroboam appointed two royal sanctuaries, one at Bethel and the other at Dan, in opposition to the chosen sanctuary (1 Kgs 12:26—13:10; cf. Amos 7:13); and Judaean kings, from Solomon onward, who were noted for having done "right in Yahweh's sight,"[30] were also cited as having tolerated "high places" that continued to flourish throughout the Southern Kingdom (1 Kgs 3:2; 11:6–7; 14:23; 15:3, 14; 22:43; 2 Kgs 12:2–3; 14:3–4; 15:3–4, 34–35; 16:4; 21:3, 21–22). The third period, out of which the redaction evolved, was the Hezekiah–Josiah period of "reform," during which "high places" were delegitimized in the interest of the one central sanctuary. Initiated in the reign of Hezekiah (2 Kgs 18:4, 22), but thwarted and reversed in the Manasseh–Amon succession (2 Kgs 21:3–5, 21), the program of centralization and reform was revived, intensified, extended and completed in the reign of Josiah (2 Kgs 23:4–16).[31]

---

28. The coupling of leadership that characterized the Josianic redaction allows for an earlier Deuteronomy–Kings composition that had ended with the editorial reflection on the Fall of Samaria (2 Kgs 17:7–18, 20–23), which was based, not on the structural design of the Josianic redactors that extended the earlier composition into 2 Kings 18:1—23:28—an addendum by the Josianic redactors that projected the period of reform and centralization of the cult—but on the sequence of Orations noted by Noth, to which the Josianic redactors made additions e.g. Deuteronomy 33; Joshua 24; I Samuel 2:1-10; 2 Samuel 7:1-17, 18-29; 23:1-5; 1 Kings 8:15-53; 13:2-3.

29. J. Roy Porter, "Succession of Joshua," 117–26 also, has drawn attention to striking affinities between the Moses–Joshua and the David-Solomon succession ritual, which seemed to him to be more than coincidence.

30. Seven kings not so reported were Rehoboam (1 Kgs 14:21–30) and his successor Abijah (1 Kgs 15:30), Jehoram (2 Kgs 8:18) and his successor Ahaziah (2 Kgs 8:27), Ahaz (2 Kgs 16: 2–4), Manasseh (2 Kgs 21:2–11), and his successor Amon (2 Kgs 21:20–22).

31. The structure seems to be further highlighted by the relationship of each of the

2 SAMUEL 7:1-17 IN PRE-CANONICAL REDACTION

The primary objective of the Josianic redaction, therefore, was to project the temple at Jerusalem as symbolic of cultic integrity and national unity in a period of political uncertainty, social disorientation and disorder,[32] and to institute regular seasons of covenant renewal for the recommitment of a chosen people to the precepts of the Mosaic law (cf. Deut 29-30; 31:9-13; Josh 24:2-25), as the way to recovery of divine favor and hope for the future (Deut 28:1-14). That hope, though frustrated by the tragic death of Josiah and the deposition of Jehoahaz, the chosen successor, in the reassertion of Egyptian hegemony, and the appointment of Jehoiakim as vassal-ruler, was not completely crushed (2 Kgs 23:29-24:7).[33] Though recognizing that, politically, Judah had entered a twilight period, the redactors did not envisage an abolition of the monarchy, an invasion of Jerusalem or a destruction of the temple (1 Kgs 8:45; Jer 7:1-15; 28:1-6),[34] but hoped that, with the rise and expansion of the neo-Babylonian empire (with whom Josiah, evidently,

---

periods to a preceding anti-period—the Moses–Joshua Period of "conquest" and the promulgation of the law of the one sanctuary, preceded by the wilderness period of unfaithfulness and rebellion (Deut 1-4; 9:7-25; 31:25-32:42), the David–Solomon period of "rest" and the building of the one sanctuary, preceded by the period of the Judges when there was no king (i.e. Davidic) in Israel (Judg 2:11-23; 17-21; cf. Deut 12:8-9), and the Hezekiah–Josiah period of "reform," preceded by the period of a proliferation and persistence of "high places" (במות) (1 Kgs 11:7-11; 2 Kgs 17:7-23; 21:3-11).

32. That this was an objective as well as a result of the Josianic reform seems to be suggested by Jeremiah's sermon, preached in the temple precincts at the beginning of Jehoiakim's reign, in which the prophet deplores the misplaced confidence in the temple as a security of last resort (Jer 7:1-15; cf. 26:1-6).

33. The Chronicler's account of the death of Josiah as a casualty of war in a hopelessly unequal engagement on which Josiah insisted (2 Chr 35:20-24) is an unlikely interpretation. A more plausible explanation is that, with the withdrawal of the Assyrian presence in Syria-Palestine, the Pharaoh Necho, an ally to Assyria, having reasserted overlordship (2 Kgs 24:7), summoned Josiah to Megiddo, who went hoping to negotiate a truce, but was executed for the anti-Egyptian tendencies of the reformation (2 Kgs 23:13: cf. 1 Kgs 11:7-8).

34. It is significant that, when Jerusalem was besieged by the Babylonian army in response to Jehoiakim's rebellion, Jehoiachin capitulated and went into exile with his family and so spared Jerusalem of the imminent invasion and, following his deportation, a third son of Josiah, Zedekiah, was appointed by the Babylonians as vassal-ruler (2 Kgs 24:1, 11-12, 15-17).

had cast his lot),³⁵ the regime might have been reestablished and the reform program further consolidated.³⁶

2 SAMUEL 7:1–17 IN THE DEUTERONOMIC REDACTION (JOSIANIC)

Situated in the Davidic-Solomonic period, the Nathan narrative (2 Sam 7:1–17), in the Josianic interpretation, marked the zenith of Israelite ascendancy in Canaan as anticipated in the Mosaic law (Deut 12:9–11; cf. 2 Sam 7:1b), and therefore also signaled the propitious period for building a sanctuary in a place chosen by YHWH. The major objective of the narrative, however, was to highlight the special significance of David in and for the dispensation of "rest," and his indispensable contribution to the building of the chosen sanctuary; for although hindered from undertaking the project because of external conflicts and internal unrest, it was the success of his earlier exploits that ushered in the "rest" that made possible the undertaking and completion of the project (2 Sam 7:1b, 5–7; cf. 1 Kgs 5:17 [MT]; Ps 132:1–5). Accordingly, under a duality pattern of "commencement and completion," the building of the temple, as the chosen sanctuary, was represented as the joint undertaking and achievement of predecessor and successor (2 Sam 7:11b–13a; 1 Kgs 8:15–21). As Moses, forbidden to enter the promised land (Deut 1:37–38; 3:23–28; 4:21–22; 31:2; 32:48–52), began the conquest in Transjordan (Deut 2:1—3:20), which Joshua's victories continued on the other side of the river and completed in his settlement of the

---

35. Jeremiah's pro-Babylonian leaning (Jer 27–29) and his high regard for both Josiah (Jer. 22:15–16) and Jehoahaz, his successor (Jer 22:10–12), and, on the other hand, Pharaoh Necho's support for Assyria in its decline, prior to the Chaldean ascendancy, and therefore his antipathy to Josiah (2 Kgs. 23:29) and Jehoahaz his chosen successor (2 Kgs 23:31–33), suggest a pro-Babylonian alignment of the Josianic regime, to which Jehoiakim, notwithstanding his vassal-status, for a brief period, also inclined (2 Kgs 24:1). It was, most likely, in the prospect of an Egyptian collapse and of a Babylonian hegemony, prior to the exile, that encouraged a Josianic redaction (2 Kgs 24:7; cf. Jer. 27:1—28:17; 37:15—38:2).

36. Evidently such expectations were focused initially on Jehoahaz, who, like his father-predecessor was made king by the עם־הארץ, the rural gentry of Judah, in the hope that he would continue his father's policies. That may also have been the reason that his reign was cut short by the Egyptian Pharaoh Necho, on whose instructions he was deported (2 Kgs 23:30–33; cf. Jer 22:10–12; Ezek 19:1–4). The hopes were, however, frustrated by the execution of Zedekiah's sons and the nobility, and the blinding and deportation of Zedekiah (2 Kgs 24:1—25:21). By that time the Josianic redaction may have been completed (cf. 2 Kgs 24:7; Jer 37:5).

2 SAMUEL 7:1-17 IN PRE-CANONICAL REDACTION

tribes on both sides (Josh 6:1—12:24; 22:1-9; cf. Deut 3:16; Josh 1:12-17; 12:6), and as the reforms, to be initiated by Hezekiah (2 Kgs 18:3-8, 22) and, though reversed by Manasseh and Amon (2 Kgs 21:3, 20-22), would be resumed, intensified, extended, and completed by Josiah (2 Kgs 23:1-20), so the building of the chosen sanctuary, completed indeed by Solomon (1 Kgs 6:38; 7:51), was represented as a Davidic initiative (2 Sam 7:1-3) to whom, also, the commission was first communicated (2 Sam 7:5-13a).

It is, however, unlikely that the Nathan narrative in 2 Samuel 7:1-17 was a free and original composition of the Josianic redactors, but was rather an integration of traditions that had, until then, been separate and independent, viz., the tradition of a commission to build a "house" (sanctuary) for YHWH (2 Sam 7:1-4a, 5b-7, 13-15; cf. 1 Kgs 3:1-5; 9:1-5), the tradition of a promise to David of a "house" (lineage), from which should come the rulers of Israel (2 Sam 7:8-12, 16; cf. Pss 89:1-4, 19-37; 132) and the tradition of Israel's entitlement to the land they occupied in Canaan as a divine gift in fulfillment of a promise to the ancestors (2 Sam 7:10-11a; cf. Deut. 6:10-12; 8:7-9; 12:10-11; 25:17-19; 26:5-9). The establishing of the Jerusalem temple as the only legitimate Israelite sanctuary required an integration of the traditions for the recognition of David as spiritual successor to Moses, as progenitor of the royal lineage and beneficiary of the promises, and as founder of the YHWH cult in Jerusalem. Consequently David, having retrieved the ark of the covenant from obscurity in Kiriath-jearim, and brought it ceremoniously to Mount Zion (2 Sam 6:1-19), became the recipient of the revelation that commissioned the central sanctuary (2 Sam 7:1-7, 12-13, 27). Prefaced by a prohibition (2 Sam. 7:1-7), the promise to David, YHWH's chosen servant, of a house—dynasty—for the security of Israel, his chosen people (2 Sam 7:8-11) was climaxed by the promise of a biological heir who was designated as the builder of the temple, his chosen sanctuary (2 Sam 7:12-16).

The incorporation of the ark traditions in the account of the commissioning of a sanctuary may also have been occasioned by the suppression of the ark sanctuary on Mount Zion and the transfer of the ark of the covenant into the temple in keeping with the centralization program (1 Kgs 8:1-10). Also, to achieve the integration of the traditions, the role of Nathan who, originally, may have been that of a royal counselor (2 Sam 7:1-3; cf. 1 Kgs 3:4-5; 9:2-6), was re-cast as mediator of a prophetic revelation that legitimized the Davidic regime in Israel, and designated Solomon as the heir and successor and the builder of the sanctuary (2 Sam 7:4-17). As Noth has commented, it was David's removal of the ark to Zion that eventually brought the temple at Jerusalem into the mainstream of Israelite cultic traditions (2 Sam 6:1–7:16; cf. Pss 42–43, 46, 48, 76, 87, 122, 125, 132, 137).[37]

THE DEUTERONOMIC REDACTION (HEZEKIANIC)

In the preceding chapter note was taken of some of the more recent studies of *Samuel–Kings*, in which the discussion was taken beyond the conclusions reached by Cross. However, to the extent that they were focused mostly on *Kings* (MT), to that extent their contribution to an elucidation of the place of 2 Samuel 7:1–17 in the Prophets was limited.

The structural analysis proposed above for a Josianic redaction must therefore raise questions not for Cross' dual redaction hypothesis only, but for Provan's delineation of two editions of *Kings* and Campbell's isolation of a "Prophetic Record."[38] From the formulaic material, Provan conjectured that a preexilic edition of *Kings*, ending at the latest in the early period of Josiah's reign, may have been the attempt of a nationalist and proto-Dtr group to justify their religious and political position.[39] The conclusion was reached partly from a close analysis of regnal formulae that introduced and closed the accounts of the reigns in the Southern kingdom, from which the formulae relating to the reigns following Hezekiah's showed marked deviations in style,[40] and partly of the attitude of the rulers to the cult,[41] among whom Hezekiah stood out because of the extent of his reform measures.[42] Provan also noted a consistency of reporting in the burial notices from Rehoboam to Ahaz, with the exception of Abijam's burial, and the change from Manasseh's onward, which also indicated a post-Hezekianic and exilic redaction (2 Kgs 21–25).[43]

So far as the Nathan narrative (2 Sam 7) was concerned, Provan saw a connection with passages in Kings that characterized David as a promissory

---

37. See Noth, "The Jerusalem Catastrophe," 262.

38. The studies of Iain Provan and Antony Campbell have been chosen from those discussed in the preceding chapter because they included an examination of the implications of their respective hypotheses for 2 Samuel 7:1–17.

39. See Provan, *Hezekiah and Books of Kings*, 155.

40. Ibid., 134–41.

41. Ibid., 57–90.

42. Ibid., 120–30

43. Ibid., 134–35, 136–38.

2 SAMUEL 7:1–17 IN PRE-CANONICAL REDACTION

figure (1 Kgs 11:32, 36; 15:4; 2 Kgs 8:19), in which the continuance of the Davidic monarchy was secured in the preservation of one of the tribes from the secession, so that David might always have dominion—נִיר—before YHWH in Jerusalem—a promise that seemed to concur with the assurances in 2 Samuel 7:11b–16.[44]

Notwithstanding the detailed examination of the evidence, Provan's analysis has left some basic questions unresolved. One has to do with his approach, which seems to have proceeded on the assumption that a concurrence of phraseology sufficed for the identification and dating of the sub-compositions. Thus conclusions regarding David as a "comparative figure" for faithfulness, drawn from the recurrence of the phrase "as David his father was," was therefore indicative of a date prior to the abolition of the monarchy. However, for such a conclusion, the argument can hardly be reliable unless, included in the redaction, was a record of David's faithfulness, with which the references cited were both chronologically appropriate and factually consistent. Otherwise the phrase could have been no more than an attempt at idealization, injected into a later redaction and for a quite different purpose.[45] Another question concerns the Manasseh pericope (2 Kgs 21:1, 17–18, 25–26) which, though excluded from the first edition of *Kings* that he identified seems, from the criteria he applied to the regnal formulae, to show, on the one hand, no firm basis for its exclusion from the preexilic redaction he proposed,[46] and, on the other hand, a much clearer affinity for that redaction, than for the corresponding formulae relating to the later reigns in the exilic redaction he identified and to which the *pericope* was consigned (2 Kgs 22–25). This observation prompts the broader question of plausibility regarding a document completed, for the latest, in the early period of the reign of Josiah partly for the encouragement of his centrist

---

44. Ibid., 94–97.

45. It is curious that it is Hezekiah, whom Provan recognizes as portrayed as the ideal ruler (ibid., 153), but in whose characterization, supposedly in the same edition, David was cited in the comparative formula (2 Kgs 18:3).

46. There is, for instance, little to choose, authorship wise, between the introductory formulae of Manasseh's reign (2 Kgs 21:1–3) and Jehoash (2 Kgs 12:1–3). Furthermore, Jotham's reign of sixteen years (2 Kgs 15:32–38) stands out, authorship wise, more glaringly than Manasseh's consisting, it seems, entirely of regnal formulae. Essential differences pertaining to authorship seem to be, therefore, less of form or style than of circumstances. For the same reason changes in burial notices seem to be less of authorship than of circumstances that did not need repetition, e.g. an assassination, execution or fatal accident already reported.

and nationalist policies,[47] but, ending with the reign of Hezekiah, omitted the intervening Manasseh–Amon regime, during which Hezekiah's program of centralization was so thwarted (2 Kgs 23:26; cf. 21:3, 19–20) as to have necessitated the later attempt.[48] As was noted above, the reigns of the reforming kings, Hezekiah and Josiah, seem to have been deliberately and systematically coupled in a Josianic redaction, precisely in order to enclose, and render innocuous the irregularities of the Manasseh–Amon regime, and thus mitigate the retribution they provoked (2 Kgs 21:12–15; 22:16–17; 23:26–27). Therefore, by identifying 2 Kings 18–23 as a Josianic addendum, the theological reflection on the fall of the Northern Kingdom (2 Kgs 17:7–18, 20–23) stands out the more clearly as the epilogue to an earlier historical account, upon which the Josianic redaction was constructed.[49]

Note has also been taken of Antony Campbell's hypothesis of a "Prophetic Record"—a ninth century composition of northern provenance, which was incorporated into a Josianic redaction.[50] The pertinent question for discussion, however, concerns the auspices under which such extensive material was incorporated, especially as its provenance and more prominent features could hardly have favored its inclusion in a late seventh century redaction which was, in part, a castigation of the Northern Kingdom for perpetuating of the "sin of Jeroboam ben Nebat," viz., the rejection of the Jerusalem cultus (1 Kgs 13). Suffice it to note, therefore, that such a document, dated in the ninth century, would have been both more readily available to, and ideologically more compatible with, an eighth century composition, also of northern provenance, and thus account for its

---

47. Ibid., 154–55.

48. If there was not a reformation, was there ground for distinguishing Hezekiah above his predecessors as a ruler who, like them, had tolerated the "high places," and thereby deprive Josiah of a distinction that only he deserved? Provan seems, however, to have accepted that there was an earlier reformation, which was reported to give inspiration to the Josianic program. Why then, were the irregularities of the intervening reigns of Manasseh and Amon omitted from a document completed, for the latest, early in the reign of Josiah, that was designed partly to further the second attempt or why, if the post-Hezekiah material in Kings was of Exilic edition, were the irregularities of the reign of Jehoiakim omitted, which were comparable and, chronologically, more appropriate to the purpose (2 Kgs 24:9; cf. Jer. 22:13–19; 26—27; 36)?

49. 1 Samuel 12 must therefore have originally been composed in the light of the fall of the Northern Kingdom, as an earlier reflection, and "your king" (v. 25) must have referred to Hoshea who was deported (cf. 2 Kgs 17:4).

50. See Campbell, *Of Prophets and Kings*, 14–15, 79–80.

2 SAMUEL 7:1-17 IN PRE-CANONICAL REDACTION

incorporation in the Josianic redaction not in isolation, but as an integral component of traditional material more amenable to the later redaction.

The foregoing observations suggest, therefore, a pre-Josianic composition of Deuteronomy–Kings that ended with a theological reflection that was typical of a Deuteronomic composition (2 Kgs 17:7–18, 20–23; cf. Deut 28:36; Judg 2:11–23; 1 Sam 12). Completed in Jerusalem after the fall of the Northern Kingdom, it may have also been influenced by the political and religious ferment that marked the reign of Hezekiah who, above all his predecessors, appeared to epitomize the Deuteronomic ideal of fidelity (Deut 17:14–20; cf. 2 Kgs 18:3–7),[51] and was probably completed in the reign of his successor, Manasseh (cf. 2 Kgs 17:13–19; cf. 21:2–6). It was, essentially, a critical review of the Israelite occupation of Canaan and, in particular, of monarchical rule, from the perspective of the Mosaic law. Accordingly, the reigns of the Northern Kingdom and Judah were deliberately synchronized, each ruler being evaluated from a common perspective, unprejudiced by obsession with a centralization program that gave the Jerusalem sanctuary a monopoly (Deut 12:10), or an idealization of the Davidic monarchy that tended to a disparagement of the northern regimes (Deut 17:14–20).

A distinguishing feature of that edition of Deuteronomy–Kings was, as noted by Martin Noth, a sequence of orations that punctuated the composition at significant junctures,[52] the foremost of which must have been the promulgation by Moses of the covenant law (Deut 5:1—30:20), whose continuing relevance was reaffirmed at the critical transition-periods of the history that unfolded (Deut 32; Josh 23; Judg 2:11–23; 1 Sam 12; 2 Kgs 17:7–23); and a prophecy-and-fulfillment *schema*, as identified by Gerhard von Rad, showing how the prophetic word invariably attained fulfillment in the same plane of the history,[53] the prototype being the prophetic word spoken Moses, and fulfilled in the fall of the Northern Kingdom (Deut 18:15; 28:15-68; 30:15-20; cf. 1 Sam 12:25; 2 Kgs 17:1–7).

While, therefore, a detailed literary critical analysis, which might more precisely differentiate the two preexilic Deuteronomic redactions,

---

51. Although the claim made for Josiah was similar, there was a subtle but important distinction in that whereas Josiah's uniqueness among the kings was his penitence, his "turning" (2 Kgs 23:25), Hezekiah's was his faith, his "trust" (2 Kgs 18:5–6).

52. See Noth, *Deuteronomistic History*, 5–6. From this sequence the oration of Solomon's dedicatory prayer (1 Kgs 8:23–55) must be excluded as a predominantly Josianic insertion, whereas the prayer of David (2 Sam 7:18–29) might be included as part of a liturgy of the Davidic sanctuary.

53. See von Rad, *Studies in Deuteronomy*, 78–81.

cannot be pursued here,⁵⁴ it can be shown that, when the particular emphases consistent with the subsequent redactions—Josianic, Exilic, and Canonical—have been duly identified, what remains of Deuteronomy–Kings is appreciably more than random traditional material that were injected piecemeal in the redaction process, or unrelated compositional blocs pertaining to the period of the monarchy which were incorporated; but a continuous and coherent historical narrative of the Israelites' sojourn in Canaan, from Deuteronomy to 2 Kings 17, which not only retained its form and content in, but gave shape and substance to, the subsequent redactions. More consistently than them, however, it was that earliest redaction that took its departure from the continuing relevance of the Mosaic law, of which the orations identified by Noth, and the prophecy-fulfillment schema highlighted by von Rad,⁵⁵ were demonstrably supportive.⁵⁶ In that respect also, it exemplified most closely von Rad's definition of a "Deuteronomistic" history, viz., that norms for its judgment of the past were the standards laid down in Deuteronomy.⁵⁷

In attempting a differentiation between the two preexilic redactions, a critical study of the twin-emphasis that distinguished the Josianic redaction, viz., the monopoly that was accorded the Jerusalem cultus, and the unique status conferred on the Davidic monarchy, might assist. While the building of a sanctuary at a location to be chosen by YHWH, was stipulated in the Deuteronomic law (Deut 12:10–11; cf. 1 Kgs 8:15–29), simultaneously, provision was also made for a sanctuary "in each of your tribes" (Deut 12:13–14), in terms that seemed not merely to have envisaged a plurality

---

54. Such a differentiation has been attempted at one level in the book of Deuteronomy by G. Minette de Tillesse "Sections 'tu' et Sections 'vous' dans le Deutéronome," 29–97, with respect to the use of the pronouns in the second person, singular or plural. Other indicators are references to the exile as deportation to a strange land not known by the ancestors (Deut. 28:36), which must therefore have excluded both Babylon and Egypt (cf. Deut 26: 5; Jos. 24:2) and pointed to Assyria (2 Kgs 15:28); and also the exile as dispersion (Deut 28:69; 2 Kgs 17:6), whereas deportation proper is referred to as a return to Egypt or captivity in another land (Deut. 28:68; 1 Kgs 8:46–48; cf. 2 Kgs 23:33). Finally, post-Cross investigations into preexilic compositions in Deuteronomy–Kings also point in that direction.

55. The story of the denunciation of the Bethel sanctuary by the unnamed prophet from Judah in 1 Kings 13, and its fulfillment in the Josianic reformation (2 Kgs 23), was obviously a Josianic injection.

56. That is to say, neither the orations identified by Noth, nor the prophecy-fulfillment schema traced by von Rad, had as much relevance for the subsequent redactions as they did for the redaction now being proposed.

57. See von Rad, *Studies in Deuteronomy*, 75.

of tribal sanctuaries, but to have disqualified Jerusalem which was, until the Davidic occupation, a Jebusite stronghold situated outside all the tribal enclaves (Josh 15:63; Judg 1:21; cf. 2 Sam 5:6-9). The discrepancy seems therefore to suggest that an exclusive centralization program, far from being a Mosaic stipulation, may have been a much later innovation, prompted initially by a national emergency that required centralization as a national policy and therefore, because of the cultic implications, was promulgated also as Mosaic law (Deut. 12:14; cf. 2 Kgs 18:4, 22; 21:3). The provision was, however, further radicalized for a more aggressive program of cultic centralization, and became established as substantive law to legitimize one central sanctuary (Deut 12:5, 10–11; cf. 2 Kgs 23:7-8).

The anachronisms are therefore unmistakable. Solomon makes a pilgrimage to "the great high place" at Gibeon (1 Kgs 9:1-6) immediately following his dedication of the temple at Jerusalem—"the only legitimate and chosen sanctuary" (1 Kgs 8:12-19; 9:1-2; cf. 3:4-5). The secession, instigated by a notable YHWH prophet, is consolidated by Jeroboam ben Nebat with the building two sanctuaries on traditional sites, in opposition to the temple at Jerusalem (1 Kgs 11:29-33; 12:26-29; 14:8-9).[58] Elijah, a fervent YHWH prophet, laments the widespread destruction of the YHWH sanctuaries and, without compunction, rebuilds the fallen shrine on Mt. Carmel (1 Kgs 18:31-32; 19:10, 14: cf. 2 Kgs 4:22-25). Notwithstanding the explicit prohibition in the Mosaic law against the "high places" (Deut 12:2-4), rulers in Judah, who tolerated them, were nevertheless approved as "having done right in YHWH's sight" (1 Kgs 15:11, 14; 22:43; 2 Kgs 12:2-3; 14:3-4; 15:3-4, 34-35).

Further evidence of a pre-Josianic composition might be gathered from the ark narrative in Samuel (1Sam 4:1—7:1; 2 Sam 6) and, in particular, from an examination of the reference to a twenty year sojourn of the ark at Kiriath-jearim (1 Sam 7:1-2; cp. 14:18). In Antony Campbell's judgment, the ark narrative, being contemporary with the events narrated, was designed to celebrate the Davidic-Solomonic regime as a revolution of the epochs,[59] in which was commemorated the end of the Old Israel of the Judges, dramatized by the fall of the Shiloh temple where the ark had been housed, and the inauguration of the New Israel in the establishment

---

58. The prophet Ahijah's disapproval was not of Jeroboam's building of sanctuaries in rivalry to the Jerusalem temple, but because of the calf-images that he installed in them (1 Kgs 14:9; 2 Kgs 10:29; 17:16; cf. Deut 9:12-17).

59. See Campbell, *Ark Narrative*, 213.

THE NATHAN NARRATIVE IN 2 SAMUEL 7:1-17

of the Davidic monarchy, and the installation of the ark at the dedication of the new temple at Jerusalem.[60] Consistent with that interpretation, the break of a Philistine captivity (1 Sam 5), followed by a twenty-year respite at Kiriath-jearim (1 Sam 7:1-2), marked the crucial turning point.[61] The suggestion of a two decade interval at Kiriath-jearim might, however, have originated not in a tenth century account, as Campbell proposed, nor yet in a later Josianic redaction, as Cross assumed,[62] but more likely in an earlier Deuteronomic interpretation that urged steady adherence to the Mosaic law, rather than reliance on the ark as a *palladium*, as the guarantee for success in battle (1 Sam 7:2-13; Josh 6:1—8:29; cp. Num 10:35; Deut 10:1-3, 28; 1 Sam 4:5-11).[63] Furthermore, in *Samuel* might also be discerned an even earlier tradition of the movements of the ark, approximating primary material, which suggests that, before the rise of the monarchy (Judg 20:23-27; 1 Sam 1:10-12; 3:3; 7:1), and throughout the reign of Saul (1 Sam 14:18),[64] the ark, as a mobile sanctuary, circulated between the major Israelite cult-centers—Shechem (Josh 8:33), Bethel (Judg 20:26-27; 21:2), Shiloh (1 Sam 1:3, 10-12; 3:3; cf. Josh 22:9; Judg 21:19), Mizpah (1 Sam 7:5-6), Gilgal (1 Sam 11:15; 12:3; 14:18; cf. Josh 4:17-19), Kiriath-jearim/Nob/Gibeon

---

60. Ibid. 200-210.

61. It is the view of Peter R. Ackroyd in *1 Samuel*, 65, that the natural sequel, so far as the narrative is concerned, should have been a new story of the ark, perhaps David bringing it to Jerusalem (2 Samuel 6). What follows, however, is an account of the inauguration of the monarchy and the appointment of Saul as the first King of Israel, following the victory of Ebenezer (1 Sam 7:3-14).

62. See Cross, *Canaanite Myth*, 97.

63. Clements, "Deuteronomy and the Jerusalem Cult Tradition," 300-301, has argued that the definition in the book of Deuteronomy of the ark as merely a receptacle for the tables of the law was in reaction to its mythologization in the Jerusalem cultus as a cherubim throne. He did not, however, extend to an investigation of the Deuteronomic History for corroboration of which the reference in 1 Samuel 7 may have been a pointer, seeing that it was brought into the battle at Ebenezer Aphek as a *palladium* to secure victory, but failed (1 Sam 4:1-22).

64. Arguments for the changing of the ark to the Ephod in I Samuel 14:18—cf. Driver, *1 & 2 Samuel*, 110, and Ackroyd, *2 Samuel*, 114—are for the most part circular, i.e., in defense of the claim of a two decade sojourn at Kiriath-jearim (itself debateable), which may also have influenced both the late insertion of 1 Samuel 14:3 and the Septuagint (LXX) substitution at 1 Samuel 14:18. Against Driver's supporting argument that the ark was not used as an organ of divination, see Judges 20:27 and 2 Kings 19:14-21, and that הגישׁ was the word properly applied to the bringing of the Ephod into use, see 2 Samuel 15:24 in which the verb was also used in connection with the ark, in the same sense and, seemingly, for the same purpose.

2 SAMUEL 7:1-17 IN PRE-CANONICAL REDACTION

(1 Sam 7:1; 21:1-6; cf. 2 Sam 21:1-10; 2 Chr 1:13)[65] and Mamre-Hebron (2 Sam 5:3)[66]—before its final removal to Zion (2 Sam 6:12, 16-17)—in a relatively unbroken itinerary that could not have accommodated such a long period of respite at any cult center.[67] Thus, it appears that even before the rise of the Deuteronomic movement or the implementation of a centralization program, there seems to have been a tradition of the ark's movements between the major tribal sanctuaries, which was acknowledged in an earlier Deuteronomic history, and was therefore an even further cry from the exclusive status, bestowed on the Jerusalem sanctuary in the Josianic redaction, whereby cult centers that had traditionally been adopted and frequented as YHWH shrines before the inception, and for the greater part of the period of the monarchy, became delegitimized and downgraded to "high places" (cf. 1 Kgs 3:4; 2 Kgs 18:4, 22; 21:3).[68]

Secondly, while the specially favored status of the Davidic monarchy was emphasized in *Samuel–Kings* (1 Sam 2:10; 13:14; 15:28; 16:13; 24:20; 25:28; 2 Sam 7:13-15; 1 Kgs 11:32, 36, 38-39; 15:4; 2 Kgs 8:19), a divergent ideology was advocated in the Deuteronomic law-code which, while

---

65. Blenkinsopp, *Gibeon and Israel*, 65–67, has argued for an identification of "the house of Abinadab on a hill" in Kiriath-jearim (1 Sam 7:1), with the sanctuary at Nob (1 Sam 21:1-6) and the "great high place" at Gibeon (1 Kgs 5:3), as signifying the same cult center in different stages of development.

66. The movement of the ark to the Mamre sanctuary at Hebron at the time of David's appointment (2 Sam 5:1-5) might account for the references to Ephra-tah in Psalm 132:6 (cf. Ruth 4:11; Mic 5:2), in connection with its recovery, and to Baale-Judah in the account of its removal to Zion *via* Kiriath-jearim (2 Samuel 6:2-3a).

67. The conclusion is reached from a close examination of the oft-recurring phrase in the Samuel corpus, לפני־יהוה which, following a lead given by Noth, cf. "David and Israel" 256, may be interpreted as a redactional device in the light of the claim of a twenty year lull at Kiriath-jearim (1 Sam 7:1-2), and thus a dissociation of the ark from the reign of Saul, but was subverted by an explicit reference in 1 Samuel 14:18. Alternatively, it may have been a shorthand colloquialism for the presence of a worshipper (or a cult object) before the ark of the covenant, whether as installed in a sanctuary, or carried in procession (cf. Num 10:35-36; Josh 6:4, 7-8; 7:6, 23; 1 Sam 4:4-8; 6: 13-20; 2 Sam 6:4-5; 7:18), which was then adopted in redaction (1 Sam. 21:6; cf. Exod 25:10-23; 34:34; 40:21-23). Moshe Weinfeld, *Deuteronomy and Deuteronomic School*, 192, has opted for a literal interpretation of לפני־יהוה that pointed to anthropomorphism which, while conceivable for an earlier period, would have presented a major difficulty for the Josianic editors (cf. 1 Kgs 8:27-29a). Also, in other contexts, which do not envisage the ark, as in 1 Samuel 16:6, another expression נגד יהוה, with a preposition of more secular and more flexible definition, was used.

68. This might also go some way in resolving the conundrum of Judaean rulers who tolerated the "high places," but were also cited as having done "right in YHWH's sight."

THE NATHAN NARRATIVE IN 2 SAMUEL 7:1-17

approving the principle of hereditary succession, rested regime-approbation less upon hereditary claims than upon a faithful adherence to the Mosaic law; and therefore did not exempt delinquent rulers from rejection and removal, however legitimate otherwise (Deut 17:14-20; cf. 1 Kgs 2:2-4; 8:25; 9:6-9; 11:36; 2 Kgs 10:30).

It was probably for support of such an ideology that the prophetic material identified by Campbell was incorporated. Committed as they were to the paramount status of the Mosaic law (Deut 5:6-7; 18:18-19; 33:4; 1 Sam 8:1-7), YHWH prophets, more numerous and vociferous in the Northern Kingdom than in Judah, confronted rulers over flagrant violations, pronounced sentences against them and, by designating a replacement, set in motion the process of regime-change, which invariably resulted not merely in a removal from office, but a liquidation of the discredited regime (cf. 1 Kgs 19:15-17). A regular pattern of indictment, prefaced by a recital of YHWH's gracious actions in election, elevation and protection, included also a citation of offences, and was climaxed by a sentencing (1 Sam 15:17-23; 2 Sam 12:7-10; 1 Kgs 14:7-11; 16:2-4; 21:20b-25; cf. Deut 32:1-43). The pattern, be it noted, also applied to the Solomon-Rehoboam regime (I Kgs 11:31-34; 12:1-16), save that "removal" and "liquidation" took the form of disaffiliation of the northern tribes from the House of David, resulting politically in a massive disruption of Israel.

Understandably, the recurring pattern of violence accompanying regime changes in the Northern Kingdom remained prominent in the later redaction because of the ammunition it lent to the blanket-condemnation of the secession (1 Kgs 12:26—13:10; cf. 14:14-16; 15:25-26; 16:2-4; 21:20b-22; 2 Kgs 3:2-3; 10:28-31). However, within the blanket condemnation, might be traced a more discriminating pattern in the varied and reasoned indictment of discredited regimes that pointed to an earlier redaction (1 Kgs 14:11; 16:4; 21:24). Moreover, contrary to the indiscriminately negative evaluation in the later redaction of the rulers of the Northern Kingdom, there was an endorsement of the secession by Ahijah the Shilonite, a YHWH prophet, whose explicit designation of Jeroboam ben Nebat as ruler in Israel included the promise of "a house as sure as David's" (1 Kgs 11:29-38).[69] The conditional legitimization of the Israelite monarchy, typically Deuteronomic (Deut 17:14-20), also points to an earlier redac-

---

69. It is significant that, whereas in the prophecy of Ahijah the Davidic ruler is demoted in secession to נשיא (prince), the rebel-leader is promoted to מלך, king over Israel (1 Kgs 11:34-37).

2 SAMUEL 7:1-17 IN PRE-CANONICAL REDACTION

tion, and might account for a phrase כסא ממלכתו in the Nathan narrative as a relic of that earlier redaction also found only in the Deuteronomic royal Law and in Solomon's post-dedication oracle (2 Sam 7:13; Deut 17:18; 1 Kgs 9:5; cf. 1 Kgs 2:2-4; 8:25; Ps 132:11-12). An earlier tradition, including such a conditional promise, might therefore be assumed for the making of the Nathan narrative.[70]

With respect to the Judaean monarchy, material evidence for a pre-Josianic redaction is less forthcoming because of the later investment in the unique status of the Davidic monarchy. However, the evidence is not altogether irretrievable. A more impartial approach might be discerned not only in a systematic synchronizing of the reigns in the two kingdoms, but also in the common evaluation of each ruler, throughout, as having done, or not done, "right in YHWH's sight." It is also striking that, in the evaluation of the Judaean reigns from Jehoshaphat to Jotham, legitimacy seemed more decisive by that test than a claim to the Davidic pedigree or approximation to the Davidic model (1 Kgs 15:9-15; 22:42-43; 2 Kgs 12:2; 14:3; 15:3, 32-34).[71] Having thus linked the fall of the Northern Kingdom to a decline in monarchical rule generally, and particularly so in deviations from the Mosaic law and repeated rejections of prophetic admonition (2 Kgs 17:7-23), the redaction, viz., the book of the law, became a salutary and urgent warning to the surviving monarchy in Judah and Jerusalem (2 Kgs 17:19; cf. 18:9-12; 22:11-20).

---

70. Provan, *Hezekiah and the Book of Kings*, 108, has suggested to the contrary that the oracle to Solomon may have been a reinterpretation of the oracle in the Nathan narrative. A similar conditionality, reflecting the Mosaic law (Deut 17:18), also evident in the king's admonition of Solomon (1 Kgs 2:4) in Solomon's prayer of dedication (1Kgs 8:25), seems to point instead to an earlier and Deuteronomic redaction.

71. In a number of cases—Jehoshaphat (1 Kgs 22:43), Amaziah (2 Kgs 14:3), Azariah (2 Kgs. 15:3), and Jotham (2 Kgs 15:34)—it is to the influence and example of the immediate predecessor that their virtues were credited. Indeed, the case of Amaziah carries a dissociation from David that is explicit (2 Kgs 14:3), and in the case of his father, Joash, it is the priest, Jehoiada who was cited as the worthy mentor (2 Kgs 12:2; cf. 2 Chr 24:22). "Doing right in YHWH's sight" as against "doing right in one's sight" (cf. Deut 12:8-9), was the characteristic Deuteronomic expression for a responsible attitude to the cult, for the furtherance of which the king's authority and commitment were critical (cf. Judg 17:6; 21:25). The naming of David as exemplar in the cases of Asa (1 Kgs 15:11) and Hezekiah (2 Kgs 18:3) may have been also due to an attempt at distancing them from their immediate predecessors—Abijah, Rehoboam, and Solomon in the case of Asa and, in the case of Hezekiah, Ahaz. Northern alliance and, in particular, Tyrian affiliation were noted among the shortcomings Jehoram (2 Kgs 8:16-18) and Ahaziah (2 Kgs 8:26-27), and northern influence cited in the indictment of Ahaz (2 Kgs 16:3-4).

THE NATHAN NARRATIVE IN 2 SAMUEL 7:1-17

Moreover, behind a veneer of hereditary continuity, the account of the Judaean monarchy gives evidence of sharp reversals in policy (1 Kgs 1:5—2:25; 15:8-13; 2 Kgs 8:15-16; 11:1-2, 12-16; 12:20-21; 14:3, 19-21), especially noticeable in changes from "unrighteous" regimes to "righteous" (cf. 1 Kgs 15:1-15; 2 Kgs 11:1-16), and *vice versa* (1 Kgs 22:41-43; 2 Kgs 8:16-18; 18:1-6; 20:21—21:3). Evidence of such a pattern must considerably narrow the difference between a dynastic continuity claimed for the Davidic monarchy and the short-lived regimes and frequency of regime-changes that destabilized the Northern Kingdom. A less orderly pattern of the successions marked the transitions in Judaean monarchy, beginning with the Solomon-Abijah regime, judged to be "evil" (1 Kgs 11:1-11; 14:22-24; 15:3), and leaving in its wake an irreparable schism (1 Kgs 12:1-16, 26-29). This was followed by the "righteous" Asa-Jehoshaphat regime during which reforms of cultic abuses were implemented, including the dismissal of the Queen Mother who seems to have been implicated, and auspicious signs of a maturing statesmanship in a cessation of hostilities and a peace alliance with the Northern Kingdom (1 Kgs 22:4, 43-44; 2 Kgs 8:16-18). The fragile accord was, however, derailed by the rise of a Tyrian-Israel axis, spawned initially by a Jezebel-Ahab marriage alliance (1 Kgs 16:29-33; cf. 18:1-18; 19:1-16), but was extended further by a Jehoram-Athaliah marriage (2 Kgs 8:16-18), which brought the Southern Kingdom, as it had the Northern, under a Phoenician hegemony (1 Kgs 18-19; 2 Kgs 9:1—10:28), exposing both kingdoms to an aggressive Tyrian religious offensive. It was at that point that monarchical rule in both Kingdoms reached the nadir of Deuteronomic disillusionment, provoking an reaction of the Israelite militia, instigated by prophetic initiative, in a violent revolt that obliterated the Omri-dynasty and, with it, Tyrian Baalism in gruesome massacre (1 Kgs 19:15-17; 2 Kgs 9:1—10:28). Then Athaliah, the Queen Mother of Judah, consequent on the assassination of her husband, the King Ahaziah, ordered the massacre of the remaining Judaean princes, usurped the throne and ruled for six years (2 Kgs 11:1-2; cf.10:13-14).[72] Following her overthrow and execution (2 Kgs 11:14-18, 20), the accession of Joash inaugurated the longest period in the succession of Judaean rulers whose approbation rested less on a Davidic ancestry or on adherence to a Davidic model, than on having done "right in YHWH's sight" (2 Kgs 12:2; 14:3; 15:3, 34), and was

---

72. The Athaliah massacre of the royal princes may have been a preemptive strike for self protection against the spreading of the Jehu revolt over the border, thus inflaming the disaffection that was already simmering in Judah (cf. 2 Kgs 11:1-20; 2 Chr 21:4-6; 22:10).

2 SAMUEL 7:1-17 IN PRE-CANONICAL REDACTION

broken by the reversion of Ahaz to the idolatrous practices of the northern rulers (2 Kgs 16:3-4). It was against that wider, clearer, objective and balanced historical backdrop of monarchical instability and decline in both kingdoms of Israel, and later, in the recovery of confidence because of the character of Hezekiah's rule, that the earliest Deuteronomic history, viz., the book of the law, was composed.

2 SAMUEL 7:1-17 IN THE DEUTERONOMIC REDACTION (HEZEKIANIC)

The relevance of the foregoing exploration for conclusions regarding the shaping of 2 Samuel 7:1-17, and its place in the Deuteronomy–Kings corpus, may already have become apparent. It has been shown that, notwithstanding its importance for the Josianic redactors, it is unlikely that the Nathan narrative in 2 Samuel 7:1-17 was entirely their creation, but was rather the reinterpretation of a position that had been reached in an earlier redaction. It was also noted, in the preceding chapter that, although the narrative seemed formally to fulfill the criteria, it was omitted from the sequence orations identified by Noth, because of its explicit rejection of the temple (2 Sam 7:5-7) and its extraordinary zeal for the monarchy (2 Sam 7:11b-16).[73] Disqualification notwithstanding, the prophetic oracle (2 Sam 7:8-16) reflected the typical pattern of a Deuteronomic covenant formulation in which the promise to a beneficiary, invariably conditional (Deut 1:6—4:24, 5; 29:2-13; Jos. 24:2-25; 1 Sam 12; cf. Exod 19:4-5; 20:2-3), was prefaced by a recital of YHWH's gracious acts (2 Sam 7:8-9). Alternatively, in prophetic invective, the promise, invariably consistent with Deuteronomic theology of accountability, was invoked against beneficiaries who failed in their obligations (1 Sam 2:27-33; 15:17-19, 28; 2 Sam 12:7-11; 1 Kgs 14:7-11; 16:2-4; cf. Deut 5:7-10; 32:1-43; 1 Sam 12; 2 Kgs 17:7-23; Amos 2:6—3:2). A Deuteronomic input is therefore evident.

If, therefore, the verses identified by Noth were incompatible with the theology of divine transcendence that distinguished the Josianic redaction (2 Sam 7:5; cf. 2 Sam 7:13a; 1 Kgs 8:27-29a),[74] and with the anti-Solomonic

---

73. See Noth, *Deuteronomistic History*, 55. To judge however, from 2 Samuel 7 that the building of a temple was prohibited, or the value of a monarchy was excessive, and therefore alien to the Deuteronomistic spirit, might be somewhat exaggerated (cf. 2 Sam 7:13-14; Deut 12:5; 17:14-15, 19-20).

74. The "name theology" is a Deuteronomic, and more specifically Josianic

perspectives which, as Marvin Sweeney has suggested, drove the Josianic reformation and informed the ensuing redaction (2 Kgs 23:13–14; cf. 1 Kgs 11:1–13; cf. 2 Sam 7:12–15);[75] and were even less compatible with an exilic redaction, which was a response to the abolition of the Davidic monarchy, the most feasible explanation of the verses in the Prophets, viz., 2 Samuel 7:5–7, 11b–16, is that they must have been the result of an unusual redaction process that alternated between an unfavorable and a favorable characterization of Solomon, and was, in any case, either unaware of, or disinclined to, the theology of divine transcendence that was uppermost in the later redaction.

Another unusual feature in the making of the narrative is the formulation of a promise (2 Sam 7:11b–16) prefaced by a history of YHWH's gracious actions (2 Sam 7:8–11a), which did not include a record of meritorious service that warranted a reward, nor the imposition of an obligation on the beneficiary consistent with the promise (2 Sam 7:11–16; cp. 1 Kgs 2:3–4; 6:12–13; 8:25; 9:4–5; 11:38; Ps 132:1–5, 11–12). It suggests that a conditional promise that, in typically Deuteronomic formulation (2 Sam 7:11b–12, 16), had obligated the beneficiaries, viz., David's successors—זרע—to observance of the Mosaic law (Deut 17:18–20; cf. 1 Kgs 2:2–4; 25; 9:4–6; 11:38; Ps 132:11–12),[76] but in which Solomon had signally failed (1 Kgs 11:1–13, 33), was overtaken by a later, but still pre-Josianic, re-editing that singled out Solomon—זרק—as sole beneficiary and builder of the temple (2 Sam 7:12–14), superseding the earlier conditionality, to render the promise immutable and the favored regime secure.

In the narrative, therefore, was preserved an early legend of a nocturnal revelation, by which המלך, viz., Solomon was commissioned to build a divine abode (2 Sam 7:1a, 2–3, 4a, 5b–7; cf. 1 Kgs 3:1–5; 9:1–6), the successful completion whereof, legitimized his succession and established his rule in Israel (2 Sam 7:13–15; cf. 1 Kgs 9:1–5). Also preserved was the cultic tradition of an annual festival in celebration of the deity's victory over alien

---

interpretation of the nature of the divine presence in the earthly sanctuary. It accentuates the divine transcendence which makes his literal presence in the local sanctuary incompatible with his nature. However, his presence with the worshipping community is realizable through his identification with his "name" (cf. 1 Kgs 8:27–29a).

75. See Sweeney, "Critique of Solomon," 607–22.

76. This may account for the Deuteronomic relic, noted by Provan, *Hezekiah and the Books of Kings*, 108, in the phrase "...the throne of your kingdom"—כסא־ממלכתך—found, apart from the royal law in Deuteronomy (Deut 17:18) only here (2 Sam. 7:13) and in 1 Kings 9:5, in the Deuteronomic corpus.

2 SAMUEL 7:1-17 IN PRE-CANONICAL REDACTION

forces of chaos (1 Sam 4-6). The deity, symbolized by the ark carried in cultic procession, was also represented by the king as a leading participant (2 Sam 6:1-19). That ancient cultic tradition, which in Israelite celebration identified the deity as YHWH, was climaxed in the early Deuteronomic redaction with a re-affirmation of YHWH's commitment to the Davidic monarchy as a whole—זרע—and a recommitment of his successors to faithful observance of the Mosaic law (2 Sam 7:8-16; cf. 1 Kgs 2:2-4, 8:25; 1 Kgs 9:1-6; Ps. 132:12). Thus the two cultic traditions, while still in separation, were then further re-interpreted in a Hezekianic redaction to establish the reformed temple as YHWH's earthly dwelling (2 Sam 7:5-7; 1 Kgs 8:12-13 cf. 2 Kgs 18:4-6), and Solomon's exclusive status as David's immediate successor—זרק—and the builder of YHWH's house (2 Sam 7:11b-15). It was these two co-existing traditions that were amalgamated by further reinterpretation in the Josianic redaction, not only because of the misgivings deriving from Solomon's apostasies (1 Kgs 11:6-13), but also to project David's superior status as progenitor of the royal lineage (2 Sam 7:8-16), his distinction as founder of the YHWH cult in Jerusalem (2 Sam 6:1-19; Ps 132), his initiatives in, and indispensable contribution to the building of the temple (2 Sam 1-7, 13a; cf. 1 Kgs 6:16-18 MT), and to re-define the temple as the only legitimate sanctuary where YHWH may be known and invoked by his Name (2 Sam. 7:13a; 1 Kgs 8:27-30 ; 13:1-3).

All the available evidence points to the period of Hezekiah's reign (715—687 BCE) as that which offered the conditions most conducive to the re-presentation and formation of both legends. In the first place it was, in W.F. Albright's view, an extraordinary period in the cultural evolution of Israel,[77] to which R.B.Y. Scott has added that it also marked a transition from oral traditions to the written compositions (cf. Prov 25:1).[78] Eduard Nielsen has also observed that such transitions usually occurred not when the cultural summits were attained, but when the culture, as such, was under threat.[79] It might be added that such compositions not only preserved oral traditions, archive-wise, as J. Roy Porter seems to have suggested,[80] but by reinterpretation in the later composition in response to the crisis that deepened.

Secondly, as the first monarch, since Solomon, to rule in Israel without a northern counterpart, Hezekiah may have attempted a recovery of the

---

77. See Albright, *From Stone Age to Christianity*, 315–21.
78. See Scott, "Solomon and the Beginning of Wisdom," 96.
79. See Nielsen, "Role of Oral Tradition," 88.
80. See Porter, "Old Testament Historiography," 137–38.

Davidic-Solomonic kingdom (cf. 2 Kgs 18:8) or, at least, taken responsibility for the Israelite population left back from the Assyrian deportations, some of whom were seeking asylum in Judah and Jerusalem, bringing with them their traditions (2 Sam 7:10–11a; cf. 2 Kgs 15:29; 17:6; 18:11).

Thirdly, in his pro-Egyptian policy, as part of his strategy of resistance to Assyrian aggression (2 Kgs 18:21; cf. Isa 30:1–7; 31:1–3; cf. 1 Kgs 3:1; 7:8b; 9:14), as well as his patronage of the Wisdom movement (Prov 25:1; cf. 1 Kgs 4:29–34) and his commitment to the Jerusalem temple as YHWH's abode (2 Sam 7:5-7, 13; cf. 1 Kgs 8:12–13), Hezekiah promoted and personified a Solomonic renaissance. While, therefore, the ark narrative, a product of the Deuteronomic movement preserving earlier pre-monarchy traditions had become adapted to the Solomonic legend as builder of the temple, that legend may have been shaped by the impact of external influences, particularly the Egyptian *Königsnovelle*.

Fourthly, the unprecedented socio-political conditions of the eighth century, resulting from Assyrian incursions, were also represented in the narrative as a crisis of un-settlement that threatened to put in reverse the traditional *Heilsgeschichte* of election, rightful inheritance and secure possession (2 Sam 7:10–11a; cf. 2 Kgs 15:29; 17:6; Isa 10:5-32). Consequently, hope of salvation (מנוחה) (v. 11a), became yoked to the legitimacy of the surviving monarchy. The narrative also reflected Israelite anxieties, following the absorption of the Northern Kingdom in the Assyrian Empire and the transplantation of settlers into Samaria.

Fifthly, reference in the narrative to the chastisement and security of David's descendants (2 Sam 7:14–15) might similarly be interpreted. Nelson interpreted the threat as pertaining to the disaffiliation of the ten tribes from the Davidic monarchy in the secession.[81] It is, however, difficult to interpret as "chastisement" the withdrawal of the allegiance of peoples on whom the rejected regime had no proprietary claim, and over whom rule could be maintained only with their consent (1 Kgs 12:1–17; cf. 2 Sam 5:1–3; 2 Kgs 11:17). If there was a historic ordeal that could be reckoned as chastisement by plunging the regime into dire straits of peril, affliction and near collapse, but from which it was delivered, it was, as Leonhard Rost has argued, the Assyrian siege of Jerusalem and the euphoria that followed its lifting (2 Kgs 18–19).[82]

---

81. See Nelson, *Double Redaction*, 101–105.
82. See Rost, *Succession to the Throne*, 49.

2 SAMUEL 7:1-17 IN PRE-CANONICAL REDACTION

The nucleus of the Nathan narrative may therefore be read as an early seventh century re-presentation of the legend of a revelation to Solomon regarding the building of the Jerusalem temple (2 Sam 7:1a, 2–3, 4a, 5b–7, 10–11a, 13–15; cf. 1 Kgs 9:1–9), to reflect the conflicting moods of relief in the lifting of a siege and lingering apprehensions about the future. Although the Southern Kingdom had suffered extensive devastation, massive deportations and the crushing burden of indemnities, it could be claimed that Jerusalem was not invaded, the monarchy was not overthrown, its citizenry had not capitulated, nor was the temple desecrated (2 Kgs 19:20–37). Nevertheless the Assyrian presence on the northern frontier remained the disquieting reality, which neither Hezekiah's reliance on Egyptian support (2 Kgs 18:21; cf. Isa 31:1–3), nor Manasseh's subservience to Nineveh could allay (2 Chron 33:11). However, the recollection of the grandeur the Solomonic era, encouraged by the Wisdom movement and grounded in the status of the Jerusalem temple as YHWH's dwelling place, offered an anxious people a measure of security in their homeland (1 Kgs 8:12–13; cf. Jer 7:4; 9:23–24).

It is therefore unlikely that the positive image of Solomon, presented in the narrative (2 Sam 7: 13–15), derived from either the Deuteronomic traditional material, or the later Josianic redaction, especially as, in both accounts, it was to the cultic abuses of his reign that the onset of national decline was traced. It could only have been a Hezekianic input, drawn most likely from an extra-Israelite parallels of regime-legitimization, in which was highlighted the legend of Solomon, the builder of the Jerusalem temple, and supported by his imperial sway and the unparalleled splendor of his reign. It also reported a reformation of the temple cultus and a program of cultic centralization (2 Kgs 18:4, 22; cf. 21:3) which, while stopping short of a suppression of the Davidic sanctuary, initiated the movement that culminated, in the Josianic period, in the transfer of the ark into the temple, the suppression of the Davidic sanctuary and the integration of the two traditions in a prophetic revelation that recognized the legitimacy of Solomon, and reaffirmed the primacy of his father David. (2 Sam 7:4–16).

The Assyrian siege had brought Jerusalem to the brink of defeat, and left Judah devastated and in subjection to Assyria; but the legend of a revelation to Solomon (2 Sam 7:4a, 5b–7, 13–15; cf. 1 Kgs 3:4), and the Deuteronomic covenant tradition of election of Israel (2 Sam. 7:10–11a) and its monarchy (2 Sam. 7:8–9, 11b, 16) offered the citizens of Judah, Jerusalem and the survivors of the deportations from the fallen kingdom a haven of emotional security in the temple as YHWH's abode (Isa 28:16; Pss 46, 48, 125), and the reassurance of a viable future under the legitimate monarchy (2 Kgs 19:15–37; cf. Ps 132).

CONCLUSION

In the chapter a redactio-critical review of the Nathan narrative in 2 Samuel 7:1–17 has been attempted. Its composition has been retraced from its place in the Prophets, to an early seventh century reflection on the failure of the people of Israel and their rulers in faithful response to the Mosaic law to which was attributed the decline and fall of the Northern Kingdom in 721 BCE (2 Kgs 17:7–18). Inspired by the Hezekianic reforms, and the relief from the long siege, but shaken by Manasseh's apostasies, it was a warning to the monarchy and the people who were left in Judah and Jerusalem (2 Kgs 17:19).

The historical review was re-configured, augmented and re-interpreted in a Josianic redaction to project the centrality of the Jerusalem cultus as a Mosaic stipulation, and denounce the secession led by Jeroboam ben Nebat and the persistent schism it engendered as cultic aberrations that caused the fall of the Northern Kingdom (2 Kgs 17:20–23). It was in that later redaction that the Nathan narrative (2 Sam 7:1–17), having originated, partly as an ancient legend in the traditions of the Jerusalem cultus, and partly as cultic tradition connected with the ark, was reinterpreted to project the building of the temple as a Davidic initiative (2 Sam 7:1–3) and its commissioning as a prophetic revelation. Thus the commission included a promise to David which, at the first, had obligated David's successors to obedience to the Mosaic law but, in the amalgamation, had been superseded by the legitimization of David's successor and the builder of the temple. The objective, therefore, was to project the temple as the central and only sanctuary for all Israel, David as the founder of the YHWH cult in Jerusalem and Solomon, the builder, as the legitimate heir.

An exilic redaction has also been proposed. This redaction reflected on the meaning of the overthrow of the Davidic monarchy (2 Kgs 24:12; 25:5–7, 27–30), notwithstanding the guarantees that had been enshrined in the Nathan narrative (2 Sam 7:11b–16). Its fall was attributed to David's culpability in the matter of Uriah the Hittite (1 Kgs 15:5; cf. 2 Sam 11–12). 2 Samuel 7:1–17, having marked the zenith of David's ascendancy in the earlier Josianic redaction, became a backdrop to the grave offence that had consequences as far-reaching as the decline and fall of the monarchy.

A Deuteronomic denomination has featured in the subtitle of each of the redactions, for whatever may have been the particular emphases, each reflected upon the unprecedented upheavals that overwhelmed Israel resulting in the abolition of the chosen monarchy, the destruction of the chosen sanctuary, the dispossession and dispersion of the chosen people and the gentile occupation of the Promised Land. The calamities were interpreted in the perspective of failure in covenant fidelity to YHWH and in adherence to the Mosaic law. It was to that end that the orations identified by Martin Noth, the prophecy-and-fulfillment schema delineated by Gerhard von Rad and the prophetic material mapped out by Antony Campbell were incorporated. The royal law in Deuteronomy and the dangers and temptations inherent in kingly rule, retrojected into the Mosaic law (Deut 17:14–20), were accentuated at the inauguration of the monarchy in Israel, as a forewarning to rulers and subjects alike (1 Sam 12:14–25).[83] There is also evidence to suggest that, in the earliest covenant formulation, the promise to David (2 Sam 7:8–16), like the promises made to Solomon (1 Kgs 2:2–4; cf. 6:12; 8:25; 9:4–9) and to Jeroboam ben Nebat (1 Kgs 11:38) carried, as a condition, an obligation to steadfast observance of the Mosaic law (Deut 17:18–20; cf. Ps 132:11–12).

The exclusive status accorded to the Jerusalem temple though, as a Mosaic stipulation, anachronistic, was important not only for a program of reform but also as a witness against the dangers of syncretism in the homeland (2 Kgs 17:24–33) and the temptations of the strange cults faced by the exiles in the dispersion (1 Kgs 8:46–50). It was also supportive of the monotheism that undergirded the Mosaic law (Exod 20:3–6; Deut 5:7–10; 12:1–14).

Finally, as Deuteronomic law did not subscribe to a theory that rendered the monarchy sacrosanct and exempt from punishment, so the fall of the house of David—the theme of the exilic redaction—confirmed a principle of retribution, with respect to the monarchy, which was consistent with Deuteronomic theology (Deut 28; 30:15–20; 2 Kgs 17:7–23). In the earlier Deuteronomic composition, precedents such as Moses and Aaron (Deut 32:48–52), Samson (Judg 13–16), the Eliade priesthood (1 Sam 2:27–36),

---

83. Clements, "Deuteronomic Interpretation," 398–410, has suggested that the abuses listed both in Deuteronomy 17:16–17 and in 1 Samuel 8:11–17 may originally have been a reflection on the abuses perpetrated during Solomon's reign, which became precautions against the dangers inherent in the monarchical system.

THE NATHAN NARRATIVE IN 2 SAMUEL 7:1-17

Saul (1 Sam 15:17–23), Jeroboam ben Nebat (1 Kgs 14:7–11) and Baasha (1 Kgs 16:1–4), all prominent figures, elected by YHWH, having erred, had fallen beyond recovery (cf. Deut 32). From that perspective not only was the captivity of Jehoiachin in Babylon reminiscent of the fallen House of Saul, but David's moving lamentation on the deaths Saul and Jonathan included, in historical retrospect, the irony of prophetic utterance. "How [indeed were] the mighty fallen!!" (2 Sam 1:17–27; 11–12; cf. 2 Kgs 25:27–30).

The inclusion of Deuteronomy in the canonizing of the Law necessarily eclipsed the original character and thrust of the earlier redactions of Joshua–Kings. However, the promises to David recorded in 2 Samuel 7:11b–16, unfulfilled in history, became the key-factor in the making of a prophetic canon (Joshua–Malachi), in which hope in the coming of a Davidic ruler was aroused (Isa 7:10–14; 9:1–7; 11:1–9; Jer 23:5; 30:9; 33:14–26; Ezek 37:15–24; Hos. 3:5; Amos 9:11–15; Mic 5:2).

It was partly the fusion of three originally independent themes of chosen monarchy, chosen sanctuary and chosen people, each bringing their independent and characteristic traditions; and partly the further adaptation of the narrative for different purposes in the successive stages of redaction, which account for the dissonances that have survived in the text. Among them are:

The nameless king המלך (vv. 1–3) and the naming of David as נגיד (vv. 5, 8).

The prophet's acquiescence (v. 3) that was subsequently vetoed (vv. 5–7).

The sanctuary was rejected (vv. 6–7) but a builder was promised (v.13).

The promise mediated (v. 11b) and the promise directly given (v. 27).

While, therefore, literary-critical analyses might take account of the more obvious discrepancies, it is the traditio-historical method that must research the pre-literary history of the composition in oral transmission, as also critical for the elucidation of the text, especially in cases where the inconsistencies, might not be immediately apparent or, even when recognized, might be misconstrued.

CHAPTER V

2 SAMUEL 7:1–17—A LITERARY CRITICAL ANALYSIS

THAT A LITERARY-CRITICAL ANALYSIS of 2 Samuel 7:1–17 should precede an exploration of the oral history reverses the chronological sequence. The relationship between two stages—the writing and the oral—in the evolution of the Biblical text has so often been set in antithesis as to have provoked Lapointe's description of the transition as a "qualitative jump" which, in the majority of the actual cases, as has been noted, might, however, be an exaggeration inasmuch as the traditional material immediately preceding the literature could hardly have been the pristine form of the tradition but an advanced stage of its evolution towards the literary composition.

Moreover, precisely because it is in biblical text, and nowhere else, that the oral traditions of Israel are accessible, literary-critical analysis is a prerequisite for their recovery, since it is unlikely that the oral forms and content of the traditions have remained unchanged up to the final shaping of the text, or that the literary shaping could have departed so radically as to have retained nothing that was essential in the tradition from its earliest stages of transmission. Therefore a text, as complex in structure as 2 Samuel 7:1–17, bears witness as much to the variety of the traditions that coalesced in the oral stages as to its checkered history in the redactional re-shaping.

THE NATHAN NARRATIVE IN 2 SAMUEL 7:1-17

THE PROBLEM OF UNITY IN 2 SAMUEL 7:1-17

The claim of compositional unity has been made for 2 Samuel 7:1–17 by McCarthy,[1] Cross,[2] and others. Closer attention must, however, also be paid to cracks and fissures that appear to have resisted and survived the redaction process of integration, up to the final shaping of the text. The more conspicuous of these have been noted by Noth, viz., verses 5, 11b and 13a.[3] The significance of each of these verses will be examined presently. It is also important, however, to note other characteristics of the narrative, not as conspicuous, but which raise questions for the claims of a unified composition.

2 SAMUEL 7:1-17 AND 2 SAMUEL 6

In the first place it is important to note that although the Nathan narrative (2 Sam 7:1–17) follows hard upon the ark narrative (2 Sam 6), is introduced by an observation on the arrangements made for its accommodation (2 Sam. 7:2; cf. 6:17) and the dominant character is YHWH Sabaoth, the deity enthroned upon the ark (2 Sam 7:8, 26–27; cf. 6:2) it is difficult to make a case for continuity on literary-critical grounds. While the two narratives appear to be bridged by the David-Michal episode (2 Sam 6:23; cf. 7:15), for which Roy Porter has recognized a pre-literary cultic connection in terms of *hieros gamos*,[4] the ark narrative seems to have reached a logical conclusion in the placing of the ark in the tent prepared for it and a liturgical blessing and dismissal of the people (2 Sam 6:17–19). Thus the proximity of the two narratives, the role of David as the prime mover in both and the ark as an object of common interest are not sufficient to outweigh what seems to be the deliberate attempt at discontinuity in the time-lapse between the two events.

Furthermore, as noted in Gesenius-Kautzsch Hebrew Grammar, the copulative—ויהי—"and it happened"—that introduces the second narrative (2 Sam 7:1) usually indicates both a change of subject and a loose connection with the preceding narrative.[5] Also, Francis Brown et al. have noted

1. See McCarthy, "2 Samuel 7," 131.
2. See Cross, *Canaanite Myth*, 246–49.
3. See Noth, "David and Israel," 251.
4. See Porter, "Interpretation of 2 Samuel 6," 165–67.
5. See Kautzsch, *Gesenius' Hebrew Grammar*, 327, 2f-h.

2 SAMUEL 7:1-17—A LITERARY CRITICAL ANALYSIS

that the verb used for the ritual placing of the ark in the tent—יצג—"he fixed," though synonymous with the more commonly used—שׂם—"he placed," includes a more forceful definition of deliberate and permanent arrangement.[6] Carlson has noted that the situation described in 2 Samuel 7:1-2, "as the king dwelt (sat) in his house" referred not to 2 Samuel 6:20 but to 2 Samuel 5:11.[7] The disappointment implied in the remark "the ark of God dwells in the tent" (2 Sam 7:2) seems, therefore, to be in contention with the arrangement made in 2 Samuel 6:17 by suggesting that what had been considered a permanent arrangement was, on reflection a judged to be an unsatisfactory provision that called for amelioration.

Also the report, "I have never dwelt in a house since the time I brought up the children of Israel out of Egypt until this day but I have been moving about in a tent and tabernacle." (2 Sam 7:6), seems to be in contention with the ark narrative, in which was implied that, from the time of its removal from the Shiloh-temple into battle at Ebenezer Aphek (1 Sam 4:3-5), the ark had been housed in relatively stable structures,[8] except for those intervals of removal from house to house (2 Sam 7:6; cf. 1 Sam 3:3; 5:2; 7:1; 2 Sam 6:10). However, while it appears that 2 Samuel 7:1-7 may not have been designed originally as a sequel to the ark narrative, the dynastic theme in 2 Samuel 7: 8-16 may, in the history of the tradition, have been in continuity with the ark narrative (cf. Ps 132).

2 SAMUEL 7:1-17 AND 7:18-29

Although the prayer of David seems to be a logical response to the Nathan narrative, closer examination will reveal the complications; for while the transitional passage (2 Sam 7:17-18), was an editorial attempt at a connection, it also seems clear that, whereas the prayer of David recalled a revelation (v. 27; cf. v. 11b), there was nothing in the narrative that anticipated a prayer-response.[9]

---

6. See Brown et al., *Hebrew and English Lexicon*, 426.

7. See Carlson, *David, the Chosen King*, 97.

8. See Porter, "Interpretation of 2 Samuel 6," 169-72, has suggested that the houses of Abinadab (1 Sam 7:1; 2 Sam 6:2) and Obed Edom the Gittite (2 Sam. 6:10-12) may also have been local sanctuaries.

9. It is unusual that a prophetic revelation to a ruler, unsolicited, unexpected, and however auspicious or inauspicious, should evoke such a response (cp. 2 Kgs 19:20-34; 20:16-20; 22:15-23:2). Ackroyd, *2 Samuel*, 81, has compared it with the Samuel speech (1 Sam 12), as marking a significant stage in the evolving history.

Furthermore, it is to be noted that the prayer responded not to the whole of the narrative preceding but only to the dynastic theme—a house for David (2 Sam 7:8-11, 16, 27), which in the narrative was made subsidiary. On the principal theme, viz., the building of a house (temple) for YHWH (vv. 5-7, 12-15), the prayer was silent. Moreover, the key verse in the narrative to which the prayer was a response stands out awkwardly, having been couched in the only form that could have overcome an ambiguity caused by the mediating role of the prophet (v. 11b). Thus, unlike the narrative, the prayer bore witness to a direct revelation (v. 11b), and a response to one subject (v.27).

The prayer is also not as structurally coordinated as the narrative. This might have been due partly to the fact that in the attempt to structure the prayer on the latter part of the narrative (vv. 8-16), it was made to carry the latent tension between a humble and grateful acknowledgement of the promised blessings (vv. 18-28; cf. vv. 8-11) and fervent supplication for the same blessings (v. 29). It would seem, therefore, that whereas the narrative had woven a number of independent themes arising from a complex process of reinterpretation over a longer period of transmission, the prayer, responding to the dynastic theme, reflected also a particular situation of crisis that created anxiety about the monarchy and the people, in contrast with the optimism of the narrative.

2 SAMUEL 7:5-7 AND 7:8-16

Perhaps the sharpest cleavage, dividing the narrative into two equal parts, runs between verses 7 and 8. The cleavage is marked by nuances designed to overcome the discontinuity. The addressee is consistently identified as "David. My servant" (vv. 5, 8). The messenger formula, "Thus says YHWH," is repeated (vv. 5, 8). The narrative-structure has also remained unbroken. A revelation, intended for David, is mediated in the one revelation through the same prophet (vv. 4, 5, 8). Last, but not least, the building of a house (temple) for YHWH has remained the dominant theme (v. 13).

However, a shift in focus seems to have been intended by the rhetorical formula "but now" which, as André Laurentin has argued, points not merely to a change of subject but frequently to a reversal or, at least, a drastic modification of the position that was earlier taken, or condition that was earlier described.[10] It is also of some significance that to the personal name

---

10. See Laurentin, "*Weʿattah—kai nun*," 164-97. It might have sometimes also preceded a statement of the logical consequences, with a meaning almost identical with לכן

2 SAMUEL 7:1–17—A LITERARY CRITICAL ANALYSIS

of the speaker, YHWH, was added the honorific title of "Sabaoth," a designation that pointed to YHWH's association with the ark of the covenant (1 Sam 4:4; 2 Sam 6:2; cf. also 2 Sam 7:26–27).[11]

Above all, whereas the burden of the first paragraph appeared to be the questioning of a plan to build a house for YHWH, the second paragraph was a declaration of YHWH's plan for his people, Israel, to give them a secure foothold and to make a steadfast house (dynasty) for David his servant and bless him with an heir who would build a house (temple) for YHWH. In search for a unifying theme Noth noted the three crucial verses that stand out in the narrative, each of which is beset with literary-critical problems. They are:

Verse 5 האתה תבנה־לי בית לשבתי
(Will you build me a house for my dwelling?)

Verse 11b והגיד לך יהוה כי־בית יעשה־לך יהוה
(And YHWH declares to you that he, YHWH, will make you a house)

Verse 13a הוא יבנה־בית לשמי
(He will build a house for my name).[12]

Taken together, the verses encapsulate the gist of the narrative. David, though prevented from building a house (temple) for YHWH, has been promised a house (lineage) and a biological heir who will build the house (temple). Furthermore, each verse depends on the others for interpretation. The temple theme, broken off at verse 8, and superseded by the dynastic theme up to verse 12, giving "seed" a collective interpretation, is revived by the intrusion of verse 13a to give זרע an individual rather than a collective interpretation. Furthermore, without verse 13a, recognized by most commentators including Rost, Tsevat, Mauchline, Ackroyd, and Nelson as a gloss,[13] verses 8–29 would have been monopolized by the dynastic theme.

("therefore").

11. See Noth, "David and Israel," 253–56. In the elaboration of the title Noth has also seen as significant the link between the two themes in the narrative, viz., the dynastic and the ark themes, as well as the oracle and the prayer. It also defined the people of Israel, as the sacral confederation of the tribes, and was therefore evidence for the persistence of the ark-sanctuary theme throughout the chapter.

12. Ibid., 251.

13. See Rost, *Succession to the Throne*, 42; see also Tsevat, "Studies in Samuel," 73; Mauchline, *Samuel*, 238; Ackroyd, *2 Samuel*, 78; and Nelson, *Double Redaction*, 107, and

THE NATHAN NARRATIVE IN 2 SAMUEL 7:1-17

How the two parts of the Nathan narrative (vv. 1–7) and (vv. 8–16) were brought together is the main question underlying the composition.

2 SAMUEL 7:8-11, 16 AND 7:12-15

There is, also, in the dynastic oracle (7:8–16), a latent tension between the promise of an enduring dynasty (vv. 8–9, 11b, 16) and the promise of a successor (vv. 12–15), underlined by the noun זרע (v.12), which is capable of both an individual and a collective definition (cf. Gen 4:25; 15:4; 1 Sam. 1:11; 2 Sam 16:11). Furthermore, the disturbed condition of verse 11b and intrusion of verse 13a, crucial as both verses are for a determination of priority of the themes, betray a late date for the composition. The disturbance of the narrative-flow seems, however, to be more pronounced in verse 13a, in that the insertion necessitated a repetition (cf. vv. 12b and 13b). It is also likely that 13a carried "for my dwelling" to correspond with verse 5, before it was amended to "for my name" (v. 13) to make the hieros logos blend with the theology of the Josianic redaction (cf. 1 Kgs 8:27–29a).

The promise to David may have also been couched originally in the pattern of a conditional covenant (vv. 8–16; cf. 1 Kgs 2:3–4) which, by the inclusion of verses 1–7, was readapted and reinterpreted to establish David's priority as the founder of the YHWH cult in Jerusalem and Solomon's legitimacy as his successor and the builder of the temple. The anthropomorphism in verses 5–7 was also re-defined by the more distinctive Deuteronomic (Josianic) name-theology.[14] It is the inclusion of an earlier Davidic covenant in (cf. vv. 8–12, 16), and its alteration by, the *hieros logos* of the temple (vv. 1–7, 13–15,) that might also explain the absence of a temple-theme from the prayer that follows in verses 18–29 and from the poetic paraphrase in Psalm 89:1–4, 19–37.

---

among those who take a contrary view, Labuschagne, "Remarks on Prayer of David," 32; Carlson, *David, the Chosen King*, 109; and Mettinger, *King and Messiah*, 53–54.

14. The anti-Solomon tendency of the Josianic redaction (cf. 2 Kgs 23:13) makes it unlikely that the *hieros logos* in 2 Samuel 7, was *ab initio*, a Josianic creation. It is more likely that the tradition of Solomon as builder of the temple had become so deeply entrenched, that it was not possible for the Josianic redactors to omit it.

2 SAMUEL 7:1-17—A LITERARY CRITICAL ANALYSIS

2 SAMUEL 7:8-9 AND 7:10-11A

As well in the dynastic oracle (7:8–16) as in the prayer of David (vv. 23–27) the recital of YHWH's past blessings on David (7:8–9; cf. vv.25–27) and a brief recital of Israel's *Heilsgeschichte* (7:10–11a; cf. vv. 23–24) are associated. This association is more suggestive of Deuteronomic redaction than of an original Davidic ideology. The changes of tense between verses 8–9a and verses 9b–11 (cf. Is 14:1–3; Amos 9:15), and also between verses 10–11and 23–24, as well as the more glaring discrepancy between verses 1 and 11a, suggest changes that were later intended to address a deteriorating situation.[15]

A recital of past favors normally prefaced a "covenant" of fealty with obligation (cf. Exod 19:3–5; Josh 24) or a prophetic indictment (cf. Deut 32:1–25; 1 Sam 15:14; 2 Sam 12:7–9; 1 Kgs 14:7–9; 16:2; Amos 2:9—3:2; Is 5:1–7; Ezek 16:1–40). Such an obligation might therefore be presumed for the Davidic covenant, which may have been superseded in the process of its adaptation to *hieros logos* (2 Sam 7: 8–16; cf. 1 Kgs 2:2–4).

The association of the dynastic and the communal were not, however, ideologically incompatible. The "Israel" identified as "my people" and beneficiary (v. 10–11a, 23-24) referred, as Martin Noth has argued, to a sacral community that transcended the political definition.[16] Similarly David, in relation to YHWH, was referred to, in both the narrative and the prayer, not as "king"—(vv. 1–3), but as "servant"—(vv. 5, 8, 19, 20, 21, 25, 26, 27, 28, 29), a distinction also accorded to Moses (Num 12:7; Josh 1:2). Also, in relation to Israel David is designated—"chieftain"—(v. 8), a designation the shared with other rulers raised up by YHWH to inaugurate regimes—Saul, Jeroboam ben Nebat and Baasha (1 Sam 10:1; 2 Sam 5:2; 1 Kgs 14:7, 16:2; cf. Deut 17:15). Finally, the identification of the God of Israel, in both narrative and prayer, as יהוה צבאות (2 Sam. 7:8, 26–27), points to the ark (cf. 1 Sam 4:4; 2 Sam 6:2) which, from the pre-monarchy period, symbolized YHWH's presence among his people. The promises suggested to Otto Eissfeldt the origin of a trend towards democratization to which, after the fall of the monarchy, the people of Israel became heir (cf. Isa 55:3; 61:8).[17]

---

15. Mulder, "Prophecy of Nathan," 39–40, argues that the verbs indicate the waw-copulative, referring to events that have transpired. Driver, *Notes on Hebrew Text*, 275, has taken the contrary view proposing that the verb "and I will make" (v. 9b) indicates a turning of attention to the future. So also has Rost, *Succession to the Throne*, 44–45.

16. See Noth, "David and Israel," 253–55.

17. See Eissfeldt, "Promises of Grace," 203–4.

THE NATHAN NARRATIVE IN 2 SAMUEL 7:1-17

2 SAMUEL 7:1-3 AND 7:4-7

While the verses 4-7 appear, at first sight, to be continuous with verses 1-3, linked by the transitional phrase, "and that night" and interpreted as a second response to the royal observation (cf. v. 2), traditio-historical examination suggests a secondary redaction rather than an original connection between the two scenes. There is nothing in verses 1-3 that anticipated a further revelation, but rather action on the part of "the king" nor was there anything in verses 5-7 that required the preceding dialogue (vv. 1-3). Discontinuity, in fact, outweighs the linkages which may be reduced to three words "House" (vv. 1, 2, 5, 6 and 7), "Nathan" (vv. 2 and 4) both of which were incidental and, in a sense, unavoidable and "Cedars" (vv. 2 and 7)—the description of the House (vv. 1-2). The last suggests an attempt at linkage in a later redaction since, from a rhetorical point of view, "cedars" seems to have replaced the more feasible "for my dwelling"(v. 7 cf. v. 5) in the ring-composition of direct speech.

Kenneth Craig has explained the obscurity of the relationship between the two segments as a deliberate design of the redactor, whose skill in withholding the vital information left the interpretation to the intuition and imagination of the reader.[18] A more plausible explanation might lie in the nature of the traditional material, and the technique of integration in the process of redaction, since it would otherwise be difficult to explain the anonymity of המלך in the introductory dialogue (vv. 1-3), who would presently be named (vv. 5, 8) if, in the traditional material underlying verses 1-3, David had been recognized as "the king." However, another named king in the traditional material, e.g. "Solomon," would be sufficient explanation of the anonymity, as David was to be named in verse 5. That the subject matter of the traditional material underlying verses 1-3 and the later redaction was identical must therefore remain a debatable proposition.

It may, therefore, have been the case that 2 Samuel 7:4a, 5b-7 preserved the early tradition of a response by "the king" (not David) to the prophet's suggestion (v. 3), and of a nocturnal revelation that commissioned the building of a sanctuary and not a prohibition (vv. 5b-7. cf. v.13a). It further suggests that there was not an original connection between verses 4a, 5b-7 and verses 8-12, 16, and that it was the bringing together and fusion of the two parts of the oracle—the temple theme and the Dynasty theme—that necessitated the royal anonymity in verses 1-3, and the insertion of

---

18. See Craig, "Character(-ization) of God," 161-62.

2 SAMUEL 7:1–17—A LITERARY CRITICAL ANALYSIS

verse 13, in order to re-interpret verses 5b–7 as well as the anonymity of "the king" in verses 1–3 as referring to David.

Carlson's argument that verse 1 referred to 2 Samuel 5:11[19] may have overlooked the personal name that might have been retained, since it would reappear in 2 Samuel 7:5, 8. In sum, the anonymity in verses 1–3 must raise formidable questions for a claim for an original continuity of verses 1–3 with 4–7, or the unity of the pericope as a whole, since in verse 8 David is designated נגיד not מלך (cf. 2 Sam 6:21; 1 Kgs 8:13–14). The suggestion, therefore, that verses 1–3 originally concerned David's wish for the ark, to which verses 4–7 were the response, is by no means self-evident.

Last, but not least, the hiatus at verse 4 must also further weaken the interpretation of verses 4–7 as originally a prohibition on David. Three conclusions may be drawn:

1. The unity claimed for the narrative was not original.
2. The narrative is a composite of originally independent traditions, drawn from different periods and situations of Israel's history.
3. As Leonhard Rost has argued,[20] only verses 11b, 16 may, with any confidence, be dated in the reign of David (cf. v. 27; 2 Sam 23:5).

2 SAMUEL 7:1–17—A COMMENTARY

On the basis of the foregoing analysis, the following commentary will show, verse by verse, the complex nature of the composition of the Nathan narrative in 2 Samuel 7:1–17, and that the unity achieved was a much later effort.

Verse 1:

ויהי כי־ישב המלך בביתו ויהוה הניח־לו מסביב מכל־איביו

Kenneth Craig has observed that the two statements stand not so much in a parallel, as in a cause-and-effect, relationship; thus improving the interpretation of the second conjunction ו to כי "because," in which interpretation, the order of the statements might also be reversed to read "(Seeing that) YHWH had given him rest from all his enemies roundabout, (therefore) the king sat in his house."[21] It is, however, likely that the second

---

19. See Carlson, *David, the Chosen King*, 97.
20. See Rost, *Succession to the Throne*, 44–46
21. See Craig, "Character(-ization) of God," 162.

THE NATHAN NARRATIVE IN 2 SAMUEL 7:1-17

part of the statement was added in the Josianic redaction so that David, having been given the principal role in the building of the sanctuary, might be included in the מנוחה "rest" period. The absence of that clause from 1 Chronicles 17:1 might be explained as consistency (cf.1 Chron. 17:9-10a) or the existence of an independent *Vorlage*.

Ackroyd has interpreted בביתו ישב המלך i.e. "the sitting of the king in his house," as "having been established," suggesting an interpretation that might extend to enthronement.[22] The anonymity of המלך, "the king" if originally a reference to Solomon, suggests that the narrative that would logically have followed the condition described in 1 Kings 2:46 (cf. 1 Kgs 5:18(MT)). A court-scene with the formalities of an enthronement ceremony, including a celebration of the king's victory over his foes (2 Sam 7:1b; cf. I Kgs 2:15-46: Pss 2:2-6, 9-10; 89:22-23; 110:1) has been proposed by Siegfried Herrmann.[23]

יהוה הניח־לו מסביב מכל־איביו. The statement is typically Deuteronomic, but the idea of divine deliverance from the enemy, and of salvation as "rest," is not exclusive to Deuteronomic literature (Deut 12:10; 25:19; Josh 23:1; 1 Kgs 5:18(MT); cf. Pss 2; 95:11; 110:1-2, 5-6; 132:8, 14). In Deuteronomic usage it recalled the completion of the conquest under Joshua and the settlement of the tribes (Deut 3:20; Josh 1:12-18; 22:1-9; 23:1) and also anticipated the annihilation of the Amalekites (Deut 25:17-19; cf. Exod 17:8-16; 1 Sam 15:1ff; 30:1-17; 2 Sam 1:1-15; 8:12)[24] and, in the Josianic redaction, it included the propitious time for the building of a sanctuary at a location that YHWH should choose and a ban on all other cult centers (Deut 12:10-11, 14; cf. 16:2, 6, 15; 26:2; 1 Kgs 8:16-21).

Verse 2:
ויאמר המלך אל־נתן הנביא ראה נא אנכי יושב בבית ארזים וארון האלהים ישב בתוך היריעה

נתן is given as the personal name of הנביא, who, contrary to the normal pattern, is not identified by either pedigree, address or place of origin (cf. 1 Sam 1-3; 1 Kgs 11:29; 16:1; 17:1; 19:16; 22:8, 11; 2 Kgs 19:20; 22:14). The appearance of prophets in the presence or company of rulers was not an unusual feature of ancient Near Eastern society. All the four occasions in

---

22. See Ackroyd, *2 Samuel*, 74.

23. See Herrmann, "The Royal Novel," 58.

24. It would appear that, in the case of David, the Amalekites also included the Philistines in the interpretation of the traditional foe (cf. 2 Sam 1:1-16; cf. 5:17-25).

2 SAMUEL 7:1-17—A LITERARY CRITICAL ANALYSIS

Samuel-Kings in which Nathan is mentioned were in a court-setting—in 2 Samuel 7:1-17, as a seer (ראה) of whom a divinatory oracle was requested, in 2 Samuel 12:1-15a, as an interventionist messenger who, uninvited, denounced the king's abuse of power, in 2 Samuel 12:25 as the custodian of Solomon, the new-born prince, and 1 Kings 1:8, 10-11, 22-24, 32, 38 as an activist who initiated the intrigues that secured the succession for Solomon. For the most of the narrative (2 Sam 7:4-16), he was the passive recipient of a nocturnal revelation (חזיון) that prohibited David from building a sanctuary for YHWH and, obliquely, repudiated the prophet's earlier acquiescence in the plan (v.3).[25]

ראה נא. This expression, usually interpreted as an interjection, virtually equivalent to הנה, הן "behold!" (so 1 Chr 17:1; but cp. Jer 1:9-10), must, in the original context, have been uttered as a royal directive to ראה, "seer," for a favorable omen (cf. Num 22-24; 1 Sam 9:9; Jer 1:9-10; Amos 7:1, 4, 7-8; 8:1-2). Such a directive could hardly, therefore, have been met with the instantaneous response given in the dialogue, but normally required at least an overnight interval for חזיון—"revelation" (vv. 4, 17; cf. Num 22-24; 1 Sam 9:14-20; 1 Kgs 22:15-23; Jer 28; 42). On the other hand the spontaneity may have arisen from the prophet's counsel that the king might follow his inclination to seek for himself an incubatory oracle, in which case the distinction between a "seer"—ראה and a "counselor"—יועץ would, at some point, have become blurred.

בבית ארזים, "in a house of cedars," (cf. 2 Sam 5:11) is descriptive of the superior quality of the material to be used in the construction. The reiteration in verse 7, as well as the unusual description, by way of contrast, of the accommodation of the ark as היריעה—"the cloth," implies that the suitability of the accommodation for the ark may have been an issue. The plural form ארזים indicates that the material used for construction was to be entirely cedar. A deeper significance of בית ארזים is that cedar was considered to be the material most suitable for the construction of temples for the gods and palaces for the kings.[26]

וארון האלהים (cf. 2 Sam 6:2, 6), also ארון ברית יהוה (Deut 31:9), refers to a cult-object which, designed as a receptacle for the tables of the law (Deut 10:1-4), became a mobile sanctuary of the Israelites up to the period

---

25. See Craig, "Character(-ization) of God," 165, who has noted that it was unusual for David to have taken the initiative in a consultation with a prophet in the matter of a divination.

26. The obligation resting on rulers for the building/renovation of sanctuaries, and the significance of it, will be discussed presently.

THE NATHAN NARRATIVE IN 2 SAMUEL 7:1-17

of the monarchy (Exod 25:10–22; 26:1–34; 37:1–9; 40:21; Num 10:33–36; Deut 10:13; 31:9; Josh 3:1—4:9; 8:33; 2 Sam 6). It was traditionally housed in "a sacred Tent" אהל (2 Sam 6:17; cf. Ps 78:60–69), and this arrangement seems to have continued beyond the nomadic period whether or not a more stable and substantial structure—בית/היכל, "house/temple" (1 Sam 2:22; 3:2–3)—was also available for accommodation. The ark was symbolic of the Presence of YHWH, for which the phrase לפני־יהוה may have been either a colloquialism or a technical term the Deuteronomic redactors preferred in establishing a case for its long sojourn at Kiriath-jearim, during the reign of Saul (1 Sam 7:1-2; cf. Judg 20:23, 27–28; 1 Sam 1:12, 15, 19, 22; 3:3; 4:4–7, 7:2, 6; 10:25; 11:15; 14:18; 21:6; 2 Sam 5:3; 6:16; 7:18; 2 Kgs 19:15).

בתוך היריעה, literally, "in the centre of the curtain," has been paraphrased by John Mauchline[27] as denoting "the tent" (cf. 2 Sam 6:17). Samuel Driver has suggested, however, that היריעה might be interpreted collectively, as is suggested by the plural form in the Chronicles denoting intensity (1 Chr 17:1).[28] Its substitution for the more commonly used אהל (cf. 2 Sam 6:17; 7:6) might therefore have been intended to accentuate the contrast with the solidity and stability of בית־ארזים—"a house of cedar" (v.2).

Verse 3:
ויאמר נתן אל־המלך כל אשר בלבבך לך עשה כי יהוה עמך

The two idiomatic expressions כל אשר בלבבך and יהוה עמך have been listed by Cross as typically Deuteronomic phrases.[29] The vagueness of the response, in its present literary setting, suggests partly evasion, partly cautious assent and partly recognition of the royal prerogative and competence. The diplomatic language in the dialogue also indicates a quantum leap in Hebrew rhetoric (cp. 1 Kgs 22:13–17), and hints at a precarious situation brought on by cultic innovation that may have had wider ramifications than the provision for a cult-object.[30]

The phrase יהוה עמך though prevalent in Deuteronomic literature (Deut 31:8, 23; Josh 1:5; Judg 2:18; 6:12, 16) is not exclusively Deuteronomic, but

---

27. See Mauchline, *Samuel*, 228.
28. See Driver, *Notes on Hebrew Text*, 274.
29. See Cross, *Canaanite Myth*, 252.

30. The crisis brought on by the threat of Assyrian expansion, as well as the political ramifications of the cultic innovations he introduced, would make the reign of Hezekiah, already recognized as a new age of political sophistication, also a period in which deftness in speech and an economy of words (cf. Amos 5:13) had become a growing tendency. Though addressed as ראה, Nathan responded as a typical courtier—a counselor.

2 SAMUEL 7:1–17—A LITERARY CRITICAL ANALYSIS

abounds in the Joseph narratives (Gen 39:3, 21, 23), the Psalter (Pss 23:4; 46:7, 11) and the history of David (1 Sam 16:18; 18:12, 14; 2 Sam 5:10; 7:3, 9).

Read against the background of the preceding narrative (2 Sam. 6), it seems unlikely that either the dialogue in 2 Samuel 7: 1–3 or the revelation that followed in 2 Samuel 7:5-7 was originally preceded by the ark narrative, even though in the revelation in verses in 2 Samuel 7:5–7 the more usual אהל was used (cf. 2 Sam 6:17). It also seems strange that the king, who had "permanently fixed" יצג the ark "in the centre of the Tent"—האהל בתוך (2 Sam 6:17), should appear to question the arrangement; only to learn that, having scorned the "cloth" in favor of the cedar, it was the "cloth" that YHWH preferred, both in the—מנוחה—"rest" period as in the—התהלך—"wandering" (2 Sam 7:5–7). It is therefore unlikely that, originally, המלך—"the king" in verses 1–3 was דוד—"David" of 2 Samuel 6:2 or that in the history of 2 Samuel 7:5–7 a veto was always intended. It is curious that in 1 Kgs 3:4, in which the pilgrimage to Gibeon is reported המלך is also anonymous and the anonymity is inconsistent with the rest of the narrative.

Verse 4:
ויהי בלילה ההוא ויהי דבר־יחוה אל־נתן לאמר

The verse appears to be transitional, and that the intention of v. 4b was to connect verses 1–3 with 5–7, implying a more explicit response to verse 2. It introduces an revelation concerning a plan for a house for YHWH who is identified with the ark of the covenant (2 Sam 7:5–7; cf. Num 10:35–36; Josh 3:3–17; 1 Sam 4:4–8; 2 Sam 6:16, 21). It is therefore worthy of note that the unusual construction of verse 4 suggests a connection that was not original but the result of a later redaction.

The space between the two parts of the verse, which appears in most of the texts, has been reckoned by Ackroyd to be the provision made for a cross-reference with Psalm 132, viewed as a commentary,[31] and therefore a suggestion that is the more compatible with the argument for a disconnection from verses 1–3, the case for an interpretation of verses 5–7 as a commission (cf. Ps 132:1–2), and המלך—"the king" in verses 1–3 as referring not to David but to Solomon to whom a commission was given. The suggestion of a nocturnal revelation must raise further questions for verse 3, in that it confirms a divinatory oracle (vv. 5–16) as the more appropriate response to the royal request ראה נא—"See, now"—(v. 2), rather than the prophet's spontaneous response in verse 3.

---

31. See Ackroyd, *2 Samuel*, 75.

THE NATHAN NARRATIVE IN 2 SAMUEL 7:1–17

Verse 5:

לך ואמרת אל־עבדי אל־דוד כה אמר יהוה האתה תבנה־לי בית לשבתי

This is a key verse as well for the recovery of the history of the composition, as for interpretation. The interrogation in verses 5b–7 seems to convey the rhetoric of an altercation in reaction to the dialogue in 2 Samuel 7:2–3, and therefore suggests a veto on the king's initiative and, obliquely, a reprimand on the prophet's compliance. This is made even more explicit in the Greek translation (LXX) not only by the omission of the interrogative sign (;) but by the inclusion of the negative οὐ—"not."

Such a conclusion is based largely on the assumption that המלך (vv.1–3) originally and always referred to David as it does in the sequel (2 Sam 7:4–16). However, without the transitional verses of the narrator (2 Sam 7:4b–5a), verses 1–3, 5b–7 might have read quite differently in the Hebrew version (MT).

The Greek translation might have reflected, as Samuel Driver has noted, the influence of I Chronicles 17:4.[32] Alternatively, both may have been drawn from a *Vorlage* of the Samuel text that carried לא אתה—"you shall not" which the Masoretic editors sought to clarify by replacing לא—"not" with the ה-interrogative rendering 2 Samuel 7:5b, האתה—"Shall you...."? On the other hand, לא אתה interpreted as a prohibition would also seem consistent with the Chronicler's theological position (cf. 1 Chr 28:3; 2 Chr 6:8–9). However, as a prohibition, לא אתה provokes some further considerations.

The symmetry of repetition in the Hebrew rhetoric of altercation demands an interrogative at verse 5b, consistent with verse 7, rather than an explicit prohibition. It therefore follows that if in an earlier recension, as was reflected in 1 Chronicles 17:4 and 2 Βασιλείων 7:5, לא אתה was the original construction, a prohibition might, rhetorically, still have been an unlikely interpretation. For the same reason, the argument for dittography in the ה—interrogative must be excluded as a possibility.

Gesenius-Kautzsch has cited instances where the ה—interrogative did not always connote a negation.[33]

Geoffrey Driver[34] and Peter Ackroyd,[35] in commenting on Amos 7:14, an analogous case, have argued that a seemingly negative construction, לא־

---

32. See Driver, *Notes on Hebrew Text*, 274.
33. See Kautzsch, *Gesenius' Hebrew Grammar*, 474, d–e.
34. See Driver, "Amos 7:14," 91–92.
35. See Ackroyd, "Amos 7:14," 94.

2 SAMUEL 7:1–17—A LITERARY CRITICAL ANALYSIS

נביא אנכי may, in some instances and especially direct speech, have been an interrogative connoting an affirmative.

If, therefore, 1 Chronicles 17:4 (MT) preserved such a version of 2 Samuel 7:5 of which MT was an attempt at clarification and the LXX a mistranslation, further insight into the history of the narrative may be gained.

Disconnected from verses 1–3, therefore, or connected by means other than verses 4b–5a,[36] verses 5b–7 may originally have been a commission urging the king to proceed with the building of the sanctuary (made stronger by the rhetoric of interrogation), confirming verse 13 as intrusive. The counterpoint to האתה of verse 5 would have been not הוא—"he"—of verse 13a but שבטי ישראל—"the tribes of Israel"—of verse 7.

Verse 6:

כי לא ישבתי בבית למיום העלתי את־בני ישראל ממצרים ועד היום הזה ואהיה מתהלך באהל ובמשכן

This is the first of the reasons given for YHWH's rejection of the plan for the building of a house for him. He had not lived in one, since the Exodus from Egypt, but had been moving about with the Israelites in a tabernacle-tent—an explanation that flies in the face of the itinerary of the ark narrative (cf. 1 Sam 3:3; 4:3; 5:2; 7:1; 2 Sam 6:10–11). This reason might, however, have equally justified a commission to build a house.[37] The children of Israel were no longer moving about, but were settled in the land that had been promised to their fathers. They had built permanent houses for themselves (Deut 8:12; 2 Sam 5:11; 7:1a). As well for YHWH, therefore, as for his people the התהלך—"wandering"—period was over, and the time had come for YHWH to have a permanent abode (cf. Ps 132:13–14).

Campbell's argument that the verse was a later insertion has already been discussed. There is also an indication that YHWH in verses 5–7, may not have been identified with the ark as might be concluded from Psalm 132:3–8, since verse 6a, without 6b, might be hinting at the claim to transcendence (cf. 1 Kgs 8:27).[38] The case may not have been, however, one

---

36. A possibility is that originally המלך in verses 1–3 was the recipient of the oracle in verses 5b–7.

37. Engnell, "The Science of Religion," 19, makes reference to "*deus otiosus*" (the resting God) of Canaanite religion. This made obligatory the building of a house for the deity who had arrived.

38. Clements, "Deuteronomy and Jerusalem Cult Tradition," 301–2, has argued that Deuteronomy was, among other objectives, a demythologization of certain aspects of the Jerusalem cult, including the theology of the ark, from a representation of, and

THE NATHAN NARRATIVE IN 2 SAMUEL 7:1-17

of transcendence since, as Richard Clifford has pointed out, there was not so much difference between בית, היכל and אהל as dwellings for Canaanite deities as to draw conclusions regarding transcendence or immanence.[39]

Verse 7:

בכל אשר־התהלכתי בכל־בני ישראל הדבר דברתי את־אחד שבטי ישראל
אשר צויתי לרעות את־עמי את־ישראל לאמר למה לא־בניתם לי בית ארזים

The repetition of ארזים (cf. v. 2) may have been a redactional device for connecting verses 5-7 with verses 1-3 or, alternatively, a commission to build a permanent sanctuary; ארזים being understood as the specification of בית in verses 5-6, thereby disqualifying the (temporary) houses in which the ark may have been accommodated and overcoming the discrepancy between verse 6, and the ark narrative. The repetition (see verse 2), may also have been the rhetorical flourish of a ring composition that was intended to bind verses 1-3 to 5-7 (cf. 1 Kgs 3:4-5; 9:1-2).

There being no record of any one tribe having been accorded superior status in pre-monarchy Israel, שבטי—"tribes"—has generally been recognized as a scribal error for שפטי—"judges" cf. 1 Chr. 17:6).

This question raised in verse 7 might also advance the case for a commissioning rather than a prohibition since such a prohibition should have precluded the designation of a builder (v. 13a). On the other hand with the emendation drawn from the rendering in 1 Chronicles 17:6, the thrust of a commission would be that David, not being שפט but עבד־יהוה—YHWH's servant (v. 5a), he represented a unique category of leadership that raised him above the disqualification.

While, therefore, the sequence of rhetorical questions in final text, followed by the designation of a builder (v 13a) suggests a prohibition, the altercation character of the rhetorical interrogation might equally point to an earlier stage of the tradition in which the building of a house for YHWH (though not necessarily an accommodation for the ark), far from having been prohibited, had been commissioned as a matter of urgency.

---

identification with, YHWH SABAOTH (1Sam 4-8; 2 Sam. 6), to being a wooden casket that contained the tables of the law (cf. Deut 10:1-5). That such a differentiation between the symbol and the thing symbolized was possible in antiquity is, however, a theory that is not easily established.

39. See Clifford, *Cosmic Mountain*, 54.

2 SAMUEL 7:1–17—A LITERARY CRITICAL ANALYSIS

Verse 8:

ועתה כה־תאמר לעבדי לדוד כה אמר יהוה צבאות אני לקחתיך מן־הנוה מאחר
הצאן להיות נגיד על־עמי על־ישראל

The conjunction, ועתה—"but now"—introduces a new subject. The prohibition (vv. 5–7) is thus mitigated by a review of YHWH's gracious acts towards David in blessing and succor. The verb לקחתיך—"I took you …," expressive of divine initiative in election (cf. Deut 32:10–13; Amos 7:15), interprets the events of David's earlier career as divinely ordered, invests his ascendancy with an aura of legitimacy, and projects his achievements and attainments as a divine gift.[40]

The repetition of the prophetic messenger formula and the repetition of the emphatic pronoun אני—"I"—accentuate, and also prescribed limits to, the messenger-role of the prophet, by emphasizing that YHWH, not the prophet, was the benefactor. The recurrence of the personal pronouns throughout (vv. 2, 5, 8, 13) is indicative of the status of the characters so identified.

The designation of David in the narrative was עבד—"servant"—in relation to YHWH and נגיד—"leader"—in relation to YHWH's people. Both terms are suggestive of the importance of the ruler's responsibility for, and the interest of YHWH in, the people over whom he ruled. While, however, David at the first (2 Sam 5:2; cf. 7:8), and Saul before him (1 Sam 10:1), and Jeroboam (1 Kgs 14:7) and Baasha (1 Kgs 16:2) after him were each designated נגיד, the only other Israelite leader whom YHWH also recognized as עבד was Moses (Josh 1:2). Thus when YHWH spoke as צבאות יהוה—"YHWH Sabaoth—the God of the covenant people, who was represented by the ark (1 Sam 4:4; 2 Sam 6:2), both the status and function of David in relation to Israel were established in terms of responsibility, which excluded autocracy.

Verse 9:

ואהיה עמך בכל אשר הלכת ואכרתה את־כל־איביך מפניך ועשתי לך שם גדול
כשם הגדלים אשר בארץ

---

40. The propaganda value is apparent when weighed against the disaffection between David and the house of Saul (1 Sam 21; 23:5–18), the acts of disloyalty and subversion (1 Sam 27), and, above all, the genocide (2 Sam 21; cf. 2 Sam 9:1; 16:5–8) and the disaffection of the Benjaminites who remained loyal to the fallen house of Saul (2 Sam 16:3–11; cf. 20:1–2).

THE NATHAN NARRATIVE IN 2 SAMUEL 7:1–17

David's successes have been ascribed wholly to YHWH (cf. 1 Sam 17:31–53; 18:25–28; 20:13; 23:1–2; 2 Sam 2:1; 5:12, 23–24).

The verse has also taken the prospective view of an even more auspicious future, which is compressed in the phrase ועשתי לך שם גדול, referring to the titles conferred on the potentate and his increasing fame, abroad and at home. נגיד—"captain, or "chieftain," which is not—שם גדול—"a great name," is destined for the grandeur attained by—הגדלים אשר בארץ—"the great ones who are on earth." His international renown inspires, therefore, a new ideology. The exalted view reflects the earlier period of the monarchy, preceding the break-up of the empire.

A contrary exegesis has interpreted the verbs from ועשתי onwards as cases of *waw coniunctivum* rather than of *waw consecutivum*. The recital would thus extend Israel's *Heilsgeschichte* to verse 11a, accentuate the break at verse 11b and remove the contradiction between verses 1b and 11a. However, the conditions described make a *waw coniunctivum* unlikely since freedom from harassment by outside forces was not part of Israel's *Heilsgeschichte*.

Verses 10–11a

ושמתי מקום לעמי לישראל ונטעתיו ושכן תחתיו ולא ירגז עוד ולא־יסיפו בני־עולה לענותו כאשר בראשונה : ולמן־היום אשר צויתי שפטים על־עמי ישראל והניחתי לך מכל־איביך

These verses do not easily cohere with the rest of the narrative, not only because the focus has been shifted from David (YHWH's servant) to Israel, (YHWH's people), but also because the promises to David have been interrupted. More importantly, the association of—עמי—"my (i.e. YHWH's) people"—with the fortunes of the monarchy suggests an adaptation of elements from the ancient *Heilsgeschichte* to the dynastic covenant. Such an adaptation may have featured in the Jerusalem cultus (cf. Exod 15:1–18; Ps. 78) where the achievements of David climaxed YHWH's salvation-blessing of his people. Here, in verses 10–11a, a disintegration of the *Heilsgeschichte-genre* is apparent in that it subjoins, rather than prefaces, the Davidic covenant. If, moreover, the waw consecutivum is accepted, Israel's uncertain future, rather than their celebrated past, becomes the focus of the *Heilsgeschichte*. It addresses a mood of profound anxiety. The verses represent neither an original connection (Ps 78) nor the Josianic view of the blessing that lay in the integral connection between the Chosen People and the Promised Land, as emphasized by Clements.⁴¹ In this case, YHWH is again preparing מקום—"a place," for his people against the time when they shall have become displaced and dispossessed. The unspecified מקום, given a cultic reference (cf. Pss 78:68; 132:5), suggests a period when the law of one sanctuary was unknown or, if in force, had become problematic. In that light Polzin expounds the crisis of an altar built in the Jordan valley (Josh 22:10–34).⁴² Expulsion notwithstanding, מנוחה—"rest"—might be found elsewhere (cf. Ezek11:16).

Preferably, מקום might be a reference to Jerusalem, the chosen city where was located the sole legitimate sanctuary, and where YHWH had given David and his descendants—ניר—"a foothold" (1 Kgs 11:36; 15:4; 2 Kgs 8:9). At a time when the Northern Kingdom had fallen to the Assyrians, most of the cities of Judah had been captured and Jerusalem, still under siege, had been flooded with refugees seeking asylum, the linking of the future of Israel with the Davidic monarchy and Jerusalem must have held special importance in a new *Heilsgeschichte* (cf. 2 Kgs 19:20–37).

It also shows that the linking of the security of the people with the reign of a divinely chosen ruler had become an important aspect of Israelite kingship (Ps 72; Is. 11:1–9). This was integral to the conception of kingship in Northern Israel, whose rulers had been given the title נגיד (1 Sam 10:1; 2 Sam 7:8; 1 Kgs 14:7; 16:2) As Widengren has argued, there was no covenant between YHWH and the Israelite ruler from which the people were excluded, but the covenant between YHWH and the king also involved a covenant between YHWH and the people of which the king was mediator, and therefore, inescapably, it also involved a covenant between king and people (cf. 2 Kgs 11:17).⁴³

Verse 11b:

והגיד לך יהוה כי־בית יעשה־לך יהוה

This is a key verse for the interpretation of the narrative and, paradoxically, its mangled state in the Masoretic Text, and the variations reflected in the versions, bear witness to its importance in Jewish tradition. The promises to David are resumed after the "Israel"-interlude. In the resumption, however, the narrative-flow of the "oracle" seems to have gone awry. In verse 11b, the prophet, and not YHWH, has become the speaker, and

---

41. See Clements, *God's Chosen People*, 50–58.
42. See Polzin, *Moses and Deuteronomist*, 134–41.
43. See Widengren, "King and Covenant," 2–7.

THE NATHAN NARRATIVE IN 2 SAMUEL 7:1-17

David, rather than the prophet, is directly addressed. Furthermore, in the brief statement, YHWH now referred to in the third person is twice mentioned by name—first as the sender of a message and then as the subject of the message sent. The clumsiness of the structure results from the new subject being introduced, viz., a house for David.[44]

The LXX rendering, "You will build him a house," is a reversal of the promise as stated in MT that virtually expunges the dynastic theme from, and makes the temple theme monopolize the *pericope*. MT is, however, supported by 4Q Florilegium 174. The Lucianic Text of 2 Samuel 7 reads "A house he [YHWH] will build for himself" but interestingly, the Lucianic Text of I Chronicles 17 reads "'A house I will build for you' says YHWH" which, as a direct revelation, most closely concurs with the prayer of David that follows (2 Sam 7: 27), shifting the emphasis to the dynastic theme.

The placing of בית at the beginning of the sentence is for the purpose of shifting the focus from s sanctuary in verses 5–7 to a dynasty. Similarly, the change of verb from בנה to עשה points, by a play on the word בית—"house"—in the same direction, viz., the founding of a dynasty.[45] It is therefore evident that the original form of the promise was preserved in v. 27 but, mediated as an oracle, it could not have been reported verbatim without the risking misinterpretation.

---

44. The problem that is reflected in the structure of v. 11b is a procedural dilemma encountered in *traditio*, viz., of converting a direct unmediated revelation (cf. v. 27), in which YHWH spoke in the first person, to an oracle in which YHWH's speech was mediated through a prophet. The sender of the message, viz., YHWH, speaking in the first person (vv.5–11a) could not, at that point (11b), be confused with the messenger (Nathan). A change was therefore required in the interest of clarification to emphasize that the benefactor was not Nathan but YHWH and, for further emphasis, the verb was also changed from "build" to "make." Ironically, verse 11b, following verse 27, became the only part of the oracle that preserved the speech of YHWH, and, even so, in the Third Person.

45. Noth, "David and Israel," 251, has claimed for v. 13a closer affiliation to v. 5b than to v. 11b, since not only is the verb—בנה—"build" repeated (cp. LXX, I Chron. 17:10 and 4Q 174 Florilegium), but also because the emphatic pronoun—הוא—"he" in v. 13a, stands in the same position in the structure of the sentence as does the emphatic pronoun—אתה—"you" in v. 5b. This is not, however, the only reading of the pericope that is possible for, not only is v. 13a precluded by vv. 6-7, but, more significantly, the chiastic structure of both verses, 5b and 11b, when juxtaposed, stands out even more clearly in that the latter is seen not in content only but, even more so, in form, to be a reversal of the former and indicating more clearly the objective.

2 SAMUEL 7:1–17—A LITERARY CRITICAL ANALYSIS

Verse 12:

כי ימלאו ימיך ושכבת את־אבתיך והקימתי את־זרעך אחריך אשר יצא ממעיך והכינתי את־ממלכתו

YHWH's role as speaker has been resumed in verse 12, which is an exposition of the promise of בית—"dynasty"—(v. 11b). For that reason, notwithstanding Tryggve Mettinger's earlier dating of the Solomonic Document,[46] זרע—"seed"—capable of both an individualistic definition, viz., "descendant" and a collective definition, viz., "progeny," leans more closely towards the collective.

יצא must, for obvious reasons, be given a future perfect rendering—"who shall have come . . . ," whichever the definition of זרע.

ממלכתו must be interpreted as a continuation of the regime beyond the close of the reign and therefore a principle of hereditary succession.

את־אבותיך ושכבת. Baruch Halpern and David Vanderhooft have interpreted the clause as connoting "peaceful death."[47] That the qualification is either necessary or correct is however debatable. It might more plausibly be interpreted as colloquialism—a circumlocution for death, whatever the circumstances. Otherwise it could not have been applied, as in this case, to a prediction that was not intended, primarily or remotely, to signify the manner of David's death. On the other hand, its association with the earlier phrase ימלאו ימיך, though in parallelism, is not a tautology. The fulfillment of the days refers to an allotted span having been attained (cf. Ps. 90:19).

את־זרע "seed" is capable of both an individualistic interpretation meaning "descendant" as well as the corporate meaning of "lineage." It might have carried, in this passage, either the one meaning or the other at different stages of redaction. At one stage it might have referred to the promise to David of a dynasty (v. 11). At a later stage it might have referred to a legitimization of the immediate successor, the builder of YHWH's house (v. 13).

---

46. See Mettinger, *King and Messiah*, 52–55. Mettinger has not, however, considered the traditio-historical possibility, disclosed in Psalm 132, of the Dynastic theme in 2 Samuel 7, commencing at verse 8, being a continuation and the climax of the ark narrative in the preceding chapter 6, and 2 Samuel 7:1-7, 13 the intrusion of a temple theme

47. See Halpern and Vanderhooft, "Editions of Kings," 180–90.

THE NATHAN NARRATIVE IN 2 SAMUEL 7:1-17

Verse 13:

הוא יבנה־בית לשמי וכננתי את־כסא ממלכתו עד־עולם

The repetition of thought at 13b (cf. v. 12b) confirms verse 13 as a later insertion, the consequences of which were considerable. It resurrected the temple-theme and settled the character of verse 5 as prohibitory. It also subverted the promise of a lineage (v. 11b) and defined—זרע—"seed" as individualistic.

לשמי—"for my name"– suggests the Josianic reinterpretation of an earlier redaction that may have carried another word, probably לשבתי—"for my dwelling" or לי "for me" (cp. v. 5), which implied an anthropomorphism that the Josianic redactors eschewed (cf. 1 Kgs 8:27–29).

The emphatic pronoun—הוא—"he" recalls—אתה—"you" of verse 5, and it is likely this was intended to project Solomon, exclusively, as builder of the temple. The personal pronoun—אני—"I" in verse 8 and the repeated "YHWH" in apposition (v.11b) was probably also another response to—אתה—"you" (v. 5). This double allusion, in contention, points to the integration of what may have been two independent traditions.

את־כסא ממלכתו. Apart from this occurrence this phrase appears only in the royal law in Deuteronomy (Deut 17:18), and in the second dream of Solomon at Gibeon (1 Kgs 9:3), both in contexts of conditional promises. This suggests the residue of a conditional promise that was superseded in a later reinterpretation.

The promise of enduring rule first appears here in the phrase עד־עולם. David responds in similar terms in the prayer that follows (vv 19, 29) and, in his Last Words, makes mention of ברית עולם by which his House would be sustained (2 Sam 23:5; cf. Ps 89:29, 34–37). Thus עד־עולם makes it the more likely that verses 12 to 15, if applied to Solomon, reflected a Hezekianic rather than either a Deuteronomic, Josianic or, still less an exilic expectation.

Verse 14:

אני אהיה־לו לאב והוא יהיה־לי לבן אשר בהעותו והכחתיו בשבט אנשים ובנגעי בני אדם

The relationship of זרע to YHWH, viz.—בן—"son," more exalted than David's—עבד—"servant," raises the status of the monarchy to a new level. Whether more than an attempt at legitimization can be drawn from the "Father-Son" relationship is however arguable. What has been interpreted in biblical scholarship as Divine or Sacral Kingship, might in more rational

2 SAMUEL 7:1-17—A LITERARY CRITICAL ANALYSIS

terms be deemed an attempt at legitimization, decorated by myth and ritual (cf. Ps 2:7). Certainly the use of the preposition—ל "for" as a prefix to—אב—"father" and בן rather than the pronominal suffixes—י and ך "my" and "your"—is recognition of kingship in terms that fall far short of divinity. Properly translated it should read "I shall be [for] a father to him and he shall be [for] a son to me." זרע will, however, have come from the loins of David (v.12)[48]. The issue, in this case, is therefore one of legitimacy.

The intention of this pronouncement is that, while security of the regime is guaranteed (v. 15), immunity from retribution is not. This is the clear definition of the "Father-Son" relationship. By comparison, the expressions used in Psalm 89:26-33 in describing the relationship of the king to YHWH are exaggerated.

Verse 15:

וחסדי לא־יסור ממנו כאשר הסרתי מעם שאול אשר הסרתי מלפניך

The word "covenant" ברית does not appear in the narrative, but—חסד—"steadfast love," also representative of the faithfulness of a covenant that is steadfast and unshakeable, can be interpreted as a viable synonym.

Driver has noted that—לא־יסור—"he will not take away" (3rd. person) should more properly be rendered—לא־אסיר—"I will not take away," as in LXX and 1 Chronicles 17:13.[49]

The comparison with the Saulide regime reflects the halcyon period of imperial grandeur and a propaganda measure designed to justify David's subversive activities (1 Sam 27:1–28:2; 2 Sam 2:1–4), his liquidation of the fallen house (2 Sam 9:1; 21 :1–9), the duplicity that prompted his demand for Michal's return to him (2 Sam 3:12-16) and the rancor that fed their later estrangement (2 Sam. 6:20-23).

Verse 16:

ונאמן ביתך וממלכתך עד־עולם לפניך כסאך יהיה נכון עד־עלם

The repetition of עד־עולם re-confirms the dependability of the promises. Furthermore, with the singular verb—נאמן—"shall be made firm," the plural subjects suggest that house, kingdom and throne are perceived as an entity. Therefore, the suggestion that there should be a time in the

---

48. Such a definition of divine kingship, in terms of procreation, has been discussed by Abraham Malamat, "A Mari Prophecy," 69, in his study of a Mari text.

49. See Driver, *Notes on Hebrew Text*, 276,

foreseeable future when there would be not be a ruling House of David was not entertained. Such was the firmness of the promise.

Driver has suggested that—לפניך—"before you," probably a dittography, should have been rendered—לפני—"before me" as in the Greek (LXX) version.[50]

Verse 17:

ככל הדברים האלה וככל החזיון הזה כן דבר נתן אל־דוד

The editorial note serves as a transition to the next narrative, viz., the prayer of David and with a view to authentication. It also shows that the editorial notes in verses 1–3 were probably not part of the original narrative, for the anonymity—המלך, in the beginning is broken by the naming of the king in the editorial note at the end. It is also rare in ancient literature that a narrative of such importance should have been ended so abruptly and the discontinuity between report and response so accentuated (cp. 12:1–7; 2 Kgs 22:9–12; Jer. 26:1–19; 36:1–26). Finally, it is the dramatic silence of the prophet that remains its most curious feature. In effect the narrator/editor/redactor has become the prophet.

CONCLUSION

The literary-critical study has shown 2 Samuel 7:1–17 to be a composition of extraordinary complexity and sophistication. It shows that the dynastic theme in verses 8–29 (13a excluded) was not originally continuous with the temple theme in verses 1–7 but rather with the ark narrative in 2 Samuel 6, before verses 2 Samuel 7:1–7 were removed from an earlier cultic setting in oral transmission to their present location. Verses 4a, 5–7, originally a commission for a building of a sanctuary, became modified to a postponement in order to accommodate a Davidic covenant in the *hieros logos* of the Jerusalem temple (cf. vv. 8–12, 16), an obligation on David's lineage having already been replaced by guarantees to his immediate successor (vv. 13–15). The introductory verses 1–3 provided, therefore, the narrative setting for a prophetic oracle, which was in fact an amalgamation of two originally separate legends. Also, the severity of the chastening rod (v. 14) had, by the time of the composition of the narrative, become evident not merely in secession (1 Kgs 12:16–19), affliction (1 Kgs 15:23; 2 Kgs 15:5;

---

50. Ibid., 276.

2 SAMUEL 7:1-17—A LITERARY CRITICAL ANALYSIS

20:1–11), fratricide (2 Sam 13:25; 1 Kgs 2:24–25), execution (2 Sam 18:15; I Kgs 2:23–25), massacre (2 Kgs 10:14; 11:1) or assassination (2 Kgs 9:27–28; 12:20; 14:19) that dogged the Davidic monarchy but, above all, in invasions and threats of invasion (1 Kgs 14:25–26; 2 Kgs 14:13–14; 16:5; 18:9—19:30) that, in the end, brought about its downfall.

The analysis has also noted that, through a play on the word בית also, האתה (v. 5 MT) might have been a scribal attempt at clarification of לא אתה from an earlier recension (cf. 1 Chr 17:4; LXX 2 Bas 7:5), by substituting the ה-interrogative demanded by Hebrew rhetoric, but was preserved by the Chronicler (1 Chr 17:4; cf. 28:3) as an interpretation that was compatible with his theology, and was misconstrued as a negation in the Greek version (LXX) (2 Bas 7:5).

Finally what was reported in the prayer of David (vv. 18–29), as a direct, unmediated revelation (v. 27), was reported in the narrative (v. 11b) as a revelation through a third party, consistent with the change from a direct commission to Solomon to build a sanctuary to an injunction for postponement. Similarly the Heilsgeschichte in the prayer (vv. 23–24), represented in the oracle as a promise (vv. 10–11a), reflected the new and troubled situation of invasion, annexation, deportation, displacement and occupation, beginning with the Assyrian depredations on the Transjordan tribes in 735 BCE (2 Kgs 15:29), and ending with the fall of Samaria, the Northern Kingdom in 721 BCE (2 Kgs 17:1–6), the extensive devastation of the cities of Judah (2 Kgs 18:13), the long and harrowing siege of Jerusalem and the heavy indemnity imposed following Hezekiah's surrender (2 Kgs 18:14–16).

CHAPTER VI

2 SAMUEL 7:1–17 IN ORAL TRANSMISSION—A FORM CRITICAL STUDY

THE RECOVERY OF THE oral stages in the evolution of 2 Samuel 7:1–17, requires exploration of the typical forms of communication and the normal systems of preservation and processes of transmission of the constituent traditions before they attained literary coherence and stability. Chief among the differences from the literary stages are the settings and the objectives that were appropriate to each stage in the evolution of the traditions. Literacy, in predominantly oral cultures, was an elitist pursuit that differed from the life situation of persons among whom such traditions normally evolved. The settings of the traditions underlying the Nathan narrative (2 Sam 7:1–17) must therefore have been quite different in both character and purpose from those of the literary composition, whether as isolated units or as components of a larger composition; and therefore the characters portrayed in the narrative, viz., the king David, the prophet Nathan, and the deity YHWH, as well as the subject matter, related less to the situation described in the narrative than to the situation the composition was designed to address. The subordination of the traditional material to the various compositions—Joshua–Kings, the Psalms (Pss 89; 132) and the Chronicles (1 Chr 17:1–15)—may have been so extensive, and the traditional material may have been so successfully readapted and subordinated, that a recovery of the oral history lies well beyond the reach of literary-critical analysis.

2 SAMUEL 7:1-17 IN ORAL TRANSMISSION

Moreover, the coherence and consistency achieved in the shaping of the narrative must have considerably obscured the pre-literary character and purpose of the traditional material. Consequently, the traditio-historical exploration involves, of necessity, a systematic process of disintegration, which may yield, out of a single narrative, a plurality and variety of traditions each with a distinctive *Sitz im Leben* and purpose.

The Nathan narrative is the account of events that were reported as having occurred in the reign of David i.e. the first half of the tenth century (c.1000–960 BCE). The date of its composition, however, could hardly have been earlier than the eighth or later than the sixth century.[1] It is therefore unlikely that, apart from a surviving nucleus, the narrative, as a reliable account of events reported, can be defended. Even alternative designations of "oracle" and "prophecy" pre-empt conclusions in advance of the evidence. Its present literary setting is that of a narrative concerning a nocturnal—חזון—"revelation" (vv. 4-16), in which the speaker was the deity, YHWH. In that sense, therefore, it might be interpreted either as a myth historicized or, conversely, as a historical occurrence mythologized. In any case, as a nocturnal—חזון—"revelation" (2 Sam 7:4, 17), neither the fact nor the subject matter can be either attested or contested and, furthermore, its attestation three centuries and in an editorial note, limits the claim of the narrative to historicity.

On the other hand, notwithstanding the claims that have been made for unity in the narrative, a free composition *de novo* is debatable, not only because of fractures in it that have obviously survived, but also because the normal means of transmission and preservation of the constituent traditions were eminently available. Its main subject areas—prophecy, monarchy, and sanctuary—represent the three most stable institutions of Israelite society during the period in which the narrative evolved.[2] The Judaean

---

1. Pfeiffer, *Introduction*, 371–73, having noted the differences as well as the similarities between the narrative and Psalm 89, advocated a date for the narrative as late as the third century BCE, presupposing an exilic dating of the Psalm and the dependence of the narrative on it. The differences suggest, however, a dependence of both the narrative and the Psalm on a common tradition, but a separate development. A date later than the sixth century should have betrayed interest in, or awareness of, the re-building of the post-exilic temple, nor earlier than the eighth century, could the note on national crisis insecurity (vv. 2 Sam 7:10–11a) be explained.

2. Cf. 1 Sam 13: 15—16:13; 28:5-20; 2 Sam 7:1-17; 12:1-15, 25; 24:11-25; 1 Kgs 5:1—9:10; 11:29-39; 12:26—13:34; 14:1-16; 15:11-15; 16:1-4; 17-19; 21; 22:2-38; 2 Kgs 1:2-17; 2:1—10:31; 11:1—12:18; 13:14-21; 14::8-14; 15:35; 16:8-16; 17:2, 7-23; 18:1—20:19; 21:1-22; 22:4-23:27; 24:13; 24:18—25:17, 27-30.

monarchy, the Jerusalem sanctuary and the prophetic movement co-existed prominently and interacted vigorously between the tenth and the sixth centuries BCE. The Jerusalem temple, which became the central sanctuary, was closely related to the legitimacy of the Davidic monarchy (1 Kgs 11:32, 36; 15:4; 2 Kgs 8:19), with both institutions enjoying prophetic endorsement (2 Sam 7:1–17, 27; 24:18–25; cf. Ps 89:19–37). It is therefore more than coincidence that, when the monarchy was abolished early in the sixth century BCE, the Jerusalem-sanctuary was also destroyed and the voice of prophecy became silent (2 Kgs 25:6–30: cf. Jer. 50:1—52:34; cp. 2 Kgs 22:11–20). The inter-relationship of such factors favored the preservation and weaving of the traditional material into a shaping of the narrative.

At the same time while continuity preserved traditions, it was discontinuity through reinterpretation that created a narrative; for if without continuity a tradition could not survive the oral phase, it is also true to say that, without its interpretative capacity, whatever survived could not have been transmitted or appropriated as tradition. Consequently, evidence of discontinuity must be investigated not only in the transition-stage at which a tradition was re-interpreted in, and superseded by, literary composition, but throughout its evolution, as well in oral transmission as in later redaction.

With respect to the Nathan narrative (2 Sam 7:1–17), continuity as well as discontinuity is evident from the very beginning, in the transmission of the original revelation, since the predisposition of the recipient—חזה—"seer" affected his apprehension in the receiving and his interpretation in the reporting. The concluding editorial note on accuracy is therefore an exaggeration (v.17). In the final analysis, 2 Samuel 7:4–16 is less the exact account of a revelation, than the redactors' interpretation of earlier traditions including, but not restricted to, the revelation for purposes other than that for which the narrative seemed to address. In effect, the redactor became the "prophet," and therefore, in the larger collection of which it was as a component, that the narrative qualified as prophecy.

2 SAMUEL 7:1–17 AS PROPHECY

Of the identifiable genres in 2 Samuel 7:1–17 none is as prominent or pervasive as the prophetic; and that not only because prophetism was a phenomenon that was commonly recognized in the Near East before and during the period indicated in the narrative, but also because the unifying

2 SAMUEL 7:1-17 IN ORAL TRANSMISSION

factor of the narrative was a prophetic role. It was about a prophet's response to the king's observation (vv. 1–3), and it included YHWH's message for his servant, David, made known to a prophet by the typical medium of חזון (vv. 4–16). However, in a narrative of such complexity, the disintegrative prerogative, consistent with the traditio-historical method, must probe, as Noth has argued,[3] both the historicity of the dominant figure and the originality of the unifying genre.

The historicity of such an event is not in serious dispute. The role of prophets as *answerers* to requests for divinatory oracles, according to Malamat's description (2 Sam 7:1–3; cf. Num 22–24; 1 Sam 9:5–9; 1 Kgs 14:1–4; 22:5–28; 2 Kgs 4; 20:1–6; 22:13–20; Jer 38:14–18),[4] and as divinely commissioned messengers, as Noth has noted (2 Sam 7:4–16; 12:1; 24:11–13; 1 Kgs 11:30–31; 13; 17:1; 2 Kgs 1:3–4; 9:1–10; 19:20; 22:1–20),[5] and whom Nathan represented under both definitions, has been well attested in both biblical and extrabiblical sources. There are, however, certain features of the narrative that raise problems for the applicability of the *genre*. In the first place, the narrative is the report of a revelation received which, by its very nature, was beyond authentication. Secondly, the length and complexity of the revelation must, in the circumstances, raise questions about the accuracy attested in the editorial note (v. 17).[6] Thirdly, the prophet's only reported utterance (v. 3), and repudiated in the ensuing revelation (vv. 4–7), reflects a much later period in the evolution of the phenomenon in Israel, in which the possibility of conflicting answers or visions misunderstood was recognized (cf. 1 Kgs 22:1–22; Jer 20:7; 23:21–22; 28). This raises the question of reliability with respect to the composition (cp. Deut 18:18; 1 Kgs 22:5–23; Jer 1:9; 23:16–22; Amos 3:7).[7] Last but not least, Nathan's portrayal in the four episodes in which he appeared (2 Sam 7:1–17; 12:1–15a, 25; 1 Kgs 1:10–46), was so varied as to render hazardous, for the narrative, the single characterization of prophet.

---

3. See Noth, *History of Israel*, 135-36, and *Pentateuchal Traditions*, 156–75.
4. See Malamat, "A Mari Prophecy" 68–82.
5. See Noth, "History and the Word of God," 183–85.
6. Guillaume, *Prophecy and Divination*, 126–29, has argued, from extrabiblical examples, that, typically, חזון could not have been more than a significant word or phrase projecting a pun that could easily be retained, e.g. Jer 1:11–12; Amos 8:1–2.
7. That Nathan, in response to the royal directive ראה נא (v. 2), answered not as ראה but as a court official (v. 3), is further evidence of a disintegration of the genre in the transmission and, more likely, in the literary phase.

THE NATHAN NARRATIVE IN 2 SAMUEL 7:1-17

Old Testament literature abounds in instances of prophetic figures in encounters with, and in the entourage of, rulers (I Sam 13:6-14, 15:1-31; 2 Sam 12:1-7; 24:11-19; 1 Kgs 11:29-39; 18:17-19; 21:16-24; 22:7-28; 2 Kgs. 9:1-10; 13:14-19; Isa 7:3-25; 37:21-35; 38:3-8; 39:3-7; Jer 22:1-30; 26:10-19; 36; 37:3-10; 38:4-28; Amos 7:10-17). The designation of "court prophets" or "royal counselors" might, however, be inadequate, even misleading. The prophet as seer—ראה—whether in response to royal requests or by intervention uninvited, fulfilled a role that was *sui generis*. The directive, ראה נא (v. 2) required more than considered advice. It envisaged a divinatory rite from which an answer appropriate to the circumstances was expected (cf. Num 23-24). Both the instantaneous response and the repudiation that followed (vv. 3-7), framed in similar construction,[8] suggest therefore a later stage in transmission in which the traditional material was superseded in the reinterpretation, indicating a disintegration of the *genre*.

It would therefore appear that, far from being a typical representative of the prophetic tradition, the prophet in 2 Samuel 7:1-17 was, in large measure, a redactional device, designed more for the purpose of legitimizing a tradition than the transmission of a revelation. Therefore, it may have been as an interventionist messenger (2 Sam 12:1-7) that Nathan first appeared, was thereafter accorded the title of הנביא, and became a representative of the prophetic tradition (2 Sam 12:1, 7, 15, 25, cf. 2 Sam 7:2; 1 Kgs 1:10, 22-23, 32, 38).

It might therefore be noted that not only was it after his stern rebuke of the king that the title הנביא became attached to him (2 Samuel 12:25; cp. vv. 1, 7),[9] but also that, long before his accession, and throughout his reign, David's seer—חזה—was not Nathan but Gad—הנביא (1 Sam 22:5; 2 Sam 24:11). Tomoo Ishida has suggested that, following the confrontation, Nathan was retained at court for the protection of the interests of Solomon against the competing expectations of other royal claimants and the ambitions of Joab, the ruthless captain of the militia and, especially so, in the precarious transition to accession (2 Sam 12:25; 1 Kgs 1:10-27); and remained, thereafter, as the regime's ideologue.[10] Therefore, it must have

---

8. The prophet's advice to the king, לך עשה "go and do. . ." was matched by YHWH's admonition of the prophet, לך ואמרת "go and you shall say. . ." (2 Sam 7:3-4).

9. A chronological misplacement of the Nathan narrative has been recognized by Ackroyd, *2 Samuel*, 73-74 and Mauchline, *Samuel*, 228, who suggest that it should be placed in a later period of his reign after the conflicts had ceased (2 Sam 7:1).

10. See Ishida, "Solomon's Succession" 185-87.

been after, and not before, his confrontation with David over the matter of Uriah the Hittite and, more than likely, as ראה of המלך, who was probably Solomon (2 Sam 7:1–3), that the introductory dialogue took place, which prompted the ensuing revelation (2 Sam 7:1–7; cf. 1 Kgs 3:4–5). It is also to be noted that to his personal name was attached no pedigree, place of origin, cultic identity or affiliation, and it first appeared after David's occupation of Jerusalem as one of the Jerusalem-born princes (2 Sam 5:14) who, officially, were recognized as priests (2 Sam 8:18). Nathan, therefore, may have been a Jebusite cult prophet who, incensed by David's abuse of power in the matter of Uriah the Hittite, intervened on behalf of the wronged resident in the name of the local deity—עליון—"Most High" for, as Jimmy Roberts has argued, the accentuation צדקה (righteousness), as a human virtue or a divine attribute, was not an exclusively Israelite preoccupation, but was also characteristic of the Zion theology (cf. Pss 1, 24, 72, 101),[11] and featured prominently in personal names of the pre-Davidic Jerusalem citizenry (Gen 14:18; Jos. 10:1; 2 Sam 15:24; Ps 110:4).[12] The adoption of the name of the Jerusalem deity—עליון—"Most High" as substantive of יהוה—YHWH—(cf. Pss 91:1–2; 21:7; 47:2; 83:19; 87:5–6; 91:1–2, 9; 92:1), is also indicative of an on-going accommodation in the post-Davidic Jerusalem cultus, and especially the importance attached to—צדקה—"righteousness," which must have informed the redaction of Joshua–Kings and the stature of Nathan as a prophet.

2 SAMUEL 7:1–17 AS COVENANT

One of the more productive areas of Old Testament form-critical research has been the recovery of a covenant genre which, appropriated by the Israelites, sharpened and deepened the understanding of their relationship with YHWH. Covenant-making was an ancient custom that formalized agreements for affiliation, association, collaboration, conflict-resolution and other modes of engagement between individuals, between groups and between individuals and groups. Covenants were contracted between equal

---

11. See Roberts, "Zion in Theology of Davidic-Solomonic Empire," 104.

12. John Gray, *Biblical Doctrine of Reign of God*, 84, has questioned the translation of מלכי־צדק in Psalm 110:4 as a personal name, suggesting instead the rendering "righteous kings" to a proper noun. The suggestion, if valid, would explain even more clearly Nathan's protest, and enhance the case for Jebusite inspiration in his intervention in the matter of Uriah the Hittite.

parties or, as the case might be, between parties in spite of disparity, with a view to stabilizing relationships in loyalty and wholeness.

Such agreements sprang from the realization that, outside the intimacy of family and, in cases of marriage and adoption, even there, relationships endured, matured and were secured as they were formalized in mutual understanding, confidence and integrity, according to the prevailing traditions and social norms. In ancient Near Eastern society the importance of such engagements for social cohesion and stability invested covenant-making with sacredness. Terms of agreement included obligations and sanctions, oaths and curses, promises of reward and warnings of reprisal, the naming of witnesses and methods of preservation for future recall. For the covenants between unequal partners, the dominant party stated the terms, and prescribed penalties in the event of breach, and it was by such agreements that relationships were cemented in mutual loyalty and—שלום—"wholeness."

The cultic setting for such acts of covenanting was noted by Noth in an essay based on a tablet recovered from the archives of Zimri-lim of the ancient city of Mari (c. 1730-1700 BCE).[13] On it was inscribed a report to the king by a deputy who had presided over a ritual pact between (*bi-ri-it*) two subject peoples, the Hanu and the Idumaras, which included the slaughter of the foal of an ass. The high antiquity of the document not only lends support to the genuineness of a similar rite recorded in the patriarchal narratives (Gen 15:9–17; cf. Jer 34:18–19), but illuminates the special significance of the verb—כרת—"cut" used to dramatize the act of covenant-making, which may also have been a warning sign of the penalty a breach might incur.

Further light has been shed on covenant-making in the Old Testament from parallels found in Hittite documents dated in the latter half of the second millennium (1500-1000 BCE), i.e. about the period of settlement of the Israelites in Palestine. George Mendenhall has called attention to similarities in structure and phraseology between the documents and accounts of the Sinai-Horeb and Shechem covenants (Exod 19–24; Jos. 24:2–28), in support of his argument for Israelite dependence on Hittite models.[14] Moshe Weinfeld, in his study of the book of Deuteronomy, has also noted parallels, dated early in the first millennium (c.1000-700 BCE), which show the extent of dependence in the structure of Deuteronomy, an account of

---

13. See Noth, "Old Testament Covenant-making," in *Laws of Pentateuch* 108–17.
14. See Mendenhall, "Covenant," 717–8.

the making of the Moab covenant, on Hittite vassal treaties which were chronologically closer to the composition of Deuteronomy than the parallels cited by Mendenhall.[15]

From their researches Mendenhall and Weinfeld have been able to identify two distinct types of covenant-making found in the Old Testament. The one type, namely the "fealty" type (Exod 19–24; Deut 5–30; Josh 24:2–28), in which the subordinate partner was obligated to loyalty and faithfulness and Weinfeld was able to show how every item listed in the structure of the Hittite vassal treaties could be replicated in one or other covenant type.[16] The other type was the "promissory" type (Gen 13:14–18; 15:1–18; 2 Sam 7:1–17), of which the clearest extrabiblical example, in translation, is that cited by Roland deVaux. It was most likely a decree of the Hittite ruler, Hattusilis, announcing in favor of his faithful scribe, Ulim Teshub of Dattasa, a reward, which was probably a villa in the countryside with a sizeable property adjoining. It was an irrevocable grant. On the death of the beneficiary it would be passed down to his son and grandson after him. Should an heir be found guilty of a misdemeanor, punishable even by death, it would still remain inalienably with the family. On no account could it be transferred to a more distant male relative; and only if there was no direct descendant surviving who was male would the estate revert to the king, since it could not be passed to any female descendant.[17]

As in the Hattusilis decree so in the Old Testament parallels (Gen 13:14–18; 15:1–18; 2 Sam 7:8–16), promises were made to which no obligation was expressly attached. The difference between this type and the treaty-type has seemed so striking as to have encouraged Richard Nelson's use, in connection with them, of the distinguishing labels "unconditional" and "conditional," respectively[18]—a distinction which has, in turn, influenced discussions on, and conclusions drawn from, the covenantal character of 2 Samuel 7:1–17.

Notwithstanding the valuable insights that have accrued from their research, the findings of Mendenhall and Weinfeld, and especially their arguments for dependence on Hittite and other foreign models, have not escaped criticism. Hans-Joachim Kraus has drawn attention to the widely differing *Sitzen im Leben*, and their importance for an appreciation

---

15. See Weinfeld, *Deuteronomy and Deuteronomic School*, 59–74.
16. Ibid., 61–66.
17. See DeVaux, "King of Israel," 158.
18. See Nelson, *Double Redaction*, 99–105.

of the essential nature of the engagement. The political context of treaty ratification could hardly be compared with the cultic festivals that drew communities together for the purpose of naming, or of re-commitment to, their chosen God.[19] Maurice Andrew also, in exploring the setting for the promulgation of the apodictic laws of the Pentateuch as a covenant-making event, endorsed the caution of his co-author, Jacob Stamm, against an over-emphasis on foreign models for a determination of the origin of Israelite law which, given the priority, was apt to misconstrue the nature and significance of the Shechem covenant (Josh 24:2–28) by detaching it from its Sinai parentage (Exod 19–24).[20]

To such reservations might be added a more basic questioning of the theory regarding the extent of the impact or influence of official documents on the shaping of social customs, which appears to have influenced the conclusions reached by Mendenhall and Weinfeld, the evidence for which is, however, unlikely appear, since the theory is itself questionable. The theory suggests that patterns of covenant-making and the methods of reporting such events as have been identified in the Old Testament were beyond the natural capability of subjects under Hittite hegemony, until official documents trickled downwards or rippled outwards to give form and substance to patterns of negotiation, association and agreement between subject peoples on the extremities of the empire, or that the patterns of covenant-making, which may have been more indigenous to the Israelites and their neighbors, could have made no significant contribution to kindred models of social interaction such as have surfaced in the biblical accounts. The theory betrays a misunderstanding of the ways in which social customs emerged, persisted and spread, and how such forms of social interaction among peoples of the Ancient Near East, who shared a common cultural milieu, may have been reported. It is, in fact, unlikely that patterns of covenant-making found in the Old Testament derived only from official documents or that such documents, discovered in relatively recent times and, be it also noted, in places that have been identified as the royal archives, were as widely disseminated or as easily accessible as the theory has implies; but throughout the ancient Near East forms of covenant-making, practiced from time immemorial, and emerging patterns shaped through mobility and social interaction, would naturally have shared common features, as well as such specificities as were more or less characteristic of certain areas than of others and more

19. See Kraus, *Worship in Israel*, 138–39.
20. See Stamm and Andrew, *Ten Commandments*, 37–44.

appropriate for certain occasions than for others. It is therefore not surprising that similarities should have surfaced between accounts of Israelite covenants and contemporary Hittite treaties, as it would be strange to discover from any sampling, phraseologies, formulations and sequences that were so exactly replicated as to prove dependence.

A related aspect of the subject requiring clarification is the implied distinction in the labeling of covenants as "conditional" and "unconditional" which, not infrequently, has been pressed to antithesis. Quite apart from the fact that, conceptually, an "unconditional covenant" is a contradiction in terms, the notion of a covenant of grant (so-called) as opposed to a covenant of obligation (so-called), while conceivable in theory is, in practice, highly improbable. The covenant relationship might be more properly described. As it is inconceivable for a covenant of obligation to have been imposed willy-nilly, but must pre-suppose a substantive relationship that warranted the imposition, so a covenant of grant (so-called), could not have been entirely gratuitous, but must pre-suppose a condition having been met that justified a reward, since neither a free gift, on the one hand, nor a condition of servitude, on the other, is compatible with the definition of, or necessitated, a covenant. The notion of an "unconditional covenant" or a "covenant of grant" might therefore be misleading if it signified, as in the Ulim Teshub-case, a merited reward. Thus interpreted, the difference between the two covenant types might be significantly reduced. In both types are obligations and expectations, expressed or implied, and include benefits that have either accrued, or are expected, from a relationship and practice of faithfulness. It is the principle of reciprocity inherent in a relationship of faithfulness that appears to have been fundamental for the making and keeping of a covenant without which a covenant is inconceivable. Therefore as a covenant of obligation could not have been arbitrarily imposed, so a gift, unconditionally bestowed, could not qualify as a covenant. On the contrary, a covenant imposed, deserving of obligation, and having been fulfilled, made a "grant" either the basis of the obligation that was to be imposed, or the reward for faithfulness in service that was rendered.

Also, the promissory covenant type, as proposed by Mendenhall,[21] might not be the most helpful approach since promises informed both covenant types whether as incentive to, or in recognition of, faithfulness. Thus understood, such a definition shows how closely the covenant types corresponded, and therefore questions the tendency in discussion to treat

---

21. Ibid., 717.

them separately or in antithesis. More properly, they might be interpreted as the one covenant at different stages—obligation and reward—each stage carrying its special emphasis. A grant bestowed in advance earned the right to impose the obligation, and the obligation faithfully discharged earned the reward appropriate to the obligation imposed.

Mendenhall found Old Testament examples of the "promissory" type in the account of YHWH's covenant with Abraham, (Gen 15) and in the Nathan narrative (2 Sam 7:1–17).[22] As regards the former, the covenant was made after Abraham's separation from Lot and, in the crisis of his lack of a biological heir, Abraham was promised extensive property in Canaan and innumerable descendants (Gen 13:14–18; 15). To those promises were attached neither specific obligations nor sanctions. Thus the promise of the covenant might more properly be interpreted less as grant than as reward for faithfulness in obedience to YHWH's call (Gen 15:1–7, 18; cf. 12:1–3).

Mendenhall also interpreted the Davidic Covenant (2 Sam 7:8–16) as the example of a "promissory" covenant, because neither as response to the recital of divine faithfulness (vv. 8–9), nor as condition for reward in further blessings (vv.11b–16), was an obligation incumbent upon the beneficiary.[23] Mendenhall was therefore also able to draw parallels that suggested that the two traditions might have influenced each other with the result that the Davidic covenant in 2 Samuel 7:1–17 might be interpreted as a consummation of the promises made to Abraham, especially in the enlargement of his kingdom and the promise of a succession of biological heirs (Gen 15:2–5, 18; 2 Sam 7:9, 11b–12). Ronald Clements, in a traditio-historical study, went a step further. He traced the transmission, reinterpretation and growth of the Abrahamic covenant tradition through the settlement of the YHWH-worshipping Calebite clan in the Mamre-Hebron region, where Abram settled and founded a sanctuary (Gen 13:18) and later purchased property (Gen 23). The Calebites amalgamated with other settlers in southern Palestine to form the tribe of Judah, for whom Mamre remained the cultic center (Josh 15:13–19).[24] Clements also noted that, on the death of Nabal, a Calebite, David married his widow Abigail, a Carmelitess (1 Sam 25:28–42) and so established his place in Judah. Following the death of Saul and his sons in battle, David, at divine direction, moved out of Ziklag into Hebron where his "house" began in the birth of

---

22. Ibid., 717–18.
23. Ibid., 718.
24. See Clements, *Abraham and David*, 37–41.

his first sons (2 Sam 3:2-5) and he was made king over the house of Judah by the men of Judah (2 Sam 2:1-4) while Ish-baal, Saul's heir, reigned in Mahanaim over the other tribes (2 Sam 2:8-10). Thus David became heir to the Abrahamic promise of land, re-interpreted to encompass the tribal territory of Judah.[25] Later, on being anointed as king over the other Israelite tribes (2 Sam 5:1-5), Abraham, having been recognized as proto-Patriarch of all-Israel, the promise of land-entitlement and—זרק—"descendants" (Gen 15:3-4) was further extended to embrace the kingdom of Israel. Thus was David also legitimized as heir to YHWH's promise to Abraham (Gen 12:1-3; 13:14-18), and as ruler over the Canaanites and the neighboring states (Gen 15:18-21).[26]

An intriguing aspect of the study, therefore, is the evidence of David's earlier faithfulness, comparable to Abram's obedience (Gen 12:1-3), which became a basis of the reward that qualified David for kingship in the first place (2 Sam 5:2), and afterwards for dynastic rule and universal renown (2 Sam 7:8-9). The evidence seems to be his critical decision to renounce Philistine vassalage by leaving Ziklag with his wives at divine direction, and settling in Hebron (2 Sam. 2:1-2; cf. Gen 11:31—12:5). Another might be the faithful discharge of his role as—עבד—"servant" and—נגיד—"captain" in crushing the Philistines and delivering YHWH's people from oppression (2 Sam 5:1-2, 17-25; 7:8-9; cf. Gen 14:1-17). Thus a promise that might, at first sight, have been regarded as an "unconditional" covenant could, on further examination and reflection, be more properly be deemed reward for faithfulness.

Closer study of 2 Samuel 7:8-16 will also show, however, that the Abrahamic tradition does not exhaust the covenantal interpretation of the Nathan narrative, in which YHWH was identified not as—מגן לך—"your shield" (cf. Gen 15:1) but as—יהוה צבאות—"YHWH Sabaoth" (2 Sam 7:8; cf. 1 Sam 4:4)—the God of the ark of the covenant (1 Sam 4:3; 2 Sam 6:2), the receptacle for the Mosaic law (Deut 10:1-5; 31:26; 33:8-10; Josh 8:31-33; cf. 1 Kgs 8:9). Furthermore, David was recognized not as—אברם זרע—"progeny of Abram" (Gen 13:16; 15:3-4) but, like Moses as—עבדי—"my Servant" in relation to YHWH (2 Sam 7:8; cf. Josh 1:2) and, like Saul,

---

25. It is likely that it was at the Mamre-shrine in Hebron, where Abraham was promised by the local deity extensive property and numerous descendants (Gen 3:14-17; 15:18-21) that the nucleus of the Davidic Covenant in the promise "I will build you a house" (2 Sam 7:27), was revealed. Apparently the Abrahamic covenant was re-interpreted in the light of David's conquests.

26. Ibid., 61-63.

as—נָגִיד—"captain" in relation to Israel (2 Sam 7:8, 10–11a; cf. 1 Sam 10:1), whose ancestors entered Canaan not from Ur of the Chaldees (Gen 15:7) but from Egypt, having been delivered by YHWH from bondage (2 Sam 7:6; cf. Deut 6:20–23; 26:5–9). Thus, whereas Abram at Mamre-Hebron, having parted company with his kinsman, Lot (Gen 13:6–11), stood before YHWH at Mamre-Hebron unaccompanied (Gen 13:14–18), in the Davidic covenant Israel—עַמִּי יִשְׂרָאֵל—"my people Israel" was included with David—עַבְדִּי—"my Servant"—as joint-beneficiaries (2 Sam 7:8, 10–11a). It seems, therefore that there was another covenant tradition that had been more pronounced in the Davidic promises which, though overtaken by re-interpretation in the course of transmission, was not entirely erased.[27]

This conclusion is partly supported by an essay, in which Noth argued that the Davidic covenant in 2 Samuel 7 was an attempt at clarifying David's authority with respect to the ark of the covenant which, until its removal to Zion (2 Sam. 6), had not been under the aegis of the monarchy.[28] It projected Israel as—עַם יהוה—"YHWH's People" a socio-religious entity that transcended the political definition (cf. 1 Kgs 12:17). The Davidic covenant was therefore, in part, an attempt at resolution of a theological incongruity provoked by the dynastic kingship articulated in the Nathan narrative (2 Sam 7:14–15), by claiming that David and his successors were also Israelite rulers within a Sinai-Horeb definition. Geo Widengren has argued that the Judaean kings may, in fact, have been covenant mediators in succession to Moses (Exod 19–20; Deut 29:12–28) and Joshua (Josh 24:2–28),[29] whose status, and duties had been defined in the Deuteronomic version of the Mosaic law (Deut 17:14–20). It included the requirement that the king, upon accession, should write a copy of the book of the law and keep it as a

---

27. It might be noted, in that connection, that Psalm 132:1 refers to David's concern for a suitable place for the ark as כָּל־עֻנּוֹתוֹ i.e. the extreme austerities he underwent to achieve that end. This points to a tradition in which the blessings bestowed in the Davidic covenant in 2 Samuel 7, were neither wholly gratuitous nor was the covenant unconditional (cf., 7:12).

28. See Noth, "David and Israel" in *Laws of the Pentateuch* 254–56.

29. Widengren, "King and Covenant," 1–32. It might be argued, on the other hand, that the examples cited by Widengren were hardly typical, in that the circumstances of the investitures were, in each case, not sufficiently normal to establish a pattern for the support of his hypothesis. The particular occasions, viz., Solomon's dedication of the temple (1 Kgs 8), Joash's investiture (2 Kgs 11:12–17) and Josiah's renewal of the covenant (2 Kgs 23:1–3), might have been prompted more by attempts at legitimization after turbulent transitions to accession, than by a regular occasion for the promulgation of the Mosaic law.

2 SAMUEL 7:1-17 IN ORAL TRANSMISSION

vade mecum (Deut 17:18-19; 1 Kgs 2:2-4). David's initiative with respect to the ark (2 Sam 6:1-19; 7:8-9, 26-27; cf. Ps 132) may therefore have also redefined the Deuteronomic conception of Israelite kingship, which, in turn, radicalized the Josianic conception (cf. 2 Kgs 23:3).

Klaus Seybold's identification of the *Heilsgeschichte genre* in 2 Samuel 7, also points to a linkage of the narrative with the Sinai-Covenant tradition. He applied the genre particularly to David's rise from pastoral obscurity to national leadership, which was attributed to YHWH's sovereign freedom in his election, protection and elevation, and was reminiscent of the recital YHWH's bringing up of Israel out of Egypt, which prefaced a covenant of obligation (2 Sam.7:8; cf. Jos. 24:2-28; Exod 19:1-6; 20:1-17).[30] The initiative-motif is particularly expressive in the active verb—לקחתיך—"I took you" (v. 8. cf. Deut 32:9-12; Amos 7:15).[31] David and Israel were objects of divine favor before their response, and co-beneficiaries of the מנוחה—blessing (2 Sam 7:1, 8-11a, 18-24).

The importance of the suggestions of Noth and Seybold is that the invoking of the ark tradition by the one, and the *Heilsgeschichte genre* by the other, for a traditio-historical interpretation of the covenantal character of 2 Samuel 7, has called in question the unconditional character that has been claimed for it as well as for the Abrahamic covenant as the antecedent. Parallels drawn by Seybold have overlooked, however, even closer parallels between David's rise to leadership in Israel and the Moses–Joshua leadership in the conquest and occupation of Canaan that informed the Josianic redaction. It might even be claimed that David's portraiture in 2 Samuel 7:8-16 was a subtle re-presentation of Israelite leadership in the time of the conquest. David was called by YHWH—עבדי—"my Servant" as Moses and Joshua were (2 Sam 7:8b; Josh 1:2; 24:29; Judg 2:8 cf. Num 12:7). Like Moses, he rose from pastoral obscurity to leadership of YHWH's people (2 Sam 7:8; cf. Exod 3:1-10; Ps 78:70-71).[32] YHWH was with David as he had been with Moses and Joshua (2 Sam 7:9a; cf. Josh 1:5). YHWH annihilated the enemies (2 Sam 7:9b; Deut 2:25—3:6; Josh 6, 8, 10-12) and found a

---

30. See Seybold, "The Davidic Kingship," 29-30.

31. Ibid., 31-35.

32. For Deuteronomic acquaintance with the story of the Exodus from Egypt, see Deuteronomy 4:34; 5:15; 6:20-22; 25:17-19; and as Rendtorff, "Yahwist as Theologian?" 1-10, posited the Yahwist theologian as responsible for the Pentateuchal redaction, it is not out of place to enquire whether the "Deuteronomist" might not also be a candidate. The Exodus pericope on the call of Moses (Exod 3:1-15), shows evidence of Deuteronomic editing (cf. vv. 6, 8, 15).

THE NATHAN NARRATIVE IN 2 SAMUEL 7:1-17

place for his people Israel (2 Sam 7:10–11a; Josh 13–21; 23:1). Parallels that point exclusively to the Abrahamic covenant traditions are the promises of "a great name" (2 Sam 7:9; cf. Gen 12:2) and of a biological heir (2 Sam 7:12b; cf. Gen 15:4).

These covenantal features point, therefore, to an original promise to David of a house which, cradled in covenant *genre*, was both reward for faithfulness (2 Sam. 7:8–9), and was also the typical *Heilsgeschichte* preface to a covenant that obligated the Davidic rulers to observance of, the Mosaic law (cf. 1 Kgs 2:2–4; 6:12; 8:25; 9:4–7; 111:38; cf. Deut 17:18–20; Ps 132:12). This explicitly conditional covenant was, however, overtaken and superseded (2 Sam 7:1–7, 13–15) in that, while retaining the *Heilsgeschichte* recital, it was climaxed not with the obligations, but with further blessings on the beneficiary (2 Sam 7:8–29).

Finally, although the word—ברית—"covenant" appears nowhere in 2 Samuel 7 (cf. 2 Sam 23:5; Pss 89:3, 28; 132:12), the more expressive—חסד—"steadfast love" (v. 15), accentuates both the divine initiative in, and the unilateral and unshakeable character of, the engagement. Indeed, misdemeanors deserving of punishment would not threaten the stability of the promise. Even so, its interpretation of—עד־עולם—"forever"—as a promise of perpetual rule might be mistaken for the following reasons:

1. עד־עולם, ("forever") attached to the promise of a kingdom (2 Sam. 7:13b, 16), should be interpreted less in the sense of perpetuity than of indefinite or undisclosed duration. According to James Barr, עולם connotes an unforeseeable, as against a limited, duration.[33] It was in that sense that the rule of the Davidic house was contrasted with the brevity of the Saulide regime (2 Sam 7:15; cf. 1 Sam 13:1).

2. In the prayer of David, עולם (vv.25, 29) is defined as למרוק to mean "from a far distance" and referred to David's house,

3. The transference of עד־עולם from "house" to "kingdom" may have been a secondary development that did not feature in the original form of the tradition (cf. v. 11b, 27), and the inference of perpetual rule, may have been due to the exaggerated language of the parallel version in the Psalter (Ps 89:19–37), of which 2 Samuel 7:1–17 was not so much a paraphrase as a reinterpretation.

---

33. See Barr, *Biblical Words for Time*, 93–94.

2 SAMUEL 7:1–17 IN ORAL TRANSMISSION

2 SAMUEL 7:1–17 AS *HIEROS LOGOS*

2 Samuel 7:1–17 is also an account of the divine authorization for the building of a sanctuary. Presented in the form of a nocturnal revelation—חזון—(vv.4a, 17), it has preserved the typical character of a sacred legend or *hieros logos* that commemorated such a foundation (vv. 5–7, 13; cf. 1 Kgs 8:12–19; 9:3). Such legends were quite common in the ancient Near East, samples of which have been published by James Pritchard, D. Winton Thomas and others. An Epic of Creation legend [. . .], translated by J.V. Kinnier Wilson, described a primordial fight between the gods Marduk and Tiamat. It dramatized a Babylonian creation-myth which, in terms cultic, was the *hieros logos* of the Marduk temple at Esangila.[34] Similarly, a Ba'al-myth that served as the hieros logos of a Ba'al-temple in ancient Ugarit, dramatized a crisis in the pantheon when Ba'al, a deity of considerable prominence and potency, did not have a house of his own.[35] The description of the building of the house may also have been ritually mimed as part of the drama of the dedication and annual commemoration.[36]

The number, diversity and spread of the legends suggest that the building and renovation of the national shrines were projects of considerable importance in ancient Near Eastern society. Theologically, the celebrations in which they featured heralded the "arrival" of "*deus otiosus*." Ideologically, they legitimized the regime. Culturally, they marked the return of cosmic harmony as well as social stability and order. On the other hand, negligence regarding the condition of the sanctuaries, or a frustration of the ruler's will for improvement, must have raised questions of suitability in the one case and of legitimacy in the other.

Such legends as have been preserved in the Old Testament texts would therefore, in the period of oral transmission, have been dramatized in cultic ritual on festal occasions but, disengaged from their cultic moorings and historicized, their original character has been lost and they have been drained of their emotional content. The purpose therefore of comparing a narrative like 2 Samuel 7 with extrabiblical parallels is not only that generic similarities, reflecting the common Near Eastern environment, might be more easily demonstrated, but, having recaptured their original

---

34. See Wilson, "Epic of Creation," 12–13.
35. See Tur-Sinai, "Ugaritic Myths and Epics" 96–105.
36. Ibid., 103–5.

THE NATHAN NARRATIVE IN 2 SAMUEL 7:1-17

significance, distinctive features in each case might be more clearly recognized and the extent of the differences more confidently explored.

It is in such a comparative study that Henri Frankfort has identified differences in character and perception between the Egyptian and Mesopotamian rulers with respect to responsibility for the national shrines.[37] The aura of divinity that clothed the Egyptian pharaoh enabled him to initiate such projects out of the plenitude of his wisdom and authority;[38] whereas the Mesopotamian ruler, being a servant of the deity, required and awaited a divine revelation which, even when it was received, did not relieve his perplexity and anxiety lest precipitate action, consequent on a misunderstanding of the revelation, might provoke divine displeasure.[39] Frankfort cited the case of Gudea, Ensi of Lagash who, instructed by the god, Ningursu, in a dream to build his house, sailed upstream to the shrine of his mother goddess, Nanshe, for guidance and counsel. En route he stopped at two sanctuaries, the one sacred to Ningursu and the other to the goddess, Gatumgdug to supplicate and offer sacrifices for assistance. Arrived at his destination, he related the dream to Nanshe, seeking her interpretation and advice, and reassured, he returned to Lagash to undertake the project; but persisting doubts delayed the start until another revelation dispelled them.[40]

Notwithstanding Frankfort's claim for Hebrew independence,[41] the evidence points to a closer affinity with the Mesopotamian awareness of the divine transcendence, stirring feelings of trepidation in the devotee, than the confidence and assertiveness that distinguished the pharaohs. Certainly, the submissive spirit that animates David's prayer (2 Sam 7:18–29), show a striking resemblance to the humility and deference of the Ensi of Lagash.

It is, therefore most likely that 2 Samuel 7:1–17 has preserved traces of *hieros logos* (cf. vv. 1–7, 13a). Sigmund Mowinckel, in opening up connecting lines between the text and its cultic antecedents, has dissented from literary critics who argued for a dependence of Psalms 89:20–37 and 132 on the Nathan narrative in 2 Samuel 7,[42] proposing instead that 2 Samuel 7 was the narrative echo of portions of the annual New Year liturgy of the enthronement of YHWH, echoes of which were also to be found in the Psalter; and

37. See Frankfort, *Kingship and the Gods*, 5–12.
38. Ibid., 55–57.
39. Ibid., 267–74.
40. Ibid., 255–58.
41. Ibid., 339–44.
42. See Mowinckel, *He that Cometh*, 100.

added that such a legend of a promise, mediated through the prophet, would have been repeated at each new investiture of the Davidic ruler. While not dismissing the possibility that such a promise may have conveyed by Nathan when, after its capture, David was installed as king of Jerusalem and entered into the heritage of the ancient King Melchizedek (Ps 110:3), he nevertheless insisted that Nathan's prophecy could not be properly understood only as an independent historical tradition. From the literary and traditio-historical point of view, therefore, 2 Samuel 7 was better understood as a historicized facade of commonly observed cultic occasions.[43]

The prohibition implied in 2 Samuel 7:5-7, viewed in the light of the foregoing interpretation, suggests, therefore, an anomaly. Not only do the absolute terms, elaborated in explanation (v. 6-7), preclude the designation of a builder (v. 13a) but, directed at David, they raise the question of legitimacy. What follows, however, is a litany of blessings not merely to compensate for the prohibition, but to confirm the legitimacy of the regime (vv. 8-16; cf. Pss. 89:1-4; 132). As well, therefore, on form-critical as on literary-critical grounds, the interpretation of verses 5-7 as originally a prohibition, or even a postponement, is open to debate.

Gosta Ahlstrom has taken his departure not from the perspective of traditional Israelite belief and practice, but from the traditions that informed the pre-Davidic Jerusalem cultus.[44] He interpreted the cultic developments in Jerusalem, following David's conquest and occupation, as a particular instance of Israelite accommodation to the Canaanite environment that had been in process from the time of the settlement. Thus, the recognition of David's kingship over Jerusalem as—על־דברתי מלכי־צדק—"according to the order of Melchizedek" (Ps 110:4; cf. Gen 14:18-20) was, in Ahlstrom's judgment, but one instance of the concessions that were made to the traditions of the Jebusite cult, which did not expire with capitulation, but influenced the shaping of the imported traditions towards an emerging cultus.[45] Evidence of the persistence of the Jebusite traditions was the observance of the Serpent cult up to the time of Hezekiah (2 Kgs 18:4),[46] the Abraham-Melchizedek episode (Gen 14:18-24),[47] the continuing use of indigenous

---

43. Ibid, 101.
44. See Ahlstrom, "Prophet Nathan," 113-27.
45. Ibid., 113.
46. Ibid., 116.
47. Ibid., 114

THE NATHAN NARRATIVE IN 2 SAMUEL 7:1-17

cult-sites at En-rogel (1 Kgs 1:9) and Gihon (1 Kgs 1:33, 38),[48] and David's erection of an altar on Araunah's threshing-floor which, in Ahlstrom's view, was a Jebusite cult-site under the custodianship of the Jebusite priest-king, Araunah (2 Sam 24:18–25).[49]

It was from that direction that Ahlstrom approached an interpretation of the Nathan narrative (2 Sam 7:1-17). He rejected the characterization of Nathan as a reactionary YHWH prophet who attempted to thwart the building of a temple in favor of retention of the nomadic ideal that was symbolized in the Tent in which the ark was housed.[50] On the contrary, he argued that Nathan first appeared after David's occupation of Jerusalem when he denounced the king's abuse of power in the matter of Uriah the Hittite (2 Sam 12:1-7), and that he continued thereafter to function in the court alongside the priest Zadok, a name of unmistakably Jebusite derivation.[51] It was this Nathan who adopted Solomon, the crown-prince, Jerusalem-born, as his protégé (2 Sam 7:12-15; 12:25; 1 Kgs 1:11–45), and defeated Adonijah's initiatives towards the co-regency on the basis of his primogeniture claim to the succession.[52] In that perspective also he interpreted Nathan's objection to David's proposal. Nathan was a conservative Jebusite cult prophet who nursed reservations about the cultic innovations that were being introduced as part of the Davidic occupation, which appeared to subvert the traditional cultus and to upstage and even replace Zadok the priest by Abiathar. He therefore urged delay, suggesting that the time was not propitious. Ahlstrom also noted that it was after the triumph of the Jebusite party in the accession on Solomon and the elimination of Adonijah and his supporters (1 Kgs 2:23–34) that the temple project was undertaken.[53]

Notwithstanding the attractiveness of its insights, Ahlstrom's exposition raises certain issues that require examination. In the first place, the suggestion of a Jebusite resistance to innovations leaves unexplained Nathan's acquiescence when the plan was first mooted. (2 Sam 7:1–3) The argument also smacks of an anachronism. It does not square with either the accommodating tendency in the indigenous mentality generally nor,

48. Ibid., 114–15.
49. Ibid., 113–19.
50. Ibid., 120–21.
51. Ibid., 121–22.
52. Ibid., 122–24.
53. Ibid., 124–26.

in particular, with the natural adaptability of the Canaanite religion in the period under discussion. Indeed it was Ahlstrom who suggested that the emerging cultus in Jerusalem following the occupation was the result of precisely such an accommodation, for the shaping of which the Jebusite contribution was considerable and probably decisive.[54] Finally, Ahlstrom's interpretation assumes a radical reworking of the original *hieros logos* since in the narrative the prophet speaks not in the name of—אל עליון—"God Most High," the high god of the West Semitic pantheon, but of YHWH, who brought the people of Israel out of Egypt and journeyed with them in a tent-tabernacle (2 Sam 7:5–6, 10–11a).

Ahlstrom's difficulties appear to have stemmed from a misunderstanding of the relevance of Nathan's role in the later episodes for his characterization in 2 Samuel 7:1–17 (cf. 2 Sam 12; I Kgs 1), and his not being sufficiently critical of either the historicity of the narratives or their historical connectedness. The Nathan of tradition may have developed in directions that differed significantly from his historical role and character.

The Nathan narrative, as *hieros logos* of the Solomonic temple, raises three problems that require traditio-historical resolution. The first is that, apart from the wisdom and temple traditions, the prominence of Solomon is nowhere else supported. Evidently, his building of the temple made him legendary in a way that could not be ignored. Still, it tended to overshadow the stature of David, who was unable to implement the project. This presented a traditio-historical problem, in view of the persistent characterization of David as the exemplar for the Judaean monarchy.[55] He remained the medium of divine blessing on the monarchy. His throne became established as the seat of authority whereas Solomon, apart from a short-lived revival in the reign of Hezekiah (Prov 25:1), receded into obscurity. In his negotiations with Hiram, king of Tyre, for workmen and materials, Solomon explained David's inability to undertake the project by his citing engagement in warfare (1 Kgs 5:4)—an explanation that differed radically from that given in the Nathan narrative (2 Sam 7:6–7), though probably more consistent with the historical reality. Furthermore, the "prohibition" did not deter David from acquiring Araunah's threshing-floor, by divine direction, as the potential temple site (2 Sam 24:15–25; cf. 2 Chr 3:1) or, as was

---

54. Ibid., 113–16.

55. The anomaly might be compared with the parallel case of the Omri-dynasty in which Omri, although the founder and progenitor and who was mentioned as a ruler of note in Assyrian inscriptions (cf. the Nimrud Tablet 55 and 57 note b) was, in the Hebrew tradition, overshadowed by his successor, Ahab.

reported in Chronicles, from making elaborate preparations and leaving instructions for the building of the temple (1 Chr 22:5–19; 28:1–21). All of this suggests that David's failure to build the temple may have been due less to a prohibition that was imposed than to instability in the realm and the pressures of political office that made such an undertaking impracticable.

A second problem is the conflict of a prohibition with the persistence of a tradition that seems to have wedded the Davidic kingship to a Jerusalem sanctuary. Such a tradition underlies the repeated assertion that David was the reason for the tribal allegiance of Judah to the monarchy and their opposition to the secession, thus saving the monarchy from overthrow (1 Kgs 11:36; 15:4; 2 Kgs 8:19; cf. 2 Sam 19:9–12). Psalm 132 gives clearer evidence of such a bond. It celebrates, in triangular pattern, David's founding of a YHWH sanctuary on Mount Zion (Ps 132:2–5), YHWH's election of Zion as his dwelling place (vv. 13–14) and YHWH's blessing of David's successors on the merits of his devotion (vv. 1, 10–12, 17–18).

A third aspect of the problem is Moshe Weinfeld's claim that the account of Solomon's first dream at Gibeon (1 Kgs 3:1–15; cf. 9:2–6) might have been denuded of the original cultic character and content and replaced by a Wisdom-narrative.[56] His argument is based on patterns of temple-building in the ancient Near East, in which an incubatory oracle for the sanctioning of the project as well as a later oracle on completion was cited.[57] Weinfeld claimed that an account of the post-dedication oracle at Gibeon exists (1 Kgs 9:2–9), and recalls an earlier event, evidently of similar character (v.2) which, not being reported elsewhere, must have been the original content of the Gibeon dream reported in 1 Kings 3:1–15, and Weinfeld suspects that its removal and replacement was due to the reservations of the redactors because of the nature of its content.[58] A more plausible explanation might be that, having been re-adapted and incorporated into the Nathan narrative (cf. vv, 1–7, and 13a), the original *hieros logos* became redundant, for it is intriguing that in both 2 Samuel 7:1–3, in which the matter of the accommodation for the ark was under discussion, which was adjourned with the advice that המלך should proceed as he wished, and 1 Kings 3:4, which reports on the pilgrimage to Gibeon, המלך is anonymous and, in both cases, the anonymity is inconsistent with the rest of the narrative. The Nathan narrative (2 Sam 7:1–17), therefore, does not reflect events that transpired in the Solomonic

---

56. See Weinfeld, *Deuteronomy and the Deuteronomic School*, 246-48.
57. Ibid., 248–50.
58. Ibid., 247.

2 SAMUEL 7:1-17 IN ORAL TRANSMISSION

period, when traditional sanctuaries like Gibeon were legitimate YHWH sanctuaries, and an ark-sanctuary on Mount Zion could co-exist with the Jerusalem-temple, which did not enjoy the monopoly of the central sanctuary.

The possibility of a co-existence between the ark-sanctuary and the temple must also raise the question of 2 Samuel 7 as *hieros logos* of the ark-sanctuary. In that connection Martin Noth has made some insightful observations.[59] Some pertinent features are immediately apparent.

In the first place, the Nathan narrative was introduced by a dialogue on the condition of the ark-sanctuary (2 Sam 7:1–3).

Secondly, the nocturnal revelation appears to have identified YHWH with the ark (2 Sam 7:5–7; cf. Num 10:35–36; 1 Sam 4:6–8, 21–22; 2 Sam 6:1–11). YHWH revealed himself to David as 2) יהוה־צבאות Sam 7:8)—the divine name that was associated with the ark of the covenant, and especially so in the ark narrative: (1 Sam 4:4; 2 Sam 6:2; cf. 7:26–27; Pss 24:7–10; 132:8).

Thirdly, the strong tradition, in the Deuteronomic historical corpus and the Psalms, of the election of Jerusalem YHWH's dwelling place and of the descendants of David to be rulers in Israel, appears to have stemmed from an early tradition of David's initiative in the installation the ark on Zion (2 Sam 6–7; cf. 1 Kgs 11:13, 36; 15:4–5; 2 Kgs 8:19; Pss 78:68–72; 132:10–14).

Fourthly the notion of the temple as replacement of the Tent for the accommodation for the ark must therefore have been, like the literary composition of Nathan narrative, a later development (1 Kgs 8:1–9; cp. 12–13).

The *hieros logos* character of the ark narrative (1 Sam. 4:1—7:1; 2 Sam 6) has been explored by Antony Campbell.[60] He has argued that its composition was not only nearly contemporary with the events narrated,[61] but it was incorporated into the larger composition as an already clearly defined and self-contained narrative-unit, bounded at one end by an account of its removal from the Shiloh temple into battle against the Philistines at Ebenezer-Aphek (1 Sam. 4) and, at the other end, by its installation on Mount Zion in a tent shrine that David had prepared (2 Sam 6:1–17) and, shortly afterwards, was removed into the debir of the temple (1 Kgs 8:1–9). Between those poles was described an eventful journey of capture and

---

59. See Noth, "David and Israel," 254–59.
60. See Campbell, *Ark Narrative*, 193–246.
61. Ibid., 10.

captivity, release and return, arrival and abandonment, and finally its permanent establishment.[62] The whole itinerary, Campbell argued, indicated movements that had, for the most part, been masterminded by the ark. It permitted itself to be captured by the Philistines when the Israelite militia was routed, and submitted itself to the power of the foe (1 Sam 4:4–11). However, imprisoned in Philistia, it wrought such havoc on the idols, and afflicted its captors with a disease so loathsome, that it was hastily repatriated. It guided the oxen that drew it homeward until they halted at Beth-shemesh (1 Sam 6:1–13). Thence it was transported to Kiriath-jearim, to the house of Abinadab on the hill (1 Sam 7:1), where it remained for two decades until David, with pomp and fanfare, removed it to Zion.[63] Thus described, the itinerary of the ark, in Campbell's interpretation, was intended to dramatize YHWH's rejection of the Old Israel in the fall of Shiloh and, in the joyful procession to Zion, his recognition of the New Israel in the accession of David, his chosen servant (Ps 132:11–12) and his choice of Jerusalem as his permanent abode (Ps 132:13–14). The celebration, was therefore, not about a preference for one sanctuary, priesthood or regime over another, but a revolution of the epochs in closure on an Old Israel, represented by the Judges and the Shiloh temple, and the inauguration of a New Israel in the chosen monarchy and the new temple.[64]

Such an interpretation relies heavily on the historicity of the events narrated in 1 Kings 8, viz., that it was as early as the reign of Solomon that the ark-sanctuary on Mount Zion was dismantled and that the relocation of the ark was a prominent part of the dedication of the new temple which, from that early period, was recognized and used as a YHWH sanctuary and the only place that he had chosen for his name. That the interpretation is highly improbable is evident not only from the nature and extent of the cultic abuses that Asa and Jehoshaphat encountered and attempted to remove (1 Kgs 15:11–13; 22:43a), but also from the strength and persistence of David-traditions that required a longer period for incubation, consolidation and popularization through regular celebrations of the installation of the ark than such a brief period on Mount Zion could offer.

It is also evident that, even as *hieros logos* in the Davidic regime, 2 Samuel 6:1—7:17 shows that some measure of demythologization and historicizing had taken place by the time the narrative reached its present

62. Ibid., 198–201.
63. Ibid., 201–5.
64. Ibid., 219.

shape; and therefore, notwithstanding Campbell's suggested dating,[65] it is unlikely that the ark narrative originated in the tenth century but, rather, that it retained patterns of festal observance, which were less distinctively Israelite, and were designed to address the more basic needs and into which, as Tryggve Mettinger has surmised, Canaanite myths were fed.[66]

Explorations at that level have been undertaken separately by Aage Bentzen and J. Roy Porter who both claimed that the ark narrative reflected a New Year festival in celebration of the renewal of nature and social life. In those celebrations YHWH SABAOTH was represented by the king, whose person was therefore invested with such theological and cosmic significance as to make the Israelite celebrations continuous with kindred observances in Canaan and the rest of the ancient Near East.[67] Its captivity and subsequent release (1 Sam 5–6) was an Israelite equivalent to the myth of the dying and rising god, which dramatized YHWH's primordial combat with, and victory over, the chaos-monsters. Also, the pompous and exuberant procession into the capital, and its installation on Mt. Zion, portrayed YHWH's ascension to the heavenly throne as King supreme over all the gods (cf. Pss 2, 24, 47; 93; 95–100; 1 Chr 16:7–36), and his re-confirmation of the legitimacy and security of the Davidic monarch, his earthly representative, with pledges of support, promises of victory over the hostile forces and an era of peace, security and prosperity (2 Sam 7:9–10; 23:6–7; Pss 2:1–8; 89:22–23; 110:1–2, 5–6; 132:18).[68] Read alongside its poetic counterpart (Ps. 132), it becomes clearer that a Davidic covenant, as was intended in the Nathan narrative (2 Sam 7:8–29; cf. 1 Kgs 2:2–4), could hardly have been omitted, for it must have been the logical climax to a *hieros logos* that envisaged an auspicious future for the regime and therefore the realm.[69]

Finally, whatever may have been the impact of external patterns, or the extent of continuity with kindred *genres*, the tradition suggests that ark of the covenant was originally an Israelite institution of long and continuous usage from the pre-monarchy period (Josh 3:3–11; 6:4–11; Judg 20:27; 1 Sam 4), with traditions stretching further back into a התהלך wilderness-period (2 Sam 7:6; cf. Exod 25:10–22; Num 10:35–36; Deut 10:1–3). Therefore, although the ark narrative may have reflected, in a period later than

---

65. Ibid., 10.
66. See Mettinger, "YHWH SABAOTH," 126–35.
67. See Bentzen, "Cultic Story of Ark in Samuel" 37–42.
68. See Porter, "Interpretation of 2 Samuel 6," 171.
69. Ibid., 168–69.

the Davidic-Solomonic regime, a rejection of the Old Israel of the Judges having, in Bentzen's and Porter's judgment, accommodated features drawn from the Canaanite environment, the ark also symbolized the abiding relevance and validity of the covenant at Sinai-Horeb as well as a theological continuity of the monarchy with the Israelite tribal confederation (Deut 10:1–6; 31:9–11; 1 Kgs 8:1–9, 21).

2 SAMUEL 7:1–17 AS *DIE KÖNIGSNOVELLE*

Die Königsnovelle, translated hereafter as "the Royal Novel," is a term specially coined by Siegfried Herrmann for the identification of a literary *genre*, found in ancient Egyptian texts peculiarly designed for an etiological purpose.[70] It describes a court ceremony in which auspicious events and sensational accomplishments of the ruler, including his founding of institutions, were celebrated. On such occasions the ruler also communicated new decrees in minute detail. Herrmann was able to trace the history of the *genre* from the Middle Kingdom to the Late Egyptian period even though integrated with other forms.

"The Royal Novel" related the appearance of the king before an assembly of court officials, with whom he shared his plans and who responded with glowing expressions of commendation and pledges of support. To that basic pattern other elements might have been added. The will of the deity, made known to the king in vision, might be recalled. The discourse might have included praises to the god Re, his Father. His pre-natal election and references to his youthful exploits before accession might have also been added for enhancement of his legitimacy and were applauded.[71]

Not only from the evidence available, but also on logical grounds, Herrmann argued the case for "the Royal Novel" form in the literature of the Old Testament. He claimed that, from the period of the Old Kingdom, and well into the Davidic-Solomonic regime, Syria-Palestine had been, for the most part, under Egyptian hegemony and within the Egyptian sphere of influence; and he cited two passages from the later period, viz., the Nathan narrative (2 Sam 7) and Solomon's dream at Gibeon (1 Kgs 3:4–15), which seemed to reflect "the Royal Novel" features.[72]

---

70. See Herrmann, "The Royal Novel," 51
71. Ibid., 51–52.
72. Ibid., 52–57.

2 SAMUEL 7:1–17 IN ORAL TRANSMISSION

With respect to the former Herrmann, having reviewed the literary-critical questions that surfaced, considered whether the chapter might not, as a whole or in sections, have also provided evidence of a literary type in which the themes of ark, temple and kingship cohered, and noted that these were precisely the issues that preoccupied "the Royal Novel." He therefore concluded that their convergence in the same narrative, far from being a literary coincidence, might more satisfactorily be accounted for through form-critical research.[73]

Herrmann was not unaware of the anomalies. Whereas "the Royal Novel" assumed the ceremonial setting of an assembled court, in 2 Samuel 7 the audience consisted of an individual who, in that context, functioned less as a typical prophet than as a counselor or, as Herrmann preferred, the "King's Friend." Even so, Herrmann observed that the individualizing of the audience was not without precedent. He cited a memorial tablet of King Amosis, which depicted the court-scene of a conversation between the pharaoh and his consort. He also considered the peculiar situation reflected in 2 Samuel 7, which might have projected the actual historical circumstances of a nascent state and a royal establishment in embryo; and therefore pleaded for form-critical flexibility on grounds of cultural differentiation.[74]

Herrmann also paralleled Nathan's answer (v. 3) with the hymned response, in "the Royal Novel" scheme, of the courtiers who enthusiastically endorsed the pharaoh's plans and applauded the wisdom of his decisions. The parallels do not, however, seem to coincide; for Nathan's initial response, ambiguous rather than positive, and diplomatic rather than enthusiastic, was followed by a longer oration, which was a restraining order on the ruler from proceeding with his plans (vv. 4–7). Answering the discrepancy, Herrmann discerned a correspondence, if only in externals, in which a counter-proposal from the court merely served as a foil to accentuate the king's over-ruling prerogative to proceed regardless.[75] In the case of 2 Samuel 7, however, the objection raised (vv. 5–7) does not appear to be a mere formality that was designed for effect, but a stern injunction, couched in altercation-mode that overruled the royal will. Again, having admitted the discrepancy, Herrmann pleaded for form-critical flexibility.[76]

---

73. Ibid., 57–58.
74. Ibid., 58.
75. Ibid., 58–59.
76. Ibid., 59.

In the second part of the narrative (vv. 8–16), Herrmann cited the promise of a "great name" (v. 9b) and the exaltation of the ruler to divine sonship as further indications of the impact of "the Royal Novel" form, whose ideological purpose was the legitimization of the ruling house.[77]

Notwithstanding the linkages he was able to identify, Herrmann's study raises two basic questions regarding the *genre*, which prompts some further observations on applicability.

Was "the Royal Novel" *genre*, in origin, an oral phenomenon or was it, throughout, fixed as literature?

What are the form-critical limits on flexibility, beyond which the *genre*, however striking the linkages, is no longer viable?

So far as its applicability to 2 Samuel 7 is concerned, the minimum requirement would seem to be the setting of a court-ceremony that was unambiguously so, and the formalities appropriate to and consistent with the occasion. By no stretch of the imagination or of generic kinship might the briefest dialogue, conducted in privacy between a ruler and his counselor or consort, and devoid of the minimum requirement of a third party, be construed as the residue of, or an apology for, a court ceremony befitting the purpose of "the Royal Novel."

Secondly, "the Royal Novel" *genre* required the presence and preeminence of the ruler, whatever the status or roles that were assigned to the other characters. This was not the case in 2 Samuel 7:1–17, in which the king spoke but once (v. 2) and thereafter, by deliberate design, was not only silent but absent, and such prominence was given to the mediator of the revelation, that not even the transmission of the revelation was dramatized but was subsequently appended in an editorial note (v. 17).

Thirdly, "the Royal Novel" was so composed that the royal will should ultimately prevail. Indeed, by virtue of the aura of divinity with which Egyptian kingship was invested, it would appear to be of the essence. That royal prerogative was directly contradicted in 2 Samuel 7, in which YHWH overruled both royal will and prophetic acquiescence; and it is to that basic difference that the king's prayer of humble acceptance (vv. 18–29) also bore eloquent testimony.

In sum, with respect to the impact of official documents on kindred forms discoverable in Old Testament literature, observations made above with respect to the impact on *genre* in other areas of documents emanating from sources in metropolitan centers and presumably higher cultures seem

---

77. Ibid., 59–60.

relevant for this discussion. Claims for downward and outward influences from more advanced and sophisticated cultures, based on similarity of patterns discovered in other cultures, only to be modified by a plea for flexibility on grounds of cultural differences, provoke questions of the premise. Henri Frankfort has shown that, not in Egypt only, but also in Mesopotamia, attention to the condition of sanctuaries was given high priority on the royal agenda for much the same reasons and with much the same objectives, notwithstanding differences in conception of the ruler's person and relationship with the deity.[78] It therefore remains to be demonstrated from the evidence not only that the Egyptian influence was more pervasive and enduring than the Mesopotamian, but that either was more determinative for the shaping of 2 Samuel 7 than the autochthonous. It might also be the case that throughout the Ancient Near East basic conceptions of monarchical rule, though prevalent, were indigenous; and that where the common features in *genre* were identifiable, they were the result not so much of borrowing as of adaptation.

Whatever might be the characterization of "the Royal Novel," to propose 2 Samuel 7 as an Israelite equivalent of Solomonic dating as Herrmann has done,[79] as well as a unity of form and consistency in content, which Noth has appeared to endorse,[80] is to render a process of oral transmission unlikely, and the argument, by the very nature of the case, untenable. Such a *genre* could not have originated in literature but rather in the participation of the monarchy in the cult. As literary *genre*, therefore, such external influences as have been discovered could hardly have preceded the transitional stage from oral transmission to literary composition, that is to say, during the reign of Hezekiah who, as it happened, valued the Egyptian alliance (2 Kgs 19:9; cf. Isa 31:1–3). That traces of Egyptian ideology are discoverable in the narrative is therefore not in question; but given the peculiar character of Israelite religion in the early period of the monarchy, when YHWH was addressed by the king as—אדני—"my Lord" (vv. 18. 19, 20, 28) and the king recognized as—עבד—"servant" by YHWH (vv. 5, 8, 19, 20, 21, 26, 27, 29), the exalted conception of kingship that informed "the Royal Novel" could hardly have been accommodated, and the role of the Israelite prophet, as bearer of the divine revelation and interpreter of the divine will, even in relation to the king (1 Sam 13: 11–14; 15:10–29; 28:16–19; 2 Sam

---

78. See Frankfort, *Kingship and the Gods*, 267–71.

79. Ibid., 61.

80. See Noth, "David and Israel," 251–57.

12:1–7; 1 Kgs 11:29–38; 12:22–24; 14:7–11; 16:1–4) could not have been simulated, but only obscured, in the role of counselor, or "King's Friend" of Egyptian definition.

CONCLUSION

The foregoing exploration of the identifiable genres in the Nathan narrative has shown that, whereas "the Royal Novel" *genre* is of limited viability, Prophecy, Covenant and Hieros Logos stand out as typical patterns and appropriate settings for the shaping and growth, preservation and transmission in the oral phases of the tradition of a promise to David. For that reason, their contribution to the shaping of the narrative has been indisputable, and their impact on the final product indelible. The pericope might be interpreted as the prophetic announcement of a covenant with David that was prefaced by the hieros logos of a YHWH sanctuary or, conversely, as the hieros logos of a YHWH sanctuary, recited by a cult prophet, which reached its climax in the announcement of a covenant of promise made to David. Whichever interpretation is preferred, there can be little question that some of the problems that have surfaced from its composite nature are the result of a blending of traditions that was not so complete as to have removed all traces of their earlier independence.

Furthermore, the coordination and integration, whether in the writing stages or the oral, were crucial for the preservation of the traditions. The original revelation may have been no more than a cryptic clause "a house I will build for you" (v. 27) which, in the process of reinterpretation, amplification and re-application, whether as *hieros logos*, covenant or prophecy, attracted other traditions. The promise to David was not connected, originally, with the building of a temple, but with the installation of the ark on Mount Zion. The final shaping of the narrative was about the recognition of the Davidic monarchy as chosen by YHWH (2 Sam 7:11b–16) and the designation of Solomon to build the Jerusalem temple (2 Sam 7:13a; cf. 1 Chr 17:1–16).

An important conclusion to be drawn from the exploration is that the significance of a narrative such as appears in 2 Samuel 7:1–17, like much else in Old Testament literature is, according to the reader's perspective, disposition and interest, either more or less than narrative composition or historical excursus. Therefore, neither do the merits nor the shortcomings in either regard determine the worth of the narrative, and to assess

2 SAMUEL 7:1–17 IN ORAL TRANSMISSION

a composition in the Old Testament as modern literature, or the chain of events reported as modern history, is to run the risk of grave misunderstanding, whatever the verdict. The Old Testament is a collection of documents that were assorted, coordinated and arranged primarily for a theological purpose. Furthermore, neither the original intention nor the mode of presentation was literary. They were expressive of a people's faith who, long before the first paragraphs were written, worshipped and confessed YHWH as their God, and whose faith and worship, like the final product, resulted not from abstract speculation or fertile imagination but from sober reflection on their past. Nor did the traditions remain static, but changed and grew as they were re-interpreted in the process of transmission.

Out of that process was bequeathed a legacy that armed succeeding generations with the fortitude to meet the challenges, both perennial and unprecedented. Coping mechanisms included vows and sacrifices, seasons of exultation and lamentation, myth and ritual, memory and hope, pilgrimage and prayer, fast and festival, and above all, God, ever-present, whose name was revealed as YHWH. Many of their experiences were akin to those of their neighbors in the common political, social, cultural and physical environment they shared. It is therefore not surprising that, notwithstanding the later claims to uniqueness and attempts at distancing themselves and their forebears, another reality might be discovered beneath the surface of the text. Kings both good and bad, prophets both courageous and compliant, priests both faithful and unscrupulous, could be found as much outside of Israel as within. The same festivals were observed at the same seasons and according to the same calendar. Sanctuaries were built on the same plan and for the same purpose. In the common legal culture the crimes condemned and the penalties imposed were the same and, in the rise and spread of the Mesopotamian empires, they were all deluged by the same *Tsunami*.

What distinguished the Israelites was the commitment of a succession of scribes to the gathering of the traditions wherever they could be accessed, and to document them for the telling of a story—their own story—not for pastime and entertainment, antiquarian interests, or as legacies for posterity, but primarily for their own edification and the instruction of their children. In pursuit of that commitment they believed that they were being faithful to the best traditions of their ancestors whose names they wished to perpetuate and whose ways they tried to emulate. For the same purpose

THE NATHAN NARRATIVE IN 2 SAMUEL 7:1-17

they called to remembrance, spoke and sang, recited and rehearsed, wept and prayed long before writing became an option.

Out of that process was created a peculiar people who were able not only to survive the vicissitudes that overwhelmed them and consigned their neighbors to oblivion, but to outlive their conquerors. The alchemy that made for resilience, it appears, was the fusion of faith and ideology. "You shall be my people and I will be your God." Who they were derived from their confession of YHWH as the only God, and who YHWH was—the jealous God—explained why they were who they were. With that affirmation and self-perception they were enabled to survive the cataclysms. Political ascendancy or political decline, the rise and fall of their monarchies, subjugation by foreign powers, oppressive or lenient—it was possible to confess through the crises what their ancestors acclaimed in cultic celebration, "YHWH, our God reigns!" (Isa 52:7: cf. Pss 47:7-8; 93:1-2; 95:3; 96:10, 97:1-2; 99:1-5).

An important component of that confession was the legend of a ruler, whose characterization was so loaded with irony and contradiction that he could hardly have been a literary invention. He was the doughty warrior and the skilled strategist whose conquests, annexations and alliances created an empire, but he was also a flawed human being, the over-indulgent father of a seriously dysfunctional family, who either could not, or would not, guide or restrain his headstrong sons. As political leader he was able to win from his followers, at court and on the field, their fiercest loyalty, while his own weakness incriminated him in a most hideous form of betrayal and abuse of power. Two cult-events, however, distinguished his reign and won for him an imperishable name. Having captured Jerusalem, he made the Jebusite stronghold his capital and personal possession and, having removed the Philistine threat, he installed the ark of the covenant on Mt. Zion, making the city of David also a cultic center for the celebration of YHWH's enthronement. For a reward, a promise was made to him that his descendants would rule Israel far into the future. A unity was thus forged between YHWH's election of Jerusalem as his inviolable abode and his legitimization and blessing of the House of David.

The promise acquired special importance in the period following the rebellion of the northern tribes under Jeroboam ben Nebat. Although the tribes that seceded outnumbered and, militarily, were far more powerful than the tribe of Judah that remained loyal to the House of David, their geographical location made the Northern Kingdom a buffer for Judah against the Assyrian onslaughts in the ninth and eighth centuries. This enabled the Davidic monarchy to outlast their northern counterpart by almost a century and a half. Moreover, whereas Samaria crumbled under the Assyrian invasion, not only was Jerusalem able to survive a long and bitter siege, but Hezekiah, ruler of Judah and Jerusalem, outlived Sennacherib, the powerful and ruthless aggressor (2 Kgs 19:36–37). Above all, whereas the Northern Kingdom had been plagued by recurrent regime changes and bloody uprisings, the kingdom of David maintained a semblance of stability for a little more than four centuries and, but for a seven year interregnum (2 Kgs 11:1–4), the throne of David was occupied by a succession of rulers in smooth transition until the post-Josianic decline in 609 BCE and the final overthrow in 586 BCE.

Until the final meltdown, cherished myths of perpetual rule (Ps 89; Isa 9:7; Jer 33:15–21a) and of the inviolability of Jerusalem (Pss 46, 48; Is. 37:27–36; Jer 7:4), were kept alive in cultic celebration, psalmody and prophetic pronouncement, and it is therefore not surprising that prophets who lived through the downfall of the Northern Kingdom, having interpreted that catastrophe as the righteous judgment of YHWH could also, while the Judaean monarchy survived, find hope for a national renewal and recovery. It is such a hope that must have inspired Isaiah of Jerusalem when the city was under siege (Isa 7:1–16: 37:21–35; cf. 2 Kgs 19:20–34) and, taken up by Jeremiah in the last days of the Davidic monarchy (Jer 22:1—23:5) and Ezekiel in the aftermath of its overthrow (Ezek 34:23–24; 37:24), stirred the interest of the redactors in the post-exilic period.

Thus, as Mowinckel has argued, after the fall of the monarchy in 586 BCE, restoration was focused on the eschatological return of a Davidic ruler (Isa 55:3–5; Jer 17:25; 33:15–26; Ezek 34:23–24; 37:15–24; Amos 9:11; Hos 4:5; Mic 4:8; 5:2).[81] Such hope was, however, predicated not on the survival of the regime but on its irrevocable demise. Earlier hopes of brief duration of the Exile and a speedy return of Jehoiachin (Jer 28:3–4), or in the appointment of a descendant, Zerubbabel, as governor of Judaea (Hag 2:25–28; Zech 4:5–9), having been proven illusory, gave way to a more sober reflection on the fall of the Davidic monarchy, which was ascribed to a heinous crime perpetrated by him. Paradoxically, it was this late reflection on the history of David, including the optimistic guarantees in the Nathan narrative (2 Samuel 7), which remained as prophecy still to be fulfilled and awakened hopes of a restoration. In this way a promise, originating in the

---

81. See Mowinckel, *He that Cometh*, 165–69.

THE NATHAN NARRATIVE IN 2 SAMUEL 7:1-17

tenth century BCE, became the inspiration for a messianic hope, and the dominant perspective for the shaping of the prophetic canon, and later, for the eschatology and Judaism and of Early Christianity.

CHAPTER VII

2 SAMUEL VII: 1–17—THE EVOLUTION OF THE NARRATIVE—A SUMMARY

IN THE FOREGOING STUDY the history of the Nathan narrative in 2 Samuel 7:1–17 was traced from its origins in the David-Solomon period, through a convergence, reinterpretation and integration of traditions, to its permanent place in the canonical Prophets (Joshua–Malachi). It is important to note, however, that the chronological boundaries, thus defined, do not limit the traditio-historical span. Its significance in and for the prophetic canon, has not limited its capacity for further interpretation in the Hebrew Bible and beyond,[1] nor was the Davidic nucleus found in 2 Samuel 7:11b and 27 the earliest recoverable pattern of regime-legitimization, of royal ritual or of covenant-making. Seasonal observances, the hallowing of cultic sites, the practice of divination, the sacralization of political office and, not least, the critical importance of biological descent for the continuity of the lineage and the security of inheritance were deeply rooted traditions in ancient Near Eastern societies long before the inauguration of monarchical rule in Israel.

At the other end, the significance of the narrative for the Davidic monarchy and the Jerusalem cultus, did not expire with the destruction of

---

1. This is demonstrated by its re-appearance in 1 Chronicles 17 with sufficient differences to indicate a reinterpretation rather than a quotation and in a Qumran fragment, *Florilegium* (4Q174).

THE NATHAN NARRATIVE IN 2 SAMUEL 7:1-17

Jerusalem and the abolition of the monarchy in 586 BCE; but an idealization of these two institutions sustained the hopes of the Jewish people throughout the long period of foreign domination (Ezek 40–48; Is. 44:24–28; 1 Chr 16–17; 21–24; 26; 2 Chr 1–8; Hag 1–2; Zech 4:1–10; 9:9–15; Ps 137). The promise made to David (2 Sam 7:11b) continued to stir the imagination and the hopes of the dispossessed and dispersed people well into the Persian period, in the proclamation of YHWH's sovereignty over the nations and his jealousy for his people and his name (Isa 9:1–7; 11:1–9; 40:9–10; 42:1–4; 45:27–28; 52:7, Jer 33:15–22; Ezek 34:23–24; 36:13–28; 37:1–14; Amos 9:11–15), and the promise to David (2 Sam 7:11b), featuring prominently in an Essene commentary on the Last Days,[2] and their incorporation of a Melchizedek-legend (cf. Gen. 14:18–20; Ps 110:4), in their portrayal of the heavenly judgment,[3] show the vitality and versatility of the Davidic traditions in the eschatology of the community as well as in the Christology of the Early Christians who recognized and confessed messiahship in Jesus of Nazareth, a Davidic descendant (Rom 1:3–6), and his eternal priesthood in the order of Melchizedek (Heb 5:6–11; 7:1–25; cf. Ps 110:4).

The Prophets have, however, been used as the literary-historical setting for the Nathan narrative in 2 Samuel 7:1–17, because it was there, first of all, as a coherent and self-contained composition and integral to a historical narrative of Israel in Canaan and of kingship in Israel (Joshua–Kings), which was afterwards incorporated as prophecy, that traditions preserved therein acquired canonical significance.

2 SAMUEL 7:1-17 IN THE PERIOD OF THE UNITED MONARCHY

The Promise of a "House" (Dynasty) as Continuity

The earliest ascertainable witness to a promise made to David by divine revelation, was not the Nathan narrative, but an Ode ascribed to him (2 Sam 23:1–7). This conclusion has been reached on three grounds:

Firstly, there is no attestation to such a promise in the Nathan narrative, apart from an editorial note that was appended at least two centuries after the period recorded in the narrative (2 Sam 7:17). It cannot therefore,

---

2. Vermes, "Florilegium," 491–92.
3. Vermes, "Heavenly Prince Melchizedek," 500–502.

2 SAMUEL VII: 1–17—THE EVOLUTION OF THE NARRATIVE

unsupported, be taken as confirmation of the historicity of a narrative that also incorporated traditional elements originally and, for the most part, independent.

Secondly, the narrative is the account of a nocturnal revelation—חזון (vv. 4, 17) the content of which, by its very nature, is beyond the possibility of corroboration or confirmation.

Thirdly, the narrative lacks the indispensable prerequisite for an emerging tradition, viz., communal participation and public ownership.

The poem attributed to David (2 Sam 23:1–7) seems, on the other hand, to have satisfied the conditions. Neil Richardson and Michael Avioz, after close literary-critical examination, have arrived independently at a dating as almost contemporary with the matters it addressed,[4] a conclusion that W.F. Albright had also reached earlier but tentatively.[5] Though a Davidic composition is not inconceivable, since his talent for poetry was commemorated in Hebrew tradition (2 Sam 1:17–27; 3:33–34; 18:33; cf. Amos 6:5), it might also have been an Ode dedicated to him towards the close of his reign or shortly after his demise. Also, the valedictory mood suggests the setting of a public occasion, precedents for which might be found in the Testaments of Jacob (Gen. 49) and Moses (Deut. 33) and, like them, indicative of the passing of an era. Having delineated the qualities of an ideal ruler, David expresses optimism for his family as the ruling "house," by virtue of—ברית־עולם—an "enduring covenant" (v. 5) of which he is beneficiary. Similarities with the Nathan narrative (2 Sam 7:1–17) are as follows:

> Both compositions promise that the regime would continue far into the future (2 Sam 7:11b, 16, 19; 23:5).
>
> Both compositions confirm that a promise was given by revelation (2 Sam 7:5, 17; 23:2).
>
> Both compositions envisage discomfiture and elimination of the enemies of the regime (2 Sam 7:10–11a; 23:6).

The significant difference, however, is that whereas in the narrative the revelation reached David by an intermediary, viz., the prophet Nathan

---

4. Richardson, "Last words of David," 257–66; cf., Avioz, *Nathan's Oracle* 62–68.

5. See Albright, *Yahweh and the Gods of Canaan*, 21. Mowinckel, "Die lietzen Worte Davids," 30–58, dissented from an early dating of the poem on the ground that its idealization of the ruler was in such stark contrast to the realities of David's rule as to render such a suggestion unlikely. This argument has been countered by the suggestion that the ode may have been made public in the ensuing reign.

THE NATHAN NARRATIVE IN 2 SAMUEL 7:1-17

(2 Sam 7:5, 8, 17), in the poem David is reported as having received the revelation directly (2 Sam 23:1–3), a feature to which the prayer of David also bears witness (2 Sam 7:27).[6] The tradition of a direct revelation might also account for the mangled state of the text of the narrative at the point when the promise was made (2 Sam 7:11b).

The "building of a house" carried special connotations in Hebrew thought. It signified the critical importance of procreation, for the increase, extension and perpetuation of the lineage as well as the security and enlargement of the inheritance. The promise was not an exclusively royal boon, but a blessing that the head of every Hebrew household was entitled to expect, the social importance of which was also highlighted in provisions of the Levirate Law (Deut 25:5–10). A "house" was therefore more than the aggregate of the relatives that happened to be residing on the same site and at the same time, which consisted of the head of the household his wife/wives and the immediate progeny with their spouses, who collaborated and subsisted as an economic unit; but included the further descendants—the "children's children," living and as yet unborn (cf. Pss 127–128). Though not an exclusively royal privilege, the revelation may have come to David as early as the period of his rule in Hebron as king of Judah (2 Sam 2:1–4; 3:2–5) for, in the case of a ruler, it was the stability and continuity of the "house," and the principle of hereditary succession, which secured the throne to the family in an orderly succession. A household as dysfunctional as David's, riddled with dissension, corrupted by promiscuity, shadowed by vendetta and susceptible to ungovernable passions, furtive violence and open rebellion boded ill for the realm (2 Sam 12–15). A further frustration might have been the failure of issue from his re-marriage to Michal of the House of Saul (2 Sam 6:20–23; cf. Gen 15:1–6).

For a king of the David's caliber, who had scattered his enemies, unified the tribes in a political kingdom, extended his sway over the neighboring states and created an Israelite empire, an unstable "house" was a crisis of considerable magnitude. Ideologically, it signified divine disfavor. Politically, it fed disaffection, invited subversion and threatened usurpation. A "house" was therefore a critical matter for David, not only at the beginning of his ascendancy but at the zenith. "Except YHWH builds the house, the builders in it have toiled in vain" (Ps 127:1). It was in the face of such a crisis

---

6. The Hebrew expression used by David for the receiving of the revelation את־אזן גליתה (2 Sam 7:27) emphasizes graphically a first-hand, direct and unmediated revelation.

2 SAMUEL VII: 1–17—THE EVOLUTION OF THE NARRATIVE

that the promise, בית אבנה לך—"A house I will build for you," became a testimony of monumental importance (2 Sam 7:27).

It therefore appears that, at whatever phase in his career such a promise was made to David, it must have been publicized either towards the end of his reign, either during the brief co-regency of Adonijah and his party (1 Kgs 1:5–7) or early in the ensuing reign after the overthrow of Adonijah (1 Kgs 2:13–35). The promise, in any case, legitimized hereditary succession as the regular form of the transference of power in Israel, above military prowess or other personal qualifications. In Judah it continued as the standard pattern for the four centuries following; and, in the Northern Kingdom, in spite of the frequency and violence of the regime changes, it was also recognized as the legitimate and normal process of succession.

The Promise of a "House" (Dynasty) as Tradition

To qualify as tradition, such a promise required popularization. Its ideological claims must have gained public recognition. Unable to thrive in the privacy of the palace, it must have become democratized in, identified with and enriched by, the popular rituals. As it became part of the communal legends, so a promise to the ruler became integrated into the story of the community and thus increased in vitality. In David's case the promise of a house, however it originated, took root as it became integrated into the legend of the ark of the covenant, an ancient Israelite institution, whose installation on Mount Zion at David's initiative, was deemed meritorious, because of the zeal he applied and his austerities—ענותו—he endured to accomplish that design (Ps 132:1–8). The promise, בית־אבנה־לך—"A house I will build for you," was made by יהוה צבאות אלהי ישראל—"YHWH SABAOTH, the God of Israel" (2 Sam 7:8, 11b, 27), enthroned on the cherubim that surmounted the ark (cf. 1 Sam 4:4; 2 Sam 6:2).

The ceremonies relating to the installation of the ark, observed annually at the Feast of the Tabernacles (Deut 16:13–15; 31:9–13), highlighted the celebration of the ascension and enthronement of YHWH SABAOTH and his entering his place of "rest" (Pss 24:7–10; 95:11; 132:1–8). They also, therefore, commemorated David's faithfulness in securing the place of YHWH's sanctuary, and his diligence in bringing the ark thither. For this commitment, the blessing on his house was the reward (2 Sam 5:6–9; 6:20; 7:11b–16, 19, 25–29; cf. 2 Sam 6:11–12; Ps 132). By the regular celebrations

THE NATHAN NARRATIVE IN 2 SAMUEL 7:1-17

of the installation of the ark, the covenanted promise to David's heirs became established in Israelite tradition.

It is significant that, though the blessing of a ruler's house was implied in the sanctioning the regime, in David's case the promise of progeny—זרע—was expressly mentioned in terms reminiscent of the covenant with Abraham (2 Sam 7:12; cf. Gen 12:1-3; 15:4, 17-21). It is therefore likely that a promise to David expressive of offspring originated, like Abraham's, in the legend of an encounter with the local deity at the Mamre sanctuary, later identified with YHWH, during the period of David's residence in Hebron. Thither the ark was brought when, following the assassination of Ish-baal, Saul's successor, David was invited to become the king of Israel (2 Sam. 5:1-3). From there it was brought up *via* Kiriath-jearim to Jerusalem when it became his capital (cf. 2 Sam 6:2; Ps 132:6; cf. Gen. 13:14-18; 15:1-6). As reward for his faithfulness, such a promise to David was not only more easily integrated into the celebrations of the ark, but might also have facilitated the participation of the southern clans (cf. 2 Sam 6:2). As Abraham was rewarded for obeying the call of God in leaving Haran with his family for a new land (Gen 12:1-3; 13:14-18; 15:1-21), so David had abandoned Ziklag at divine direction, renouncing Philistine vassalage, and moved into Hebron (1 Sam 27:1-9; 2 Sam 2:1-3; cf. Gen 13:18; 23:1-20), to begin a family (2 Sam 2:2; 3:2-5). He then became king of Judah (2 Sam 2:4) and afterwards of all Israel (2 Sam 5:1-5). The promise of a "house" may therefore have originated as reward for the initiatives of faith taken at direction of YHWH at the start of his ascendancy (2 Sam 7:8-9), and was later integrated into the celebration of the transfer of the ark to Zion (2 Sam 6:1-19).

The Building of a "House" (Sanctuary) as Legitimization

A curious feature of the Nathan narrative (2 Sam 7:1-17), with the prayer of David that followed (2 Sam 7:18-29) is that, from verse 8 onwards, no further mention is made of the building of a house for YHWH, except for the intrusion of verse 13; but the narrative is taken up entirely with the future of David's house and kingdom. Since it appears that only verse 13 responded to the issues raised in verses 1-7, to accentuate not the (collective) progeny but an (individual) heir, it would also appear that traditions of the building of a house for YHWH (vv. 1-7, 13-15), and the covenant with David (vv. 8-12a, 16) were originally unconnected, and that the arrangements for the accommodation of the ark on Mount Zion had been

2 SAMUEL VII: 1–17—THE EVOLUTION OF THE NARRATIVE

adequately met by its installation—יצג—in a Tent (2 Sam 6:17-19). The suggestion of further and more appropriate arrangements (2 Sam 7:2; cf. v.6) arose therefore out of a different historical situation and was derived from another cultic tradition.[7]

It is also conceivable that a "house" (sanctuary) that was more befitting (2 Sam 7:2) should have been a Solomonic, rather than a Davidic, preoccupation. The inadequacy of a cloth-tent—היריעה (2 Sam 7:2), and the obsession with prestige projects, would have been the natural inclination for a ruler in a period of peace, prosperity and growing international renown (1 Kgs 5:17-18 MT; 10:1-10). Moreover, as crown-prince, Jerusalem-born (2 Sam 5:14), Solomon might not have been as conversant with, or committed to, the traditions of the pre-monarchy confederation of the tribes, among whom the ark was held in special veneration as David, his father, was. Above all, Solomon inherited an empire of which Jerusalem was the metropolis (Pss 48:1-3, 11-13; 87:1-6). YHWH, hitherto a desert deity (2 Sam 7:6), became identified with אל־עליון, the High God of the West Semitic pantheon (Pss 91:1-2, 9; 92:1, 8; 95:3) who, in Engnell's interpretation, was "*deus otiosus*"—(Ps 132:8, 14)[8] and, as such, required an abode compatible with his exalted status (2 Sam 7:1-3; cf. 1 Kgs 6:38—7:1; 9:1).

The ideological background underlying such concerns was, as Ronald Clements has noted, the question of legitimacy which, for Solomon, must have been a matter of urgency.[9] Though recognized as ruler *de facto*, the transition process was sufficiently flawed to arouse suspicion.[10] Adonijah's complaint, "You know that the kingdom was mine and all Israel expected me to reign" (1 Kgs 2:15), though ill-timed, may not have been entirely baseless, since Hebrew tradition, at least, supported the claim of *primogeniture* (cf. Deut 21:15-17). Solomon's accession, on the other hand, must have given rise to the widespread speculation that he was not properly named.

---

7. Clifford, *Cosmic Mountain*, 54, has argued from evidence in the Ugaritic texts that even for the Canaanite high God El (אל), the tent seemed altogether appropriate as a dwelling place. The reference in 2 Samuel 7:2, 7 to cedar (ארזים) as material necessary for the building of the sanctuary, therefore suggests Egyptian influence.

8. See Engnell, "The Science of Religion," 19.

9. See Clements, *God and Temple*, 59.

10. Ishida, "Solomon's Succession," 179-81, has offered a dissenting view, arguing that Solomon and not Adonijah may have been David's choice as successor, and that for political reasons, not least the growing power of Joab and Adonijah's dependence on him. The argument, however, lacks the evidence, and does not explain the futility of, and folly in, Adonijah's complaint.

THE NATHAN NARRATIVE IN 2 SAMUEL 7:1-17

It was a decree that was issued in the privacy of the royal bed-chamber, from which the heirs-apparent were apparently excluded, and in which all the witnesses had vested interests, especially in Adonijah's exclusion (1 Kgs 1:11–21). On the other hand, it was David's public toleration of Adonijah's initiatives towards the co-regency (1 Kgs 1:5–6), that spurred the machinations of Nathan the prophet and Bathsheba, mother of Solomon, for the naming of Solomon as successor. To the outsider there was sufficient cause for complaint that not only was Solomon was improperly designated, but he may not have been David's original or unfettered choice and that Adonijah, the rightful heir, had not only been cheated of the succession but, together with Joab, the captain of the militia and his supporter, was silenced by execution on trumped-up charges (1 Kgs 2:13–25).

Solomon's reign must therefore have begun under a cloud of disaffection. Furthermore, the theory and practice of kingship in Israel had become so well established during the reign of David, that whereas from the inauguration of the monarchy to David's accession, eligibility was assessed chiefly by military capability (2 Sam 5:1–3; cf. I Sam 18:7–8; 20:30–31), by the end of his long reign it was heredity that became the guiding principle for the transference of power. Solomon's accession seemed therefore to be either the result of a designation extracted from an ageing ruler in the last stages of decline or, worse still, a palace coup that succeeded because of the support of the foreign mercenaries who formed the palace-guard (1 Kgs 1:33–38). The long-term effects of Solomon's disputable accession might be measured by the early attempt of Rehoboam, his successor, at regularization by seeking pledges of allegiance from the alienated tribes—a requirement that was not necessary when legitimacy was above question (cf. 2 Kgs 11:1–20).[11]

In Ancient Near Eastern society the tried and proven way to legitimization in such circumstances was, so Henri Frankfort has argued, a divine revelation commissioning the building or renovation of a national shrine and success in the undertaking. Such projects enjoyed high priority among Mesopotamian rulers newly crowned[12] and might therefore explain the

---

11. A convocation was also necessary in the case of Joash whose accession (2 Kgs 11:1–20) followed a seven-year Interregnum of a usurper, who had ordered the massacre of all the potential claimants. Athaliah's shouts of "Treason!" suggest not merely her recognition of Joash, but also her knowledge of his parentage, and therefore her attempt at the exposure of an imposter (v. 14). For that reason she was quickly removed and silenced (vv. 12–18, 20b), and a ceremony of investiture, with public acclamation, legitimized the succession. This was followed by the renovation of the temple (2 Kgs 12:4–16).

12. See Frankfort, *Kingship and Gods*, 267–74.

2 SAMUEL VII: 1-17—THE EVOLUTION OF THE NARRATIVE

dialogue that introduced the Nathan narrative (2 Sam 7:1-3), indicating that Solomon was, originally, the anonymous המלך, and an incubatory oracle (vv. 4a, 5b-7; cf. 1 Kgs 9:1-2), in which he was commissioned to build a sanctuary; and, having been successful, his succession was legitimized and his regime established (1 Kgs 8:24-26; 9:2-5). The two main themes of the Nathan narrative, emerging from the period of the united monarchy, were therefore of separate origin—

The promise of a dynasty (vv. 11b, 27)

A revelation regarding the building of a sanctuary (vv. 5b-7, 13a).

2 SAMUEL 7:1-17 IN THE PERIOD OF THE DIVIDED MONARCHY

Nothing shows so clearly the depth of estrangement between David's earliest successors and their northern subjects as the encounter at Shechem that broke down at the call to the northern tribes to discontinue their allegiance to the House of David (1 Kgs 12:1-16). The ultra-monarchists, represented by the younger courtiers, to whose counsel Rehoboam was inclined, viewed the demands of the subjects as perversity and an intolerable insolence that could be brought to heel by the threat of harsh punitive measures (1 Kgs 12:8-11). On the other hand, the estranged tribes, led by Jeroboam ben Nebat, justified secession as the reasonable and proper response to oppressive rule, and a deliverance comparable to the exodus from Egyptian bondage (1 Kgs 12:16, 28). They could not, therefore, countenance a return to the *status quo ante* (1 Kgs 12:25-29),[13] but moved quickly to consolidate the rebellion by building two sanctuaries, one at Bethel and the other at Dan, in order to discourage pilgrimages to Jerusalem. A more sober and moderate position, however, represented by the prophet Shemaiah, opposed an armed response to the rebellion as futile, fratricidal and costly, and persuaded Rehoboam to desist (1 Kgs 12:17, 21-24). At the heart of the quarrel was an ideological conflict regarding the practice of monarchical rule in Israel. Among the Northern tribes the monarch, however valid the hereditary claim or however divinely chosen, ruled with the consent of the people (1 Sam 10:21-25; 2 Sam. 5:1-5; cf. Deut 17:15), whereas David's successors rested their legitimacy on a divine appointment that superseded popular endorsement or disenchantment (2 Sam 7; Pss 2; 89; 110).

---

13. A sympathetic case for the secession has been expounded by Coote, *In Defence of the Revolution*, 49-69.

THE NATHAN NARRATIVE IN 2 SAMUEL 7:1-17

THE RESPONSE OF THE MONARCHY TO THE COLLAPSE OF THE EMPIRE

The secession was the final blow in the disintegration of the Davidic-Solomonic empire that began in the reign of Solomon (1 Kgs 11:14-25). The loss of the northern tribes also left Judah isolated, vulnerable and exposed to its hostile neighbors. The Pharaoh Sheshonk encountered no resistance when he invaded Jerusalem and plundered the temple (1 Kgs 14:25-26), and Baasha, ruler of the Northern Kingdom, was able to seize the town of Ramah and so harassed the subjects of his southern neighbor in their movements along the border that Asa was compelled to seek the help of Benhadad, king of Syria, at considerable cost in compensation (1 Kgs 15:16-18). Judah became further isolated when the kingdom of Tyre, their former ally (2 Sam 5:11; 1 Kgs 5:1-7 [MT]), and still increasing in wealth and power, entered into a dynastic alliance with Omri, the ruler of the Northern Kingdom, whose crown prince, Ahab, was married to the Tyrian princess, Jezebel (1 Kgs 16:31). Therefore, when Syria began to threaten Israel's northern front and Ahab, now king, initiated a peace alliance with Judah, Jehoshaphat had little choice but to accede (1 Kgs 20:22). The accord was sealed by the marriage of Jehoram, the crown prince of Judah, to Athaliah, the daughter of Ahab and Jezebel. Baleful consequences resulted from these unions in the over-exposure to Tyrian religious penetration (2 Kgs 9:16-28). It is therefore curious that, notwithstanding his alliance with Ahab, of all the kings the most reviled by the editors (1 Kgs 16:30-33; 21:25-26), Jehoshaphat was commended for having done "right in YHWH's sight" (1 Kgs 22:43).[14]

---

14. Gray, in his commentary, passed over this verse without comment; *Kings*, 457. It might, however, be the case that, Jehoshaphat's alliance was not objectionable, because the historical Ahab was not as evil as he was made out to be by the Deuteronomic editors, for whom the dire effects of his Tyrian connections were uppermost and determinative. Otherwise, Ahab appears to have been a conscientious and able ruler who, following his father Omri's achievements, raised the Northern Kingdom to unprecedented levels of wealth and greatness. He took a leading part in the military coalition against Shalmaneser III in the battle at Qarqar in 853 BCE—an engagement whose success in thwarting an Assyrian invasion was never equalled. Even in the biblical narratives, beneath the Deuteronomic invectives, might be discerned a more objective evaluation of Ahab which, viewed from his vulnerable position as an ally to Tyre, might explain, and even justify, Jehoshaphat's positive response to his initiative (cf. 1 Kgs 17:1; 18:3-20, 38-46; 21:1-4, 28-29).

2 SAMUEL VII: 1-17—THE EVOLUTION OF THE NARRATIVE

Monarchy and Cultic Reform

The loss of empire was not without its compensations. A notable result was the commitment of the Davidic monarchy to reform. Asa, upon accession, purged the temple cultus of its grosser abuses, including the dismissal the Queen Mother, who seems to have been implicated—a program that his successor, Jehoshaphat, continued (1 Kgs 15:12–15; 22:43, 46). It is, however, not clear what the concern was that drove the reforms. It may have been that the secession had reflected so negatively on the image of the monarchy that a change in priority, towards responsibility for the cult, resulted. Also, the arrival of Tyrian Baalism and, with it, an aggressive program with syncretistic tendencies, may have become a threat to Mosaic Yahwism, and aroused resistance. Thirdly, the mounting stridency of the prophetic movement may have reached the court and influenced the princes (1 Kgs 12:22–24; 18:13; 19:10, 14, 18), for it is significant that, like his southern counterpart, Jehoram, king of Israel, also distanced himself from his predecessor, Ahab, and from his fanatical mother, Jezebel, who had taken advantage of Ahab's indifference (2 Kgs 3:2; cf. 1 Kgs 19:1–2; 21:1–18).

Nor were the objectives of the reforms enunciated. They may have been the initial and tentative steps towards a post-secession accord, not merely for the combating of the Tyrian infiltration, but for improving and deepening relationships in spite of the political division. Whatever the motivations, the early attempts at reform indicated a shift from an overpreoccupation with the dubious benefits of external alliances towards the recovery of an identity that was rooted in a common traditions; and it may have been in pursuit of that objective that the rulers were emboldened to interrogate the policies and re-arrange the priorities of their predecessors; but so entrenched had Tyrian Baalism become, so aggressive its strategy, so dominant its power and so widespread its influence, that these early attempts proved to be inadequate and, by the middle of the ninth century, they were overtaken by a more radical and ruthless reaction in the Israelite militia, led by Jehu, their captain, which annihilated the Omri-regime and purged the Northern Kingdom of the last vestiges of Tyrian domination. In Judah, in reaction to the assassination of King Ahaziah, a casualty of the Jehu-revolt, Athaliah the Queen Mother massacred all the princes save an infant who narrowly escaped (2 Kgs 9:14–25; 10:25–28). Seven years later, a *coup d'état*, instigated by the priesthood and supported by the standing

THE NATHAN NARRATIVE IN 2 SAMUEL 7:1-17

army and the rural gentry,[15] ended the Athaliah-*interregnum* and extirpated Tyrian Baalism from the kingdom; and, with the investiture of Joash, the survivor of the massacre, ushered in the longest succession of rulers who "... did what was right in YHWH's sight" (2 Kgs 11:1—12:2; 14:3; 15:3, 34).

The Deuteronomic Movement

It must have been in that period of violent contention, turmoil and carnage (1 Kgs 18:17–40; 2 Kgs 9:24–27, 30–37; 10:1–8, 12–14, 20–25; 11:1), of harassment, intimidation and persecution (1 Kgs 19:1–14; 1 Kgs 21:1–14; 22:17–28; 2 Kgs 11:16, 18, 20), that a movement for the renaissance of Mosaic Yahwism and reform of Israelite faith, worship and ethos, took root in Northern Israel. In that pursuit the ancient traditions and institutions were revisited, cultic practices and social customs were reinterpreted and a program for religious and social reform was documented in a legal code that was later identified as "a book of the law." As a movement that was essentially conservative, it looked back to the period of Moses' leadership as the ideal period of Israel's history, and to the traditions and the precepts of the Sinai-Horeb covenant for inspiration, and guidance. It traced Israel's decline from the post-Joshua period (Deut 31:28–29; Josh 24:31; Judg 2:7–11), and an acceleration with the introduction of the monarchy (Judg 8:22–23; 1 Sam 8:7; 10:18–19a; 12:7–26) when Israel, already contaminated by the Canaanite environment, became further corrupted by foreign alliances, and the infiltration of foreign values that compromised their allegiance to YHWH (Deut 7:1–5; 17:14–20). It was this decline that the promoters, known as the Deuteronomists, hoped to arrest and, if possible, reverse.

Whether the reform movement originated, as Nicholson has suggested, among the YHWH prophets in the Northern Kingdom (1 Kgs 22:6; 2 Kgs 2:2–7), whose legitimacy was defined and mission endorsed in the Code (Deut 18:15–22)[16] or, as von Rad has argued, with the Levitical priesthood who, traditionally, were the recognized exponents of the Mosaic law (Deut 31:9; 33:8–10),[17] it seems that out of the upheavals the ninth century, a desire was quickened in the Northern Kingdom to revisit the Sinai-Horeb traditions and explore their relevance for the spiritual and moral crises that

---

15. It is in this way that the term, "people of the land," 2) עַם־הָאָרֶץ Kgs 11:14, 18, 20), might best be interpreted. So suggests Gray, *Kings*, 577–78.

16. Nicholson, *Deuteronomy and Tradition*, 69–71.

17. Von Rad, *Studies in Deuteronomy*, 68–69.

2 SAMUEL VII: 1-17—THE EVOLUTION OF THE NARRATIVE

had overtaken the people. Inevitably, the exercise included an evaluation of political rule with the intent of recalling the rulers of both kingdoms to the demands of their office as outlined in the Mosaic law and, especially, their responsibility for preserving the integrity of the cult.[18]

The agenda also involved an updating and re-interpreting of the laws that were promulgated in the Sinai/Horeb covenant (cf. Exod 20–23), especially in the light of widespread syncretism, idolatry, polytheism and tendencies to absolutism which threatened the integrity of Mosaic monotheism. It therefore traced a history of Israel's occupation of Canaan, from Moses' reading of the law at Moab (Deut 4:45–48; 5–28), in order to show the course, complexity and extent of the decline that culminated in the fall of the Northern Kingdom (2 Kgs 17). Whether the two exercises—the legal codification and the historical review—were undertaken by the same group sequentially or by separate groups concurrently, it was about a century after the Fall of Samaria, in the eighteenth year of the reign of Josiah, that a Scroll, identified by Hilkiah the priest of the Jerusalem temple as the book of the law—ספר־התורה, also described as the Covenant Document—ספר־הברית—was discovered during the temple renovations (2 Kgs 22:8; 2 Kgs 23:2).[19] It was intended primarily for the ruler, especially in a period of deepening crisis that placed the future of YHWH's people in doubt (2 Kgs 22:8–20; cf. Deut 17:18–19; 1 Kgs 2:3). Whether the document discovered was the legal preface or the scroll in its entirety (2 Kgs 22:8), it is as unlikely that such a historical evaluation would have been undertaken without an enunciation of the principles and criteria on which the evaluation was based, as that ספר־התורה was a bare legal code, without a review of the situation it was designed to address.[20]

---

18. "Inevitably," because it is not likely, nor does the Deuteronomic Code indicate, that the exercise was undertaken in a historical vacuum, but was in response to practices that were viewed as deviations from, and flagrant violations of, the traditions of the Sinai-Horeb covenant.

19. It is not unlikely that ספר־תורה (the book of the law) was a legal code of Mosaic origin, to which additions were made from time to time, after the Mosaic period (cf. Exod 24:7; Josh 24:26; 1 Sam 10:25). Furthermore, in the Hebrew tradition such a legal statement, being a covenant document—ספר־הברית (2 Kgs 23:2)—that obligated the beneficiary would either be prefaced by a recital of the gracious acts of the benefactor (Exod 19:4–5; 20:2; Deut 29:2–8; Josh 24:3–13), or would preface a prophetic indictment (Amos 2:9–11).

20. Its impact on the king, Josiah, after the reading of the Document (2 Kgs 22:10–11), is a fair indication of its character and content.

THE NATHAN NARRATIVE IN 2 SAMUEL 7:1-17

2 SAMUEL 7:1-17 IN PERIOD OF THE SINGLE MONARCHY

It seems that the immediate beneficiary of the book of the law was Hezekiah, king of Judah, in whose regime the Document, concluding with a reflection on the fall of Samaria, and its implications for Judah, was completed.[21] He, of all the Israelite rulers, had seemed the most responsive to prophetic intervention and receptive of their admonitions (2 Kgs 19:20-34; 20:1-11, 14-19; cf. Jer 26:17-19). Following the deportation of Hoshea, Hezekiah was left as the only ruler in Israel (2 Kgs 17:1-6). Coming to the throne, six years after the fall of Samaria, he inherited from his predecessor a policy of subordination that seemed to work. Whatever the cost was in payment of tributes and cultic concessions (2 Kgs 16:8-18), it had purchased Judah's survival in 735 BCE when neighboring states—cities in Philistia, in Transjordan, Megiddo, Hazor of the Northern Kingdom, cities of Syria—suffered heavily from the Assyrian onslaught under Tiglath-Pileser III, and later, in 721, when the westward campaign was resumed under Shalmaneser V, and the Northern Kingdom capitulated and became absorbed in the Assyrian empire. In that sense, therefore, Hezekiah's adherence to the policy of subordination initiated by Ahaz seemed not merely feasible or convenient but politically responsible.

Ernest Nicholson has suggested that among the refugees from northern Israel seeking asylum in the Jerusalem after the fall of Samaria, may have been Deuteronomists who brought with them the book of the law,[22] in which the apostasy of rulers generally, the widespread violation of the Mosaic law and the persistent refusal to heed the warnings of the prophets, were cited as the prime causes of the social and political decline (Deut. 28:36-37; cf. 1 Sam 12:25; 2 Kgs. 17:1-4). Although updated in Jerusalem, the book of the law had ended with a theological reflection on the fall of the Northern Kingdom with the implications for Judah (2 Kgs 17:7-18. 20-23). It also seems, that the final shaping of the document was influenced by the character of Hezekiah's reign, and also the apostasies and excesses of the Manasseh regime; for the failure of the Judaean kings seems to have

---

21. Concealed or misplaced during the Manasseh-Amon regime, the Scroll, upon re-discovery, was immediately identified by the priest, Hilkiah, as ספר־התורה—the book of the law (2 Kgs 22:8; cp. Shaphan v. 10). The identification suggests not a strange object, but a previous acquaintance and recognition of a document that had already been in circulation.

22. See Nicholson, *Deuteronomy and Tradition*, 98.

2 SAMUEL VII: 1-17—THE EVOLUTION OF THE NARRATIVE

been explained by their contamination through foreign alliances, including affiliation with the Omri-regime and, by extension, the aggressive expansion of Tyrian influence (1 Kgs 11:1-6; 2 Kgs 8:18, 27: 16:3). Those not so tarnished were reckoned as having done "right in YHWH's sight"—an approval rating that was measured by their adherence to the Mosaic law (1 Kgs 15:11; 22:43; 2 Kgs 12:2; 14:3; 15:3, 34).

DEUTERONOMY AND THE REBELLION OF HEZEKIAH

In the evaluation of Hezekiah's reign, the Deuteronomic preoccupation with the cult overshadowed its distinguishing feature; viz., his rebellion against Assyria (2 Kgs 18:7b, 14-16; cf. 16:1-10) which, in terms of Realpolitik, seemed ill-conceived.[23] Granted the internal squabbles that marked regime-changes in Mesopotamia may have been a temptation to end the alliance and cast off the abject yoke, still any relief gained thereby could only be short-lived, for the new ruler, once established, would reassert his authority by imposing even stiffer penalties. Furthermore, the Assyrian empire, far from being in decline, had not attained its zenith or the full extent of its territorial expansion. Political wisdom should therefore have dictated that Hezekiah maintain the relationship with Assyria he inherited and, whatever the cost, stay the course set by Ahaz.

What then could have provoked Hezekiah to rebel? He stopped the payment of the tributes, and initiated a program of centralization and reform unprecedented in the history of the monarchy. He fortified the cities of Judah, accomplished the engineering feat of opening an underground aqueduct from the Gihon spring into Jerusalem to secure adequate water-supply in the event of a prolonged siege (2 Kgs 20:20) and he organized and led a coalition of resistance against the Assyrian response that he knew was inevitable. The only possible explanation was the book of the law, ספר־התורה, in which foreign occupation of Israel was anathematized and resistance was sanctioned as fidelity to the covenant (Deut 7:1-6, 17-26; 12:1-3; 17:15; 20:1-20; 27:15, 26; cf. 2 Kgs 16:2-3, 7-13). While therefore the unrest in Nineveh, in the succession transition, may have offered a window of opportunity and the delegation from Merodach-Baladan an added

---

23. Except that he was applauded, in a general way, for his faithfulness and trust (2 Kgs 18:3, 5-6), the only mention of the rebellion was his humble apology and submission to Sennacherib after having caused him offence (2 Kgs. 18:14-16).

incentive (2 Kgs 20:12-19),[24] Hezekiah's motivation was an imperative that lay at the deeper level of an imperative enjoined upon him by the Mosaic law (Deut 7:1-10, 17-26; 33:26-29). It stirred him up with a zeal for Holy War (Deut 20:1-9), which the re-institution of a national Passover festival could only have inflamed[25]. Hezekiah's rebellion was therefore an act of faith and faithfulness which, though political in expression, was an adventure that both confounded and transcended political realism.

THE HIEROS LOGOS OF THE HEZEKIANIC REFORMED TEMPLE

It was in the heat of that revolutionary situation, therefore, that the narrative in 2 Samuel 7:1-17 began to take shape. In the original book of the law, written out of the northern context, the Davidic-Solomonic regime had been accorded the same status as Saul's that preceded, and the northern regimes following the secession. The common Deuteronomic criterion, measured by their commitment to the Mosaic law and, in particular their regulation of the cult, was their doing "right/evil in YHWH's sight." The Davidic covenant was therefore, like the Sinai-Horeb covenant all the other royal covenants, perceived as a conditional covenant (cf. 1 Kgs. 11:38), by which the rulers in Israel were obligated to keep the Mosaic law. The accounts of the reigns must therefore have been summary in form, except for some of the special material that was identified by Anthony Campbell as a Prophetic Record. The account of David's reign must have highlighted, in addition, the capture of Jerusalem (2 Sam 5:6-9), the installation of the ark (2 Sam 6:1-19) and a Davidic covenant couched in terms of the Deuteronomic conditionality (2 Sam 7:8-12, 16). In the account of Solomon's reign, in addition to the conditional promise, given at his investiture (1 Kgs 2:3-4), there was the legend of a nocturnal revelation that had commissioned him to build a temple (2 Sam 7:5b-7; cf. 1 Kgs. 3:3-5), a brief account of its dedication (1 Kgs 8:12-13, 25) and, as a climax, a post-dedication oracle

---

24. The linking of the visit to Hezekiah's illness, and its dating after the lifting of the siege, is almost certainly a chronological misplacement in order to leave untarnished the record of Hezekiah's rebellion as an act of faith in, and faithfulness to, YHWH, and a witness to his constancy in adhering to the Mosaic law.(2 Kgs 18:5-6).

25. Though omitted by the Josianic redactors, the Chronicler recognized the Hezekianic revival of the Passover Festival and the Feast of Unleavened Bread, a nation-wide observance, as the highlight of his reign and the climax to the reformation he initiated (2 Chr 30:1-26).

2 SAMUEL VII: 1-17—THE EVOLUTION OF THE NARRATIVE

that included a conditional promise (1 Kgs 9:4-9; cf. 2:2-4; 6:12-13; 8:25; 11:38; Ps 132:11-12). In those terms the Jerusalem temple, now reformed, became sanctified as YHWH's house, and the surviving monarchy was legitimized through Solomon, both as builder and as successor to David (cf. 2 Kgs 18:3). It also included, however, a record of Solomon's irregularities and excesses, by which the Deuteronomic Code was violated, the integrity of Israel was damaged and a fatal schism was provoked (Deut 17:18-20; 1 Kgs 11:30-33).

The Davidic sanctuary on Mount Zion, in which the ark was housed, remained untouched by Hezekiah's program of reform, nor did the *hieros logos* of the Hezekianic reformed temple include the ark narrative (1 Sam 4:1—7:1; 2 Sam 6-7) or the Davidic covenant (2 Sam 7:8-9, 11b-12, 16). The two cultic institutions, with their respective traditions re-interpreted in Deuteronomic law, continued to co-exist separately as they had since the reign of Solomon, the one bearing witness to YHWH's choice of Zion as his abode and the Davidic monarchy to rule in Israel, and the other to the commissioning of Solomon, as the rightful successor, to build a house in a place that YHWH would choose and where he would dwell forever in thick darkness (1 Kgs 8:12-13).

Ronald Clements has claimed that the Deuteronomic reinterpretation of the Mosaic law was informed, partly, by a critical evaluation of the Jerusalem cultus.[26] Even so, the reinterpretation could not have been so limited as to become evident only in the Law. The Davidic monarchy and the Jerusalem cultus were also shaped by the impact of the Deuteronomic law. This became apparent in the conditions attached to the promises that were obligatory on the monarchy, excepting the special connection between the Davidic monarchy and the Jerusalem cultus (1 Kgs 11:36; 15:4; 2 Kgs 8:19) and the confirmation of the Davidic rule and the Solomonic succession (2 Sam 7:8-9, 12-16). What seems to have occurred was a more positive interaction between Deuteronomic perception of Israelite kingship and the Jerusalem cult traditions than would have been possible otherwise. This resulted in a Deuteronomic acceptance of the legitimacy of the hereditary succession without capitulating to an unconditionality that exempted offending rulers from dethronement (Deut 17:14-20; 2 Sam 7:14; cf. Pss 2:7, 12; 89:26-27). The interaction might also go some way in explaining some of the more positive features of the Northern regimes that appear in the Deuteronomic History (1 Kgs 11:38; 21:29; 2 Kgs 3:2; 10:30; 13:4-5; 14:25-

---

26. See Clements, "Deuteronomy and the Jerusalem Cult-Tradition," 300-301.

27), as well as the negative characteristics that appeared in the Davidic rulers (1 Kgs 14:24; 2 Kgs 8:18; 12:18; 16:3–4). Contributing factors to that re-evaluation may have been the positive impact of Hezekiah's rule,[27] in the cultic reforms he initiated and his courageous resistance to the Assyrian aggression (2 Kgs 18:4–12), as well as the disillusionment in the long tenure of the Manasseh-Amon regime (2 Kgs 21:1–15).

THE HIEROS LOGOS OF THE JOSIANIC CENTRAL SANCTUARY

Josiah's reign, following the apostasies of the Manasseh-Amon regime (2 Kgs 21:3–5, 20–21), saw a return to reform measures that had been initiated by Hezekiah. There were, however, differences between the two attempts at reform.

Whereas Hezekiah's reforms were part of a larger centralizing program in preparation against a foreign invasion, Josiah's signified a nation-wide renewal of the Sinai-Horeb Covenant and a recommitment to the Mosaic law, in the period of respite that followed the fall of Nineveh. The Josianic reforms, of which the centralization of the cult was a part, were undertaken in full realization that politically, the sovereignty of Judah was coming to an end; and the most that could be expected was its survival as a vassal-state, subjected to Egypt or the Babylonian empire. There was therefore need for spiritual renewal, and in that re-commitment, to draw the stamina to withstand the travail of foreign domination.

The Josianic reformation, based on a monopolistic and exclusivist interpretation of the Deuteronomic law of the Central Sanctuary, resulted in more extensive and thoroughgoing reform program. Having legalized the Temple as the only Sanctuary, the Davidic sanctuary on Mount Zion was suppressed and, consequently, the ark narrative with a Davidic covenant as its climax, and the *hieros logos* of the Hezekianic Temple were integrated in a prophetic revelation. Thus the Nathan narrative in 2 Samuel 7:1–17 came into being.

Whereas Hezekiah projected Solomon as the wise ruler and the builder of the temple, in the Josianic evaluation Solomon's stature was considerably

---

27. It was probably also during the period of crisis and anxiety in Hezekiah's reign that a creation hymn (Ps 89:1–4, 19–52) was enclosed to celebrate YHWH's ascension and victorious rule over the forces of chaos, ים and רהב (vv. 9–10), represented, politically, by the Assyrian aggressors, and to re-affirm the Davidic covenant.

2 SAMUEL VII: 1-17—THE EVOLUTION OF THE NARRATIVE

reduced. David, on the other hand, the founder of the YHWH cult in Jerusalem, to whom the prophetic revelation of the Chosen Sanctuary was given, was promoted as the only ancestor worthy of emulation.

Whereas the Hezekianic response was aimed at refurbishing the image of Solomon, through a reform of the Temple cultus (2 Kgs 18:4), a sponsoring of the Wisdom-movement (Prov 25:1) and an endorsement of the prophetic movement (2 Kgs 19:20-34; 20:4-18; cf. 2 Sam 7:1-3; Jer 26:17-19), the paramount concerns of the Josianic redactors were a redefinition of Israel as a "chosen" people (Deut. 7:7-9; 14:2; 32:9-10), the continuing relevance of the Mosaic law (Deut 5:1-3; Josh 24:26) and the Jerusalem Temple as the only sanctuary for all of Israel (1 Kgs 8:46-51, 56; cp. 2 Kgs 22:8; 23:1-9).

It was in the conquests of David that the Josianic redactors located the "rest"—מנוחה—that YHWH had given his people (2 Sam 7:1b), rather than the peace, prosperity and prestige of Solomon's reign, as the Hezekianic redactors had assumed (1 Kgs 5:3-5).

The Josianic Temple was not a dwelling place of YHWH but a place of prayer where the "name" was invoked (1 Kgs 8:17-30).[28] The anthropomorphism reflected in לשבתי—"for my dwelling" (2 Sam 7:5; cf. 1 Kgs 8:12-13) was re-interpreted and restated as לשמי—"for my name" (2 Sam 7:13; cf. 1 Kgs 8:27-30).

Above all, it seems that the outworking of the Deuteronomic theology of retribution, more clearly articulated in the Josianic redaction, spanned the generations. This may have been a result of the impact of Josiah's unexpected demise (2 Kgs 22:20; 23:29-30), and was included in the Deuteronomic Code (Deut 5:7-10; 29:19-28; 32:48-52). The covenant promises, notwithstanding a ruler's faithfulness, could be thwarted and nullified by unfaithfulness as much in his predecessors as in his successors. Therefore, as Solomon's reign, following David's faithfulness, initiated a decline, which neither his father's faithfulness could have forestalled, nor the efforts of his righteous successors reverse (1 Kgs 11:5-13, 31-32; 12:26-33; 15:11-15; 22:43), so the apostasies of the Manasseh-Amon regime (2 Kgs 21:2-16, 20-22), following Hezekiah's unprecedented faithfulness (2 Kgs 18:5), sealed the doom of Judah so irrevocably that not even Josiah's thorough-going

---

28. The Deuteronomic "name-theology" as expressive of the divine presence in the chosen sanctuary, over against earlier anthropomorphic tendencies, is one of the clearer indicators of a Josianic redaction (Deut 12:5,11; 16:2, 6, 11; 1 Kgs 8:17, 29; 9:3)

attempts at reform could avert (2 Sam 7:11b–16; cf. 2 Kgs 21:10–15; 23:26, 29–30; 25:27–30).[29]

2 SAMUEL 7:1–17 AFTER THE FALL OF THE MONARCHY

It was in an Exilic Redaction that much of the Davidic material in the Samuel corpus, viz., the History of David's Rise (1 Sam 16–2 Sam. 1), and the succession narrative (2 Sam 9–20; 1 Kgs 1–2), was incorporated.[30] However, the Nathan narrative, though unaltered, was re-interpreted to become a counterfoil-prologue to the transgression of David in "the matter of Uriah the Hittite," which was cited as the primary cause of the fall and abolition of the monarchy.

The David-tradition, preserved in 2 Samuel 7:1–17, Psalms 89:1–4, 19–51 and 132 also informed the canonical Prophets at three levels:

A hope for the restoration of the Davidic monarchy was stirred when Zerubbabel the grandson of Jehoiachin, was appointed governor of Judaea (Hag 2:3, 21–23; Zech 3:6—4:9); but it proved to be forlorn.

A democratized interpretation of the Davidic Covenant, adumbrated in the Nathan narrative (2 Sam 7:10–11a, 23–24; cf. Isa 55:3), was proposed by Otto Eissfeldt;[31] but the dispersion of the Jews and their continuing subjection to foreign overlordship and a succession of empires made it difficult for such an interpretation to gain popularity.

A Messianic Hope that influenced Jewish eschatology (Isa 9:6–7; 11:1–9; Jer 23:5; 30:9; 33:20–21; Ezek 34:23–24; 37:24; Amos 9:11–12).

It was in that third direction, out of which the Prophetic Canon was created, that the influence of the Davidic tradition overflowed the Hebrew Bible into the eschatology of Palestinian Judaism, in the commentaries and other literature of the Essene Community at Qumran, and into the Christology that was articulated in the literature the New Testament.

---

29. In the final analysis, YHWH's character, distinguished by righteousness, renders the any covenant-relationship with him, of necessity, conditional.

30. Episodes that were included in the earlier redactions may have been his election as king by the men of Judah (2 Sam. 2:4) and by the northern tribes (2 Sam. 5:1–5), his capture and occupation of Jerusalem (2 Sam. 5:6–10), his decisive defeat of the Philistines (2 Sam. 5:17–25), his transfer of the ark (2 Sam. 6:1–23), the Nathan narrative (2 Sam. 7) and the purchase of Araunah's threshing-floor (2 Sam. 24). Of the History of David's rise or the succession narrative the Chronicler makes no mention.

31. See Eissfeldt, "Promises of Grace" 196–207.

SELECT BIBLIOGRAPHY

Ackroyd, Peter R. "Amos 7:14." *ExpTim* 68.3 (1956) 74.
———. "The Chronicler as an Exegete." *JSOT* 3 (1977) 2–32.
———. *Chronicles I & II, Ezra and Nehemiah*. London: SCM, 1973.
———. *Exile and Restoration: A Study of Hebrew Thought of the Sixth Century BC*. Philadelphia: Westminster, 1968.
———. *The First Book of Samuel:* The Cambridge Bible Commentary on the New English Bible. Cambridge: Cambridge University Press, 1971.
———. "An Interpretation of the Babylonian Exile: A Study of 2 Kings 20, Isaiah 38–39." *SJT* 27.3 (1974) 439–52.
———. "Kings I & II." In *IDBSup* 516–19.
———. *The Second Book of Samuel:* The Cambridge Bible Commentary on the New English Bible. Cambridge: Cambridge University Press, 1972.
———. "The Temple Vessels: A Continuity Theme." In *Studies in the Religion of Ancient Israel*, 166–81. VTSup 23. Leiden: Brill, 1972.
Ahlstrom, Gosta W. "Der Prophet Nathan und der Tempelbau." *VT* 11 (1961) 111–37.
Albright, William F. *From the Stone Age to Christianity*. New York: Doubleday, 1957.
———. "The Impact of Archaeology on Biblical Research." In *New Directions in Biblical Archaeology*, edited by David Noel Freedman and Jonas C. Greenfield, 3–16. New York: Doubleday, 1971.
———. "Some Remarks on the Song of Moses in Deuteronomy 33." *VT* 9.4 (1959) 339–46.
———. *YHWH and the Gods of Canaan*. London: Athlone, 1963.
Alt, Albrecht. *Essays on Old Testament History and Religion*. Translated by R. A. Wilson. Oxford: Blackwell, 1966.
Amsler, Samuel. *David, roi et Messie: La tradition davidique dans l'Ancien Testament*. CahT 49. Neuchâtel: Delachaux & Niestlé, 1963.
Andreason, Niels-Eric A. "The Role of the Queen Mother in Israelite Society." *CBQ* 45 (1983) 179–92.

SELECT BIBLIOGRAPHY

Avioz, Michael. *Nathan's Oracle (2 Samuel 7) and Its Interpreters*. Bible in History 5. New York: Peter Lang, 2005.
Barr, James. *Biblical Words for Time*. SBT 33. London: SCM, 1969.
———. *Holy Scripture: Canon, Authority, Criticism*. Philadelphia: Westminster, 1983.
Bentzen, Aage. "The Cultic Use of the Story of the Ark in Samuel." *JBL* 67 (1948) 37–53.
———. *King and Messiah*. Oxford: Blackwell, 1970.
Blenkinsopp, Joseph. *Gibeon and Israel: The Role of Gibeon and the Gibeonites in the Political and Religious History of Early Israel*. SOTSMS 2. Cambridge: Cambridge University Press, 1972.
Bright, John. *Covenant and Promise*. Philadelphia: Westminster, 1974.
———. *A History of Israel*. London: SCM, 1981.
Brown, Francis, et al. *Hebrew and English Lexicon of the Old Testament*. Oxford: Blackwell, 1974.
Browne, Henry. *Triglot Dictionary of Scriptural Representative Words in Hebrew, Greek, English*. London: Samuel Bagster, 1901.
Bruggemann, Walter. *Genesis*. Atlanta: John Knox, 1980.
Bussche, H. van den. "Le Texte de la Prophétie de Nathan sur la Dynastie Davidique: II Samuel VII / I Chron. XVII." *ETL* 24 (1948) 154–90.
Calderone, Philip J. *Dynastic Oracle and Suzerainty Treaty: 2 Samuel 7:8–16*. Manila: Loyola House of Studies, 1966.
Campbell, Antony F. *The Ark Narrative, 1 Samuel 4–6 and 2 Samuel 6: A Form-Critical and Traditio-historical Study*. SBLDS 16. Cambridge: Cambridge University Press, 1975.
———. *Of Prophets and Kings: A Late Ninth-Century Document (1 Samuel 1–2 Kings 10)*. CBQMS 17. Washington, DC: Catholic Biblical Association of America, 1986.
Caquot, André. "La Prophétie de Nathan et ses Echos Lyriques." In *Congress Volume: Bonn, 1962*, 213–24. VTSup 9. Leiden: Brill, 1962.
Carlson, R. A. *David, the Chosen King: A Traditio-historical Approach to the Second Book of Samuel*. Stockholm: Almqvist & Wiskell, 1964.
Charles, Robert H., ed. *The Apocrypha and Pseudepigrapha of the Old Testament*. Vol. 2, *Pseudepigrapha*. Oxford: Clarendon, 1969.
Childs, Brevard S. *Introduction to the Old Testament as Scripture*. London: SCM, 1979.
———. *Isaiah and the Assyrian Crisis*. London: SCM, 1967.
———. *Memory and Tradition in Israel*. London: SCM, 1962.
Clements, Ronald E. *Abraham and David: Genesis 15 and Its Meaning for Israelite Tradition*: SBT 2. London: SCM, 1965.
———. *A Century of Old Testament Study*. Guildford: Lutterworth, 1976.
———. "The Deuteronomic Interpretation of the Founding of the Monarchy in 1 Sam. VIII." *VT* 24 (1974) 398–410.
———. "Deuteronomy and the Jerusalem Cult Tradition." *VT* 15 (1965) 300–312.
———. *God's Chosen People: A Theological Interpretation of the Book of Deuteronomy*. London: SCM, 1968.
———. *God and Temple*. Oxford: Blackwell, 1965.
———. *Isaiah and the Deliverance of Jerusalem*. JSOTSup 13. Sheffield: JSOT Press, 1980.
———. *Old Testament Theology: A Fresh Approach*. Atlanta: John Knox, 1978.
———. *Prophecy and Covenant*. SBT 43. London: SCM, 1965.
———. *Prophecy and Tradition*. Oxford: Blackwell, 1975.
———. Review of *Das uberlieferungsgeschichtliche Problem des Pentateuch*, by Rolf Rendtorff." *JSOT* 1.3 (1977) 46–56.

SELECT BIBLIOGRAPHY

Clifford, Richard J. *The Cosmic Mountain in Canaan and the Old Testament*. Cambridge: Harvard University Press, 1972.
Coats, George W. "Tradition Criticism, Old Testament." In *IDBSup* 912-14.
Coote, Robert B. *In Defense of the Revolution: The Elohist's History*. Philadelphia: Fortress, 1991.
Craig, Kenneth M. "The Character(-ization) of God in 2 Samuel 7:1-17." *Semeia* 63 (1993) 150-76.
Cross, Frank M., Jr. *Canaanite Myth and Hebrew Epic: Essays in the History of the Religion of Israel*. Cambridge: Harvard University Press, 1973.
Davies, Philip R. *In Search of Ancient Israel*. Sheffield: JSOT Press, 1992.
Delekat, Lienhard. "Tendenz und Theologie der David-Salomo-Erzahlung." *Das ferne und nahe Wort*, edited by Fritz Maass, 28-38. BZAW 105. Berlin: Töpelmann 1967.
De Tillesse, G. Minette. "Sections 'tu' et sections 'vous' dans le Deutéronome." *VT* 12 (1962) 29-97.
De Vaux, Roland. *Ancient Israel, Its Life and Institutions*. Translated by John McHugh. London: Darton, Longman and Todd, 1968.
———. "The King of Israel, Vassal of Yahweh." In *The Bible and the Ancient Near East*. Translated by Damian McHugh, 152-162. London: DLT, 1971.
———. "Reflections on the Present State of Pentateuchal Criticism." In *The Bible and the Ancient Near East*. Translated by Damian McHugh, 35-36. London: DLT, 1971.
Dines, Jennifer. "Septuagint." In *Dictionary of Biblical Interpretation*. edited by R.J. Coggins and J.L. Houlden, 622-25. London: SCM, 1996.
Driver, Geoffrey R. "Amos VII, 14." *ExpTim* 67.3 (1955) 91-92.
Driver, Samuel R. *An Introduction to the Literature of the Old Testament*. New York: Meridian, 1956.
———. *Notes on the Hebrew Text and the Topography of the Books of Samuel*. Oxford: Clarendon, 1960.
Eaton, John H. *Kingship and the Psalms*. SBT, 2nd ser., 32. London: SCM, 1976.
———. *Psalms: Introduction and Commentary*. London: SCM, 1967.
Ebeling, Gerhard. *Word and Faith*. Translated by James W. Leitch. London: SCM, 1963.
Eichrodt, Walther. *Theology of the Old Testament*. Translated by J.A. Baker, vol. I. London: SCM, 1961.
Eissfeldt, Otto. "The Hebrew Kingdoms." In *Cambridge Ancient History*, vol. II, pt. 2, 537-605. London: Cambridge University Press, 1975.
———. *The Old Testament: An Introduction*. Translated by Peter R. Ackroyd. Oxford: Clarendon, 1966.
———. "The Promises of Grace to David in Isaiah 55:1-5." In *Israel's Prophetic Heritage*, edited by Bernhard W. Anderson and Walter Harrelson, 196-207. London: SCM, 1962.
———. "The Prophetic Literature." In *The Old Testament and Modern Study*, edited by Harold H. Rowley, 115-61. London: Oxford University Press, 1961.
Elliger, Karl, and Wilhelm Rudolph, eds. *Biblica Hebraica Stuttgartensia*. Stuttgart: Deutsch Bibelstiftung, 1967/77.
Engnell, Ivan. "The Book of Psalms." Translated by John T. Willis. In *A Rigid Scrutiny: Critical Essays on the Old Testament*, edited by John T. Willis, 68-122. London: SPCK, 1970.
———. "The Science of Religion." Translated by John T. Willis. In *A Rigid Scrutiny: Critical Essays on the Old Testament*, edited by John T. Willis, 12-34. London: SPCK, 1970.

SELECT BIBLIOGRAPHY

———. *Studies in Divine Kingship in the Ancient Near East*. Oxford: Blackwell, 1967.
———. "The Traditio-historical Method in Old Testament Research." Translated by John T. Willis. In *A Rigid Scrutiny: Critical Essays on the Old Testament*, edited by John T. Willis, 3–11. London: SPCK, 1970.
Flanagan, James W. "Court History or Succession Document? A Study of 2 Samuel 9–20 and I Kings 1–2." *JBL* 91 (1972) 172–81.
Flusser, David. "Two Notes on the Midrash on 2 Samuel Vii." *IEJ* 9 (1959) 99–100.
Fohrer, Georg. *History of Israelite Religion*. Translated by David E. Green. London: SPCK, 1973.
Frankfort, Henri. *Kingship and the Gods: A Study of Ancient Near Eastern Religion as the Integration of Society and Nature*. Chicago: University of Chicago Press, 1978.
Fretheim, Terence E. *Deuteronomic History*. Nashville: Abingdon, 1983.
Friedman, Richard E. "From Egypt to Egypt: Dtr1 and Dtr2." In *Traditions in Transformation: Turning Points in Biblical Faith*, edited by Baruch Halpern and Jon D. Levenson, 167–92. Winona Lake, IN: Eisenbrauns, 1981.
Gray, John. *The Biblical Doctrine of the Reign of God*. Edinburgh: T&T Clark, 1979.
———. *The Canaanites*. London: Thomas and Hudson, 1964.
———. *Kings, I & II: A Commentary*. Philadelphia: Westminster, 1970.
———. *The Legacy of Canaan: The Ras Shamra Texts and Their Relevance to the Old Testament*. Leiden: Brill, 1965.
Guillaume, Alfred. *Prophecy and Divination among the Hebrews and Other Semites*. London: Hodder and Stoughton, 1938.
Gunkel, Hermann. *The Psalms: A Form-Critical Introduction*. Philadelphia: Fortress, 1967.
Gunn, David M. "David and the Gift of the Kingdom (2 Sam. 2–4, 9–20, 1 Kgs. 1–2)." *Semeia* 3 (1975) 14–45.
———. *The Fate of King Saul: An Interpretation of a Biblical Story*. JSOTSup 14. Sheffield: JSOT, 1980.
———. *The Story of David: Genre and Interpretation*. JSOTSup 6. Sheffield: JSOT, 1978.
Halpern, Baruch, and David S. Vanderhooft. "The Editions of Kings in the 7th and 6th Centuries BCE." *HUCA* 62.1 (1991) 179–244.
Harrelson, Walter. "Life, Faith and the Emergence of a Tradition." In *Tradition and Theology in the Old Testament*, edited by Douglas Knight, 11–30. Philadelphia: Fortress, 1977.
Hayes, John, and Carl R. Holloday. *Biblical Exegesis: A Beginner's Handbook*. Atlanta: John Knox, 1982.
Hayes, John, and J. Maxwell Miller, eds. *Israelite and Judaean History*. London: SCM, 1977.
Herrmann, Siegfried. "Die Konigsnovelle in Agypten und Israel." *WZ der Karl Marx Universitat der Leipzig* 3 (1953-54) 51-62.
Hicks, R. Lansing. "Perez." *IDB* 3:729.
Ishida, Tomoo, "Solomon's Succession to the Throne of David: A Political Analysis." *Studies in the Period of David and Solomon and Other Essays: Papers Read at the International Symposium for Biblical Studies*, edited by Tomoo Ishida, 175–87. Winona Lake, IN: Eisenbrauns, 1982.
Johnson, Aubrey R. *Cultic Prophet in Ancient Israel*. Cardiff: University of Wales Press, 1962.
———. *Sacral Kingship in Ancient Israel*. Cardiff: University of Wales Press, 1987.
Kapelrud, Arvid S. "King and Fertility: A Discussion of II Sam. 21:1–14." In *Interpretationes ad Vetus Testamentum pertinentes Sigmundo Mowinckel septuagenario missae*, edited by Arvid S. Kapelrud, 113–22. Oslo: Land og kirke, 1955.

SELECT BIBLIOGRAPHY

Kautzsch, E. *Gesenius' Hebrew Grammar.* Translated by A.E. Cowley. Oxford: Clarendon, 1957.

Knight, Douglas A. *Rediscovering the Traditions of Israel: The Development of the Traditio-historical Research, with Special Consideration of the Scandinavian Contribution.* SBLDS 9. Cambridge: Cambridge University Press, 1975.

———. "Tradition and Theology." In *Tradition and Theology in the Old Testament,* edited by Douglas A. Knight, 1–8. Philadelphia: Fortress, 1977.

Knoppers, Gary N. *Two Nations Under God: The Deuteronomistic History of Solomon and the Dual Monarchies.* 2 vols. Atlanta: Scholars, 1992–94.

Kraus, Hans-Joachim. *Worship in Israel: A Cultic History of the Old Testament.* Oxford: Blackwell, 1966.

Kruse, Heinz. "Psalm CXXXII and the Royal Zion Festival." *VT* 33.3 (1983) 279–97.

Labuschagne, C. J. "Some Remarks on the Prayer of David in II Sam. 7." In *Papers Read at 3rd Meeting of the O.T. Werkgemeenskop,* 28–35. Pretoria: University of South Africa, 1960.

Lapointe, Roger. "Tradition and Language: the Impact of Oral Expression." In *Tradition and Theology in the Old Testament,* edited by Douglas A. Knight, 125–42. Philadelphia: Fortress, 1977.

Laurentin, André. "*Weʿattah—kai nun*: Formule caractéristique des textes juridiques et liturgiques (à propos de Jean 17,5)." *Bib* 45 (1954) 168–97.

Lemaire, André. "Vers L'histoire de la Redaction des Livres des Rois." *ZAW* 98 (1986) 221–36.

Lindblom, Johannes. *Prophecy in Ancient Israel.* Oxford: Blackwell, 1967.

Lods, Adolphe. *The Prophets and the Rise of Judaism.* Translated by S. H. Hooke. The History of Civilization. London: Routledge, 1956.

Lundbom, Jack R. "The Lawbook of the Josianic Reform," Washington, *CBQ* 38 (1976) 293–302.

Malamat, Abraham. "A Mari Prophecy and Nathan's Dynastic Oracle." In *Prophecy: Essays Presented to Georg Fohrer on His Sixty-Fifth Birthday, September 6 1980,* edited by J. A. Emerton, 68–82. New York: de Gruyter, 1980.

Matthews, Victor H. "Kings of Israel: A Question of Crime and Punishment." In *SBL 1988 Seminar Papers,* edited by David John Lull, 517–26. Atlanta: Scholars, 1988.

Mauchline, John. *1 and 2 Samuel.* London: Oliphants, 1971.

Mayes, Andrew D. H. *Israel in the Period of the Judges.* SBT, 2nd ser., 29. London: SCM, 1974.

———. *The Story of Israel between the Settlement and the Exile: A Redactional Study of the Deuteronomic History.* London: SCM, 1982.

McCarter, P. Kyle. *II Samuel.* AB 9. Garden City, NY: Doubleday, 1984.

McCarthy, Dennis J. "II Samuel 7 and the Structure of the Deuteronomic History." *JBL* 84 (1965) 131–38.

———. "*Berît* and Covenant in the Deuteronomistic History." In *Studies in the Religion of Ancient Israel,* 65–85. VTSup 23. Leiden: Brill, 1972.

———. *Old Testament Covenant: A Survey of Current Opinions.* Atlanta: John Knox, 1978.

McKane, William. *Prophets and Wise Men.* SBT 44. London: SCM, 1966.

McKay, John. *Religion in Judah under the Assyrians.* SBT, 2nd ser., 26. London: SCM, 1973.

McKenzie, John L. "The Dynastic Oracle in II Samuel 7." *TS* 8 (1947) 187–218.

SELECT BIBLIOGRAPHY

McKenzie, Steven L. *The Trouble with Kings: The Composition of the Book of Kings in the Deuteronomistic History*. Leiden: Brill, 1991.

Mendenhall, George E. "Covenant." *IDB* 1:714–23.

———. *The Tenth Generation: The Origins of the Biblical Traditions*. Baltimore: John Hopkins University Press, 1973.

Mettinger, Tryggve N. D., *King and Messiah: The Civil and Sacral Legitimation of Israelite Kings*.Coniectanea Biblica Old Testament Series 8. Lund: Gleerup, 1976.

———. *The Mishnah*. Translated by Herbert Danby. London: Oxford University Press, 1933.

———. "YHWH SABAOTH—The Heavenly King on the Cherubim Throne." In *Studies in the Period of David and Solomon and Other Essays*, edited by Tomoo Ishida, 109–38. Winona Lake, IN: Eisenbrauns, 1982.

Mowinckel, Sigmund. "Die lietzen Worte Davids: II Sam. 23:1–7." *ZAW* 45 (1927) 30–58.

———. *He That Cometh*. Translated by G. W. Anderson. Oxford: Blackwell, 1959.

———. *The Psalms in Israel's Worship*. Translated by D. R. Ap-Thomas. 2 vols. Oxford: Blackwell, 1967.

Muilenburg, James. "The Form and Structure of the Covenantal Formulations." *VT* 9 (1959) 347–65.

———. "Form Criticism and Beyond." *JBL* 88 (1969) 1–18.

Mulder, E. S. "The Prophecy of Nathan in II Samuel 7." *Papers Read at the 3rd Meeting of the O.T. Werkgemeenskop*, 36–42. Pretoria: University of South Africa, 1960.

Murray, Donald F. "Of All the Years the Hopes: Or Fears? Jehoiachin in Babylon (2 Kings 25:27–30)." *JBL* 120.2 (2001) 245–65.

Nelson, Richard D. *The Double Redaction of the Deuteronomistic History*. JSOTSup 18. Sheffield: JSOT, 1981.

Nicholson, Ernest W. *Deuteronomy and Tradition*. Oxford: Blackwell, 1967.

Nielsen, Eduard. "The Role of Oral Tradition in the Old Testament." In *Old Testament Issues*, edited by Samuel Sandmel, 68–93. London: SCM, 1968.

Noth, Martin. "David and Israel in 2 Samuel 7." In *The Laws in the Pentateuch, and Other Studies*. Translated by D. R. Ap-Thomas, 250–59. Edinburgh: Oliver & Boyd, 1967.

———. *The Deuteronomistic History*. Translated by Jane Doull et al. JSOTSup 15. Sheffield: JSOT, 1981.

———. *Exodus: A Commentary*. Translated by J. S. Bowden. London: SCM, 1962.

———. "History and the Word of God in the Old Testament." In *The Laws in the Pentateuch, and Other Studies*. Translated by D. R. Ap-Thomas, 179–93. Edinburgh: Oliver & Boyd, 1967.

———. *The History of Israel*. Translated by P. R. Ackroyd. London: A. & C. Black, 1958.

———. *A History of Pentateuchal Traditions*. Translated by Bernhard W. Anderson. Emglewood Cliffs, NJ: Prentice Hall, 1972.

———. "The Jerusalem Catastrophe of 587 B.C. and Its Significance for Israel." in *The Laws in the Pentateuch, and Other Studies*, Translated by D.R. Ap-Thomas, 260–80. Edinburgh: Oliver & Boyd, 1967.

———. "Jerusalem and the Israelite Tradition." in *The Laws in the Pentateuch, and Other Studies*, Translated by D. R. Ap-Thomas, 132–44. Edinburgh: Oliver & Boyd, 1967.

———. "Old Testament Covenant-Making in the Light of a Text from Mari." In *The Laws in the Pentateuch, and Other Studies*, translated by D. R. Ap-Thomas, 108–17. Edinburgh: Oliver & Boyd, 1967.

SELECT BIBLIOGRAPHY

———. "The Re-presentation of the Old Testament in Proclamation." In *Essays on Old Testament Interpretation*, edited by James Luther Mays, 76–88. Atlanta: John Knox, 1979.

Ostborne, Gunnar. *YHWH's Words and Deeds*. Uppsala: Harrassowitz, 1951.

Otzen, Benedikt, et al. *Myths in the Old Testament*. Translated by Frederick Cryer. London: SCM, 1980.

Overholt, Thomas W. *The Threat of Falsehood: A Study in the Theology of the Book of Jeremiah*. SBT, 2nd ser., 16. London: SCM, 1970.

Peckham, Brian. *The Composition of the Deuteronomistic History*. HSM 35. Atlanta: Scholars, 1985.

Pedersen, Johs. *Israel: Its Life and Culture*. Translated by Aslang Moller. 4 vols. London: Oxford University Press, 1964.

Pfeiffer, Robert H. *Introduction to the Old Testament*. London: A. & C. Black, 1953.

Polzin, Robert. "'The Ancestress of Israel in Danger' in Danger." *Semeia* 3 (1975) 81–98.

———. *Moses and the Deuteronomist: A Literary Study of the Deuteronomic History*. New York: Seabury, 1980.

Porteous, Norman W. *Living the Mystery: Collected Essays*. Oxford: Blackwell, 1967.

Porter, J. Roy. "Interpretation of 2 Samuel VI and Psalm CXXXII." *JTS* 5 (1954) 161 - 73.

———. "Old Testament Historiography." In *Transition and Interpretation*, edited by G. W. Anderson, 131–52. Oxford: Clarendon, 1979.

———. "The Succession of Joshua." In *Proclamation and Presence: Old Testament Essays in Honor of Gwynne Henton Davies*, edited by John I. Durham and J. Roy Porter, 117–26. London: SCM, 1970.

Provan, Iain. *Hezekiah and the Books of Kings: A Contribution to the Cebate about the Composition of the Deuteronomistic History*. BZAW 172. New York: de Gruyter, 1988.

———. "The Historical Books of the Old Testament." In *The Cambridge Companion to Biblical Interpretation*, edited by John Barton, 198–211. Cambridge: Cambridge University Press, 1998.

Rast, Walter E. *Joshua, Judges, Samuel, Kings*. Philadelphia: Fortress, 1978.

———. *Tradition History and the Old Testament*. Philadelphia: Fortress, 1972.

Rendtorff, Rolf. "The Yahwist as Theologian? The Dilemma of Pentateuchal Criticism." *JSOT* 3.1 (1977) 2–9.

Richardson, H. Neil. "The Last Words of David: Some Notes on II Samuel 23:1–7." *JBL* 90 (1971) 257–66.

Ridout, George P. "Prose Compositional Techniques in the Succession Narrative (2 Sam. 7, 9–20, 1 Kings 1–2)?" PhD diss., California Graduate Theological Union, 1971.

Roberts, Jimmy J. M. "Zion in the Theology of the David-Solomonic Empire." In *Studies in the Period of David and Solomon and Other Essays*, edited by Tomoo Ishida, 93–108. Winona Lake, IN: Eisenbrauns, 1983.

Rost, Leonhard. *The Succession to the Throne of David*. Translated by Michael D. Rutter and David M. Gunn. Sheffield: Almond Press, 1982.

Schipper, Jeremy. "Significant Resonances with Mephibosheth in 2 Kings 25:27–30: A Response to Donald F. Murray?" *JBL* 124.3 (2005) 521–29.

Schmidt, Werner H. "A Theologian of the Solomonic Era? A Plea for the Yahwist." In *Studies in the Period of David and Solomon and Other Essays*, edited by Tomoo Ishida, 54–71. Winona Lake, IN: Eisenbrauns, 1983.

Schniedewind, William. "The Problem with Kings: Recent Study of the Deuteronomistic History." *Religious Studies Review* 22.1 (1996) 22–27.

SELECT BIBLIOGRAPHY

Scott, R. B. Y. "Solomon and the Beginning of Wisdom in Israel." In *Studies in Ancient Israelite Wisdom*, edited by James Crenshaw, 84–101. New York: Ktav, 1976.

Seybold, Klaus. *Das davidische Konigtum im Zeugnis der Propheten*. FRLANT 107. Gottingen: Vandenhoeek & Ruprecht, 1972.

Simon, Marcel. "La Prophétie de Nathan et le Temple." *RHPR* 32 (1952) 41–58.

Smart, James D. *The Strange Silence of the Bible in the Church: A Study in Hermeneutics*. London: SCM, 1970.

Snaith, Norman H. "The Historical Books." In *The Old Testament and Modern Study*, edited by Harold H. Rowley, 84–114. Oxford: Oxford University Press, 1961.

———. *Hymns of the Temple*. London: SCM, 1951.

Soulen, Richard N. *Handbook of Biblical Criticism*. Atlanta: John Knox, 1978.

Spriggs, David G. *Two Old Testament Theologies: A Comparative Evaluation of the Contribution of Eichrodt and von Rad to Our Understanding of the Nature of Old Testament Theology*. SBT 2nd ser., 30. London: SCM, 1974.

Stamm, Johann J., and Maurice E. Andrew. *The Ten Commandments in Recent Research*. SBT 2nd ser., 2. London: SCM, 1967.

Sweeney, Marvin A. "The Critique of Solomon in the Josianic Edition of the Deuteronomistic History." *JBL* 114.4 (1995) 607–22.

Tsevat, Matitiahu. "The House of David in Nathan's Prophecy." *Bib* 46 (1965) 353–56.

———. "Studies in the Book of Samuel. III: The Steadfast House; What Was David Promised in II Samuel 7:11b–16?" *HUCA* 34 (1963) 71–82.

Tucker, Gene M. *Form Criticism of the Old Testament*. Philadelphia: Fortress, 1976.

Tur-Sinai, N. H. "The Ark of God at Beit Shemesh (1 Sam. VI) and Peres 'Uzza (2 Sam. VI; I Chron. XIII)." *VT* 1. Leiden: Brill (1951) 275–86.

———. "Ugaritic Myths and Epics." Translated by H. L. Ginsberg. In *The Ancient Near East: An Anthology of Texts and Pictures*, edited by James B. Pritchard, 92–118. New Jersey: Princeton University Press, 1958.

Vermes, Geza. "Florilegium or Midrash on the Last Days (4Q174)." In *The Complete Dead Sea Scrolls in English*, 491–92. London: Penguin, 1997.

———. "The Heavenly Prince Melchizedek (11Q13)." In *The Complete Dead Sea Scrolls in English*, 500–502. London: Penguin, 1997.

Van Seters, J. *In Search of History: Historiography in the Ancient Near East and the Origins of Biblical History*. New Haven: Yale, 1983.

Von Rad, Gerhard. *Deuteronomy: A Commentary*. Translated by Dorothea Barton. London: SCM, 1966.

———. *Studies in Deuteronomy*. Translated by David Stalker. SBT 9. London: SCM, 1953.

———. *Genesis: A Commentary*. Translated by John H. Marks. London: SCM, 1961.

———. *Old Testament Theology*. Translated by David Stalker. Vol. 1. London: Oliver & Boyd, 1970.

———. "The Form Critical Problem of the Hexateuch." In *The Problem of the Hexateuch and other Essays*. Translated by E. Trueman Dickie, 1–78. London: Oliver & Boyd, 1966.

———. "There Remains Still a Rest for the People of God: An Investigation of a Biblical Conception." In *The Problem of the Hexateuch and other Essays*. Translated by E. Trueman Dickie, 94–102. London: Oliver and Boyd, 1966.

Ward, James M. "The Literary Form and Liturgical Background of Psalm LXXXIX." *VT* 11 (1961) 321–39.

Weinfeld, Moshe. "Covenant, Davidic." *IDBSup* 188–92.

SELECT BIBLIOGRAPHY

———. *Deuteronomy and the Deuteronomic School*. Oxford: Clarendon, 1972.

Weippert, Helga. "Die 'deuteronomistischen' Beurteilungen der Könige von Israel und Juda und das Problem der Redaktion der Konigsbucher." *Bib* 53.3 (1972) 301–39.

Weippert, Manfred. *The Settlement of the Israelite Tribes in Palestine: A Critical Survey of Recent Scholarly Debate*. SBT, 2nd ser., 21. London: SCM, 1971.

Weiser, Artur. *Introduction to the Old Testament*. Translated by Dorothea Barton. London: Darton, Longman & Todd, 1961.

———. *The Psalms: A Commentary*. Translated by Herbert Hartwell. London: SCM, 1962.

Wenham, Gordon J. "The Deuteronomic Theology in the Book of Joshua." *JBL* 90 (1971) 140–48.

Whybray, Roger N. *The Succession Narrative: A Study of II Sam. 9-20 and I Kings and 2*. SBT 2nd ser., 9. London: SCM, 1968.

Widengren, Geo. "King and Covenant." *JSS* 2.1 (1957) 1–32.

Willis, John T. "Redaction Criticism and Historical Reconstruction." In *Encounter with the Text, Form and History in the Hebrew Bible*, edited by Martin J. Buss, 61–89. Philadelphia: Fortress, 1979.

Wilson, J. V. Kinnier. "Epic of Creation." In *Documents from Old Testament Times*, edited by D. Winton Thomas, 3–16. New York: Harper and Row, 1961.

Wiseman, D. J., trans. "Interventions of Tiglath-Pileser III in Syria and Palestine (743-732 B.C.)." In *Documents from Old Testament Times*, edited by D. Winton Thomas, 53–58. New York: Harper and Row, 1958.

———, trans. "Sennacherib's Siege of Jerusalem." In *Documents from Old Testament Times*, edited by D. Winton Thomas, 64–69. New York: Harper & Row, 1958.

Wolff, H. Walter. *Anthropology of the Old Testament*. Translated by Margaret Kohl. London: SCM, 1974.

———. "The Kerygma of the Deuteronomic Historical Work." *The Vitality of the Old Testament Traditions*, edited by Walter Brueggemann and Hans Walter Wolff, 83–100. Atlanta: John Knox, 1978.

Wright, G. Ernest. "Biblical Archaeology Today." In *New Directions in Biblical Archaeology*, edited by David Noel Freedman and Jonas C. Greenfield, 167–86. New York: Doubleday, 1971.

———. "Cult and History: A Study of Current Problems in Old Testament Interpretation." *Interpretation* 16.1 (1962) 3–20.

———. *God Who Acts: Biblical Theology as Recital*. SBT 8. London: SCM, 1966.

———. *The Old Testament against Its Environment*. SBT 2 London: SCM, 1950.

Yadin, Yigael. "A Midrash on 2 Sam VII and Pss. I-II (4Q Florilegium)." *IEJ* 9 (1959) 95–98.

Zimmerli, Walther. *The Law and the Prophets: A Study of the Meaning of the Old Testament*. Translated by R.E. Clements,.New York: Harper & Row, 1965.

INDEX OF AUTHORS

Ackroyd, Peter R., 13n21, 29, 29n37, 38n4, 63n94, 73n15, 76n25, 88n61, 88n64, 103n9, 105, 105n13, 110, 110n22, 113, 113n31, 114, 114n34, 114n35, 130n9
Ahlstrom, Gosta, 143, 143n44, 143n45, 143n46, 143n47, 144–145, 144n48, 144n49, 144n50, 144n51, 144n52, 144n53, 145n54
Albright, William F., 3n4, 95, 95n77, 161, 161n5
Andrew, Maurice E., 134, 134n20, 135n21, 136n22, 136n23
Avioz, Michael, 58–61, 59n80, 60n82, 60n83, 60n84, 60n86, 61n87, 62, 161

Barr, James, 140, 140n33
Bentzen, Aage, 6n8, 49n52, 72, 72n13, 149, 149n67, 150
Blenkinsopp, Joseph, 89n65
Brown, Francis, 102–103, 103n6
Budde, Karl, 47n42
Bussche, H. van den, 7n9

Campbell, Antony F., 5n6, 48–53, 48n43, 48n44, 48n45, 48n46, 48n47, 48n48, 50n55, 50n58, 51n61, 51n62, 52, 52n63, 59n81, 62, 82, 82n38, 84, 84n50, 87, 87n59, 88, 88n60, 90, 99, 115, 147–148, 147n60, 147n61, 148n62, 148n63, 148n64, 149n65, 174
Caquot, André, 6n7
Carlson, R. A., 14n24, 41–43, 42n17, 42n18, 42n19, 42n20–43n20, 74, 74n18, 103, 103n7, 106n13, 109, 109n19
Childs, Brevard S., 2, 2n1, 8, 8n11, 12, 12n20, 37, 37n3, 65, 65n99
Clements, Ronald E., 2n2, 71n10, 88n63, 99n83, 115n38, 119, 119n41, 136, 136n24, 137n26, 165, 165n9, 175, 175n26
Clifford, Richard J., 116, 116n39, 165n7
Coats, George W., 23, 23n22
Coote, Robert B., 167n13
Craig, Kenneth M., 17, 17n29, 108, 108n18, 109, 109n21, 111n25
Cross, Frank Moore, Jr., 10n16, 43–46, 44n25, 44n26, 44n27, 44n28, 44n29, 44n30, 45n32, 46, 47, 61, 64, 64n95, 77, 82, 88, 88n62, 102, 102n2, 112, 112n29

Daube, David, 29
de Tillesse, G. Minette, 86n54

INDEX OF AUTHORS

Delekat, Lienhard, 13n21, 76n25
deVaux, Roland, 24, 24n24, 133, 133n17
Dines, Jennifer, 67n1
Driver, Geoffrey, 114
Driver, Samuel R., 8n13, 88n64, 107n15, 112, 112n28, 114, 114n32, 123, 123n49, 124, 124n50

Eaton, John H., 5n5
Eissfeldt, Otto, 21n12, 25, 25n25, 47n42, 70, 70n8, 107, 107n17, 178, 178n31
Engnell, Ivan, 5n5, 22, 22n21, 23, 25, 25n26, 26, 28, 62, 62n92, 115n37, 165n8

Flanagan, James W., 13n21, 76n25
Frankfort, Henri, 142, 142n37, 142n38, 142n39, 142n40, 142n41, 153, 153n78, 153n79, 166, 166n12
Fretheim, Terence E., 65n98
Friedman, Richard E., 64n97

Gray, John, 11n17, 71, 71n12, 131n12, 168n14, 170n15
Guillaume, Alfred, 129n6
Gunkel, Hermann, 5n5, 19, 19n3, 19n5, 19n6

Halpern, Baruch, 62, 62n91, 121, 121n47
Harrelson, Walter, 29, 30, 30n38, 30n39, 30n40
Hayes, John, 26, 26n29
Herrmann, Siegfried, 110, 110n23, 150–152, 150n70, 150n71, 150n72, 151n73, 151n74, 151n75, 151n76, 152n77, 153
Hicks, R. Lansing, 3, 3n3
Holloday. Carl R., 26, 26n29
Homer, 23

Ishida, Tomoo, 50n57, 130, 130n10, 165n10

Kautzsch, E. ??not spelled correctly in footnote, 102n5, 114, 114n33
Knight, Douglas, 18, 18n1, 21, 21n14, 25–26, 26, 26n27, 28, 28n34, 28n35, 29, 29n36

Kraus, Hans-Joachim, 133–134, 134n19

Labuschagne, C. J., 106n13
Lapointe, Roger, 27, 27n30, 27n31, 27n32, 27n33
Laurentin, André, 104, 104n10–105n10
Lemaire, André, 62, 62n90

Malamat, Abraham, 123n48, 129, 129n4
Mauchline, John, 73n15, 105, 105n13, 112, 112n27, 130n9
Mayes, Andrew D. H., 65n98
McCarter, P. Kyle, Jr., 56–58, 56n75, 56n76, 56n77, 57n78, 57n79
McCarthy, Dennis J., 43, 43n21, 43n22, 43n24, 59, 102, 102n1
McKenzie, John L. ?? misspelled in text, 6n7, 49n54
Mendenhall, George E., 132, 132n14, 133, 134, 135, 136
Mettinger, Tryggve, 106n13, 121, 121n46, 149, 149n66
Mowinckel, Sigmund, 5n5, 142, 142n42, 143n43, 157, 157n81, 161n5
Mulder, E. S., 107n15

Nelson, Richard D., 10n16, 43n23, 44–45, 45n31, 54, 64, 96, 96n81, 105, 105n13, 133, 133n18
Nicholson, Ernest W., 48, 48n51, 170n16, 172, 172n22
Nielsen, Eduard, 95, 95n79
Noth, Martin, 8n13, 18, 21–22, 21n13, 21n15, 21n16, 22n17, 22n18, 22n19, 36–41, 37n1, 37n2, 39n6, 39n7, 39n8, 40n14, 40n15, 45, 46, 47, 52, 58, 66, 66n101, 76, 76n24, 78n28, 81–82, 85, 85n52, 86, 86n56, 89n67, 93, 93n73, 99, 102, 102n3, 105, 105n11, 105n12, 107, 107n16, 120n45, 129, 129n3, 129n5, 132n13, 138, 138n28, 139, 147, 147n59, 153, 153n80

Otzen, Benedikt, 75n20

Peckham, Brian, 46–47, 46n36, 46n37, 46n38, 46n39, 47n40, 47n41, 47n42
Pfeiffer, Robert H., 6n7, 17, 17n28, 127n1

INDEX OF AUTHORS

Pieper, Josef, 30
Polzin, Robert, 119, 119n42
Porter, J. Roy, 6n8, 78n29, 95, 95n80, 102, 102n4, 103n8, 149, 149n68, 149n69, 150
Pritchard, James, 141
Provan, Iain, 10n16, 53–56, 53n65, 53n66, 53n67, 54n68, 54n69, 54n70, 55n71, 55n72, 55n73, 59n81, 62, 64, 64n96, 82, 82n38, 82n39, 82n40, 82n41, 82n42, 82n43, 83, 83n44, 84n47, 91n70, 94n76

Rast, Walter E., 23, 24n23
Rendtorff, Rolf, 139n32
Richardson, H. Neil, 161, 161n4
Ridout, George P., 11n17, 73, 73n16
Roberts, Jimmy J. M., 131, 131n11
Rost, Leonhard, 13n21, 40, 73, 73n16, 76n25, 96, 96n82, 105, 105n13, 107n15, 109, 109n20

Schipper, Jeremy, 76n23
Scott, R. B. Y., 95, 95n78
Seybold, Klaus, 139, 139n30, 139n31
Simon, Marcel, 16n26, 61n88
Snaith, Norman H., 5n5
Stamm, Johann J., 134, 134n20, 135n21, 136n22, 136n23
Sweeney, Marvin, 94, 94n75

Thomas, D. Winton, 141
Tsevat, Matitiahu, 105, 105n13
Tur-Sinai, N. H., 141n35, 141n36

Vanderhooft, David S., 62, 121, 121n47
Vermes, Geza, 160n2, 160n3
von Rad, Gerhard, 14, 14n23, 18–20, 18n2, 20n9, 22, 39–40, 39n9, 39n10, 40n11, 40n12, 40n13, 41, 48, 48n50, 52, 85, 85n53, 86, 86n56, 86n57, 99, 170, 170n17

Ward, James M., 6n7
Weinfeld, Moshe, 89n67, 132, 133, 133n15, 133n16, 134, 146, 146n56, 146n57, 146n58
Weippert, Helga, 61–62, 62n89
Weiser, Artur, 48, 48n49
Wellhausen, Julius, 19, 21, 66n101
Wenham, Gordon J., 65n100
Whybray, Roger N., 76n25
Widengren, Geo, 119, 119n43, 138, 138n29
Willis, John T., 11n17
Wilson, J. V. Kinnier, 141, 141n34
Wolff, Hans Walter, 41, 41n16, 47, 63, 75, 75n21
Wright, G. Ernest, 20n10, 22, 22n20

Zimmerli, Walther, 52, 52n64

SCRIPTURE INDEX

Old Testament

Genesis

2:16–17	75	13:14–18	2, 133, 136, 137, 138, 164
2:16–18	75	13:16	137
2:17	75	13:18	136, 164
2:18	75	14:1–17	137
3:3	75	14:18	131
3:16	75	14:18–20	143, 160
3:21	75	14:18–24	143
3:23–24	75	15	136
3:24	75	15:1	137
4:1	75	15:1–6	162, 164
4:25	106	15:1–7	136
9:25–27	2	15:1–18	2, 133
11:30	3	15:1–21	164
11:31–12:5	137	15:2–5	136
12:1–3	2, 136, 137, 164	15:3–4	137
12:1–5	4	15:4	3, 106, 140, 164
12:2	3, 140	15:7	138
12:6–7	4	15:9–17	132
12:10–18	75n19	15:17–21	164
12:11–19	75	15:18	136
13:6–11	138	15:18–21	137, 137n25
13:14–7 ??	137n25	16	3
		17:10–14	4
		18:9–15	3

SCRIPTURE INDEX

Genesis (continued)

18:20–33	76n22
20:1–18	75n19
22	3
22:16–18	2
23	136
23:1–20	164
25:21	3
26:1–11	75n19
26:7–11	75
26:24	2
27:1–29	2
28:13–14	2
30:1	3
31:26–30	51
31:36–42	51
35:11–12	2
37:5–11	3
37:26	3
37–50	3
38	7
38:28–30	3
39:3	113
39:5–9	75n19
39:6–9	75
39:21	113
39:23	113
42–45	3
44:14–31	3
49	161
49:3–28	5
49:8–10	3

Exodus

2:1–10	49n52
3:1–10	139
3:1–15	139n32
3:6–8	4
4:25–26	4
12:1–13	4
14:14–28	4
15:1–18	19, 118
15:13–18	3
17:8–16	110
18:13–26	49n52
19:1–6	139
19:3–5	107
19:4–5	93, 171n19
19:4–20:17	4
19:5	4
19–20	138
19–24	132, 133, 134
20:1–17	139
20:2	171n19
20:2–3	93
20:2–7	4
20:3–6	99
20:14	75
20:17	75
20–23	171
24:7	171n19
25:10–22	112, 149
25:10–23	89n67
26:1–34	112
32:9–14	76n22
34:34	89n67
37:1–9	112
40:21	112
40:21–23	89n67

Leviticus, 20:10 75

Numbers

10:33–36	112
10:35	88
10:35–36	14n22, 89n67, 113, 147, 149
11:11–13a	51
11:29	4
12:5–8	49n52
12:6–8	4
12:7	107, 139
22:1–4	4
22–24	47, 111, 129
23–24	130
24:7–9	3
24:17	3
25:1–13	4

SCRIPTURE INDEX

Deuteronomy

1:1–5	39
1–4	79n31
1:6–4:24, 5	93
1:20–46	39
1–34	60
1:37–38	80
2:1–3:20	80
2:16	81
2:25–3:6	139
2:30–3.20	41
3:1	77
3:20	41, 110
3:23–28	80
3:28 ??	77
4:21–22	80
4:25–26	39
4:34	139n32
4:45–48	171
5:1–3	177
5:1–30:20	85
5:2–3	4
5:6–7	90
5:7–10	93, 99, 177
5:15	139n32
5:17–18	42
5:18	75
5:21	42, 75
5–28	171
5–30	133
6:10–12	81
6:10–17	39
6:20–22	139n32
6:20–23	4, 138
6:20–24	19
7:1–5	170
7:1–6	39, 173
7:1–10	174
7:7–9	177
7:17–26	173, 174
8	39
8:7–9	81
8:12	115
8:12–14	60
9:6–29	39
9:7–25	79n31
9:7–29	76n22
9:12–17	87n58
10:1–3	88, 149
10:1–4	111
10:1–5	116n38, 137
10:1–6	150
10:13	112
10:28	88
11:1–32	42
11:5–6	39
11:8–15	4
12:1–3	173
12:1–14	99
12:2–4	87
12:2–14	78
12:5	87, 93n73, 177n28
12:8	45n34
12:8–9	54, 79n31, 91n71
12:8–11	58
12:9–10	14, 41, 42
12:9–11	80
12;9–14	44
12:10	14, 74, 85, 110
12:10–11	4, 42, 78, 81, 86, 87, 110
12:11	177n28
12:13–14	86
12:14	87, 110
12:28	54
13:1–5	52
14:2	177
16:2	110, 177n28
16:6	110, 177n28
16:11	177n28
16:13–15	163
16:15	110
17:14–15	4, 93n73
17:14–20	10, 52, 85, 90, 99, 138, 170, 175
17:15	107, 167, 173
17:15–20	4
17:16–17	99n83
17:18	55, 91, 91n70, 94n76, 122
17:18–19	139, 171
17:18–20	4, 94, 99, 140, 175
17:19–20	93n73

195

SCRIPTURE INDEX

Deuteronomy (continued)

17:20	4, 45n34
18:9–14	39
18:15	85
18:15–22	4, 49n52, 52, 170
18:18	129
18:18–19	90
18:21–22	68
20:1–9	174
20:1–20	173
21:15–17	165
22:22	42, 75
25:5–10	162
25:17–19	41, 42, 81, 110, 139n32
25:19	42, 74, 110
26:2	110
26:5	4, 86n54
26:5–9	19, 81, 138
26:6–9	4
26:8–9	4
27:15	173
27:26	173
28	4, 99
28:1–14	79
28:15–68	85
28–30	42
28:36	85, 86n54
28:36–37	172
28:68	86n54
28:69	86n54
29	39
29:1	4
29:2–8	171n19
29:2–13	93
29:12–28	138
29:19–28	177
29–30	79
30:11–20	39
30:15–20	85, 99
31	43n24
31:2	80
31:8	112
31:9	111, 112, 170
31:9–11	150
31:9–12	77
31:9–13	79, 163
31:23	112
31:25–32:42	79n31
31:26	137
31:28–29	170
31:29	54
32	85, 100
32:1–25	107
32:1–43	42, 90, 93
32:9–10	177
32:9–12	139
32:10–13	117
32:15–28	39
32:46–47	40
32:48–52	80, 99, 177
33	78n28, 161
33:4	90
33:5–23	5
33:7	3
33:8–10	137, 170
33:8–11	4
33:13–17	3
33:26–29	174

Joshua

1:1–15	77
1:2	74, 107, 117, 137, 139
1:5	112, 139
1:12–17	81
1:12–18	110
3:1–4:9	112
3:1–17	4
3:3–11	149
3:3–17	113
4:17–19	88
5:5–9	4
5:11–12	4
6	139
6:1–8:29	88
6:1–12:24	81
6:4	89n67
6:4–11	149
6:7–8	89n67
7:6	89n67

SCRIPTURE INDEX

7:23	89n67	6:1	54
8	139	6:12	112
8:31–33	137	6:16	112
8:33	88, 112	8:22–23	11n18, 170
10:1	131	9	11n18
10–12	139	9:5	73
12:6	81	9:7–20	11n18
13–21	5, 140	10:6	54
15:13–19	136	13:1	54
15:63	87	13–16	99
21:43–22:10	77	17:6	1, 11, 54, 58, 91n71
21:45	40	17:23–24	51
22:1–2	41	18:1	1, 11
22:1–9	110	19:1	1, 11
22:2	78	20:23	112
22:9	88	20:23–27	88
22:10–34	119	20:26–27	88
23	39, 42, 85	20:27	88n64, 149
23:1	41, 74, 110, 140	20:27–28	112
23:14	40	21:2	88
24	78n28, 107	21:19	88
24:1–18	4	21:25	1, 7n10, 11, 54, 58, 91n71
24:2	86n54		
24:2–25	79, 93		
24:2–28	132, 133, 134, 138, 139	Ruth	
24:2b-13	19	1:1–4	7, 7n10
24:3–13	171n19	2:2	7
24:6–13	4	4:11	89n66
24:26	171n19, 177	4:13	7
24:29	139	4:17	7
24:31	170	4:17–22	7n10
		4:18–22	7

Judges

1:21	87	**1 Kingdoms (1 Samuel)**
2:7	78	
2:7–11	170	16:1–3Kingdoms 2:4 7
2:8	139	
2:11–13	54	**1 Samuel**
2:11–23	39, 42, 78, 79n31, 85	
2:17–21	79n31	1:3 88
2:18	112	1–3 12, 52, 110
3:7	54	1:10–12 88
3:12	54	1:11 106
4:1	54	1:12 112

SCRIPTURE INDEX

1 Samuel *(continued)*

1:15	112
1:19	112
1:22	112
2:1–10	47, 78n28
2:1b–10	12, 13
2:2–10	1
2:10	13, 59, 89
2:22	112
2:27–33	93
2:27–34	76n22
2:27–36	99
3	49n52
3:2–3	112
3:3	14, 88, 103, 112, 115
4	147, 149
4:1–7:1	6, 6n8, 12, 14, 87, 147, 175
4:1–22	88n63
4:3	14, 115, 137
4:3–5	103
4:4	16n25, 105, 107, 117, 137, 147, 163
4:4–5	14
4:4–7	112
4:4–8	89n67, 113
4:4–11	148
4:5–7	14n22
4:5–11	88
4–6	95
4:6–8	147
4–8	116n38
4:21–22	147
5	88
5:2	14, 103, 115
5–6	149
6:1–13	148
6:13–20	89n67
7:1	14, 88, 89, 89n65, 103, 103n8, 115, 148
7:1–2	87, 88, 89n67, 112
7:2	112
7:2–13	88
7:3–14	88n61
7:5–6	88
7:6	112
7:8–9	72
7:15–17	49n52
8:1–7	90
8:7	170
8:7–19	13
8:11–17	99n83
8–15	12, 49
9	52
9:1–11:1	76
9:5–9	129
9:9	111
9–10	49n52
9:14–20	111
10:1	48, 74, 107, 117, 119, 138
10:1–25	4
10:18–19a	170
10:21–25	167
10:25	112, 171n19
11:15	4, 88, 112
12	39, 42, 84n49, 85, 93, 103n9
12:3	88
12:7–26	170
12:14–25	99
12:25	85, 172
12:26–31	76
13:1	140
13:1–23:7	76
13:6–13	49n52
13:6–14	130
13:11–14	153
13:13–14	59
13:14	1, 4, 12, 13, 74, 89
13:15–16:13	127n2
14:3	88n64
14:18	87, 88, 88n64, 89n67, 112
14:18 (LXX)	88n64
15:1–31	130
15:1ff	110
15:10–29	153
15:14	107
15:17–19	93
15:17–23	90, 100
15:28	1, 4, 12, 13, 50, 89, 93

SCRIPTURE INDEX

15:28–29	59
16–1 Kings 2	11
16:1–1 Kings 2:4	7
16:1–2 Samuel 4	76
16:1–3	50
16:1–13	4, 12, 13, 48, 50
16:1–13a	1, 7n10, 11n18, 49
16–2 Samuel 1	178
16–2 Samuel 5	48, 50, 72
16–2 Samuel 9	42
16–2 Samuel 23	59, 72, 73
16:6	89n67
16:13	89
16:18	113
17:31–53	118
17:54	42
18:6–7	13
18:7–8	166
18:12	113
18:14	113
18:25–28	118
18–27	12
19:18–22	50
20:13	118
20:14–15	59
20:30–31	166
21	117n40
21:1–6	89, 89n65
21:6	89n67, 112
21:11	13
22:3–4	7
22:5	130
23:1–2	118
23:5–18	117n40
23:20	89
24:20	1, 13
24:20–21	59
25:1	50
25:28	1, 59, 89
25:28–31	13
25:28–42	136
25:39–43	74
25:43	74
25:44	74
26:19	42
27	117n40
27:1–9	164
27:1–28	123
27:3	74
28	49
28:5–20	127n2
28:16–17	12
28:16–19	153
28:17	1
28:17–19	59
30:1–17	110
30:1–20	41

2 Bas (2 Samuel)

7:5 LXX	61, 114, 125

2 Kingdoms (2 Samuel)

7:11b (LXX)	69, 69n4

2 Samuel

1:1–15	110
1:1–16	110n24
1–7	95
1:17–27	100, 161
2:1	118
2:1–2	137
2:1–3	164
2:1–4	123, 137, 162
2:2	164
2:4	13, 164, 178n30
2:8–10	137
3:2–5	74, 137, 162, 164
3:9–10	13
3:12–16	123
3:13–16	74
3:22–34	51
3:33–34	161
4:9	12
5:1–2	137
5:1–3	13, 96, 164, 166
5:1–5	4, 5, 7n10, 12, 89n66, 137, 164, 167, 178n30
5:2	107, 117, 137

SCRIPTURE INDEX

2 Samuel *(continued)*

5:3	89, 112
5:6–9	87, 163, 174
5:6–10	178n30
5:6–11	42
5:10	113
5:11	103, 109, 111, 115, 168
5:12	118
5:12–15	73
5:13	74
5:14	131, 165
5:17–23	41–42
5:17–25	110n24, 137, 178n30
5:17–26	12
5:23–24	118
6	6, 6n8, 9n14, 14, 16, 87, 102, 112, 113, 116n38, 121n46, 138, 147
6:1–7:16	82
6:1–7:17	148
6:1–11	147
6:1–17	6, 147
6:1–19	71, 81, 95, 139, 164, 174
6:1–20	14
6:1–23	178n30
6:2	16n25, 102, 103n8, 105, 107, 111, 113, 117, 137, 147, 163, 164
6:2–3a	89n66
6:4–5	89n67
6:6	111
6–7	3, 12, 147, 175
6:10	103
6:10–11	14, 115
6:10–12	103n8
6:11–12	163
6:12	78, 89
6:16	112, 113
6:16–17	89
6:17	14, 42, 102, 103, 112, 113
6:17–19	102, 165
6:20	103, 163
6:20–23	3, 123, 162
6:21	109, 113
6:22	74
6:23	3, 102
7	6n7, 6n8, 7, 7n9, 17, 40, 41, 42, 43, 45, 46, 47, 48, 53, 58, 59, 60, 61, 73, 82, 93n73, 106n14, 120
7	121n46, 138, 138n27, 139, 140, 141, 142, 143, 147, 150, 151, 152, 153, 157, 167, 178n30
7:1	14, 41, 57, 102, 107, 108, 109, 130, 130n9, 139, 146
7:1–2	56, 73, 103, 108
7:1–3	6, 14n22, 15, 42, 49n53, 57, 58, 60, 81, 98, 100, 108, 108–109, 109, 113, 114, 115, 115n36, 116, 124
7:1–3	129, 131, 144, 146, 147, 165, 167, 177
7:1-3-7:5-7	116
7:1–4a	81
7:1–7	14, 15, 16, 40, 42, 61, 81, 103, 106, 121n46, 124, 131, 140, 142, 146, 164
7:1–7 (MT)	40
7:1a	56, 94, 97, 115
7:1b	14, 74, 78, 80, 110, 118, 177
7:2	102, 103, 108, 110, 112, 113, 116, 117, 129n7, 130, 152, 165, 165n7
7:2–3	56, 94, 97, 114
7:2–4	73
7:3	51n59, 100, 108, 111, 112, 113, 129, 129n7, 151
7:3–4	130n8

SCRIPTURE INDEX

7:3–7	130
7:4	15, 104, 108, 111, 127
7:4–7	50, 108–109, 109, 129, 151
7:4–11	57
7:4–16	15, 51, 97, 111, 114, 127, 128, 129
7:4–17	81
7:4a	94, 97, 108, 124, 141, 167
7:4b	113
7:4b-5a	114, 115
7:5	16, 51, 51n59, 52, 57, 58, 74, 93, 100, 102, 104, 105, 107, 108, 109, 114, 115, 117, 122, 153, 161, 162, 177
7:5 (MT)	125
7:5–6	116, 145
7:5–7	6, 15, 40, 51, 57, 60, 61, 78, 80, 93, 94, 95, 96, 100, 104, 104–106, 106, 113, 115, 116, 117, 120, 124
7:5–7	141, 143, 147, 151
7:5–11a	120n44
7:5–13a	81
7:5–16	113
7:5a	55
7:5b	114, 120n45
7:5b–7	56, 81, 94, 97, 108, 109, 114, 115, 115n36, 167, 174
7:6	14, 14n22, 15, 103, 108, 112, 115, 116, 138, 139n32, 149, 165
7:6–7	3, 56, 100, 120n45, 143, 145
7:6–7a	51, 52
7:6a	115
7:6b	115
7:7	15, 51, 51n62, 52, 57, 58, 74, 108, 111, 114, 115, 116, 130, 165n7
7:7b	51, 52
7:8	5, 11n18, 15, 16, 57, 74, 100, 102, 104, 105, 107, 108, 109, 117, 119, 121n46, 122, 137, 138, 139, 139n32
7:8–9	12, 56, 74, 93, 97, 107, 136, 137, 139, 140, 164, 175
7:8–9a	107
7:8–11	81, 104, 106
7:8–11a	94, 139
7:8–12	81, 106, 108, 124, 174
7:8–12a	164
7:8–16	10, 13, 93, 95, 99, 103, 104, 104–106, 106, 107, 133, 136, 137, 139, 143, 152
7:8–17	40
7:8–29	4, 16, 140, 149
7:8–29 (13a excluded)	124
7:8	147, 153, 162, 163
7:8b	139
7:9	3, 15, 113, 117, 136, 140
7:9–10	149, 176n27
7:9a	139
7:9b	107, 139, 152
7:9b–11	107
7:10	4
7:10–11	107
7:10–11a	3, 4, 14, 15, 57, 68, 69, 78, 81, 96, 97, 107, 118, 125, 127n1, 138, 140, 145, 161, 178
7:10–12	146
7:10–16	76
7:11	121
7:11–16	6, 45n34, 68, 94
7:11a	96, 107, 118

SCRIPTURE INDEX

2 Samuel *(continued)*

7:11b	15, 16, 40, 50, 51, 51n60, 68n2, 69, 74, 97, 100, 102, 103, 104, 105, 106, 109, 118, 119
7:11b	120n44, 120n45, 121, 122, 125, 140, 159, 160, 161, 162, 163, 167
7:11b-12	11, 15, 56, 94, 136, 175
7:11b-13a	80
7:11b-15	95
7:11b-16	11, 15, 40, 46, 54, 56, 68, 70, 76, 83, 93, 94, 98, 100, 136, 154, 163, 178
7:12	3, 105, 106, 121, 123, 164
7:12-13	13-14, 15, 40, 50, 55, 73, 81
7:12-14	4, 74, 94
7:12-15	73, 94, 104, 106, 122, 144
7:12-16	4, 81, 175
7:12-18	166n11
7:12b	15, 55n74, 106, 122, 140
7:13	50, 57, 61, 91, 94n76, 96, 100, 104, 106, 109, 115, 117, 121, 121n46, 122, 141, 164, 177
7:13-14	15, 93n73, 146
7:13-15	81, 89, 94, 97, 106, 124, 140, 164
7:13a	6, 15, 16, 40, 55, 78, 93, 95, 102, 105, 106, 108, 115, 116, 120n45, 143, 146, 154, 167
7:13b	15, 55, 55n74, 106, 122, 140
7:14	5, 55, 122, 124, 166n11, 175
7:14-15	96, 138
7:14-16	11
7:15	11, 12, 13, 75, 76, 102, 123, 139n32, 140
7:15-16	15
7:16	15, 40, 50, 68, 68n2, 73n14, 74, 81, 94, 97, 104, 106, 108, 109, 123, 124, 140, 161, 164, 174, 175
7:17	50, 50n56, 73, 74, 111, 124, 127, 128, 129, 141, 152, 160, 161, 162
7:17-18	103, 146
7:18	89n67, 112, 153
7:18-21	40
7:18-24	139
7:18-28	104
7:18-29	15, 78n28, 85n52, 103-104, 106, 125, 142, 152, 164
7:19	107, 122, 153, 161, 163
7:19-21	74
7:20	107, 153
7:20b	166n11
7:21	107, 153
7:22-24	40
7:23-24	3, 4, 107, 125, 178
7:23-27	107
7:25	84n49, 107, 140
7:25-27	107
7:25-29	40, 74, 163
7:26	107, 153
7:26-27	102, 105, 107, 139, 147
7:27	16, 16n25, 51n60, 81, 100, 103, 104, 107, 109, 120, 120n44, 125, 128, 137n25, 140, 153, 154, 159
7:27	162, 162n6, 163, 167
7:28	107, 153
7:29	104, 122, 140, 153

SCRIPTURE INDEX

8	3, 73n14	13:25	125
8:10–11	12	13a	42, 142
8:10–12	14	13b–15a	56
8:11–17	75n19	15–16	12
8:12	42, 110	15–20	14
8:13–14a	3	15:24	88n64, 131
8:18	131	15:31–37	12n19
9	69, 76n23	16:1–4	74n17
9:1	117n40, 123	16:3–11	117n40
9:1–13	76	16:5–8	74n17, 117n40
9–20	13, 50, 73, 76n25, 178	16:11	106
		16:20–17:14, 23	12n19
10–11a	118, 138	18:15	125
10–12	3	18:33	161
11:1b–2	73	19:9–12	146
11:2–27	74	19:9–15	5
11–12	3, 12, 42, 72, 73, 74, 98, 100	19:11–13	51
		20:1–2	5, 117n40
11–20	48	20:1–22	12
12	145	21	117n40
12:1	73, 129, 130	21:1	12
12:1–7	49n53, 130, 153–154	21:1–7	124
12:1–8	74	21:1–9	123
12:1–14	8	21:1–10	89
12:1–15	50, 127n2	22	5
12:1–15a	111, 129	22:1–23:7	12
12:5	75	23:1–3	162
12:7	73, 130	23:1–5	68, 78n28
12:7–8	74	23:1–7	1, 12, 13, 47, 59, 76, 160, 161
12:7–9	107	23:2	161
12:7–10	90	23:5	13, 16, 109, 122, 140, 161
12:7–11	93	23:6	161
12:7–12	72	23:6–7	149
12:10	73	23:18	78
12:13	73	24	178n30
12:13–14	75	24:11	130
12:15	73, 130	24:11–13	129
12–15	162	24:11–19	130
12:23	73	24:11–25	127n2
12:23–25	73	24:13–15	12
12:24–25	14, 50	24:15–25	145
12:25	111, 127n2, 129, 130, 144	24:18–25	128, 144
13–15	97		
13–20	42		

SCRIPTURE INDEX

1 Kings

1	145
1–2	13, 48, 50, 73, 76n25, 178
1:5–2:25	92
1:5–6	166
1:5–7	163
1:5–21	73
1:9	73, 144
1:10	130
1:10–11	111
1:10–27	130
1:10–46	129
1:11–21	166
1:11–25	50
1:11–30	14
1:11–45	144
1:18	111
1:22–23	130
1:22–24	111
1:29	12
1:32	111, 130
1:33	144
1:33–38	166
1:38	111, 130, 144
1:39–40	4
1:46	73
1:48	73
2:1–4	4
2:2–4	54, 90, 91, 94, 95, 99, 107, 139, 140, 149, 175
2:3	171
2:3–4	94, 106, 174
2:4	53, 54, 55, 91n70
2:13–25	166
2:13–35	163
2:15	165
2:15–46	110
2:23–25	125
2:23–34	144
2:24–25	125
2:25	94
2:46	110
3:1	96
3:1–2	78
3:1–5	81, 94
3:1–15	146
3:2	78
3:3–5	174
3:4	89, 97, 146
3:4–5	81, 87, 116, 131
3:4–15	150
3:6	71
3–12	48
4:29–34	96
5:1–7 MT	168
5:1–9:10	127n2
5:3	89n65
5:3–5	177
5:4	145
5:15–17 MT	14
5:16–19 MT	42
5:17 MT	80
5:17–18 MT	165
5:17–19 MT	61
5:18 MT	42, 78, 110
6–8	78
6:12	4, 55, 71, 99, 140
6:12–13	94, 175
6:16–18 MT	95
6:38	81
6:38–7:1	165
7:8b	96
7:51	81
8	39, 148
8:1–6	4
8:1–9	147, 150
8:1–10	81
8:1–11	78
8:9	137
8:12–13	95, 96, 97, 174, 175, 177
8:12–19	87, 141
8:13–14	109
8:15–21	80
8:15–29	86
8:15–53	78n28
8:16–21	42, 110
8:17	177n28
8:17–19	57
8:17–30	177
8:18–19	57

SCRIPTURE INDEX

8:19	3	11:6–7	78
8:20	40	11:6–13	95
8:21	150	11:7–8	79n33
8:23–55	85n52	11:7–11	79n31
8:24–25	71	11:13	147
8:24–26	167	11:14–25	168
8:25	4, 53, 54, 55, 90, 91, 91n70, 94, 95, 99, 140, 174, 175	11:15–16	3
		11:26–38	5, 49
		11:29	110
8:27	115	11:29–33	8, 87
8:27–29	122	11:29–35	4
8:27–29a	89n67, 93, 94n74, 106	11:29–38	90, 154
		11:29–39	50, 127n2, 130
8:27–30	95, 177	11:30–31	129
8:29	177n28	11:30–33	175
8:45	79	11:31–32	177
8:46–48	77n26, 86n54	11:31–34	90
8:46–50	99	11:32	83, 89, 128
8:46–51	177	11:33	94
8:56	14, 40, 177	11:34–37	90n69
8:65	12	11:36	1, 9n14, 10, 53, 83, 89, 90, 119, 128, 146, 147, 175
9:1	165		
9:1–2	87, 116, 167		
9:1–5	81, 94	11:38	45n34, 94, 99, 174, 175
9:1–6	4, 87, 94, 95		
9:1–9	97	11:38–39	89
9:2–5	167	11:39	71
9:2–6	81, 146	12:1–16	90, 92, 167
9:2–9	146	12:1–17	5, 96
9:3	122, 141, 177n28	12:8–11	167
9:4–5	53, 54, 55, 71, 94	12–13	147
9:4–6	94	12:16	167
9:4–7	140	12:16–19	124
9:4–9	55, 99, 175	12:17	138, 167
9:5	91, 94n76	12:20	4
9:5a	55	12:21–24	167
9:6–6	90	12:22–24	154, 169
9:14	96	12:25–29	167
9:20–21	3	12:26–13:10	78, 90
10:1–10	165	12:26–13:34	127n2
10:28	52	12:26–29	87, 92
11:1–6	173	12:26–33	10, 177
11:1–11	92	12:28	167
11:1–13	94	13	77, 84, 86n55, 129
11:4	71	13:1–3	95
11:4–8	78	13:2–3	78n28
11:5–13	177	13–16	48

SCRIPTURE INDEX

1 Kings *(continued)*

14:1–4	129
14:1–16	127n2
14:5–11	50
14:7	74, 107, 117, 119
14:7–9	107
14:7–11	49, 90, 93, 100, 154
14:8–9	87
14:9	87n58
14:11	90
14:14–16	90
14–16	49
14:21–30	78n30
14:22–24	92
14:23	78
14:24	176
14:25–26	125, 168
15:1–4	50
15:3	78, 92
15:3–5a	71
15:4	1, 9n14, 10, 50, 83, 89, 119, 128, 146, 175
15:4–5	53, 54, 147
15:5	45n34, 72, 74, 98
15:5b	71
15:8–13	92
15:9–15	91
15:11	45n34, 71, 87, 91n71, 173
15:11–13	148
15:11–15	127n2, 177
15:12–15	169
15:14	78, 87
15:16–18	168
15:23	124
15:25–26	90
15:30	78n30
15:34	77
16:1	110
16:1–4	49, 127n2, 154
16:2	74, 107, 117, 119
16:2–4	90, 93
16:4	90
16:17–19	127n2
16:29–33	92
16:30–33	168
16:31	168
17:1	110, 129, 168n14
17–18	49
17–19	48
18:1–16	92
18:1–18	92
18:3–20	168n14
18:13	169
18:17–19	130
18:17–40	170
18:19	77
18–19	92
18:26	77
18:31–32	87
18:38–46	168n14
19	49
19:1–2	169
19:1–14	170
19:10	87, 169
19:14	87, 169
19:15–17	52, 90, 92
19:15–37	98
19:16	50, 110
19:18	169
20:22	168
21	48, 127n2
21:1–4	168n14
21:1–14	170
21:1–18	169
21:16–24	130
21:19–24	50
21:20b–22	90
21:20b–25	90
21–22	49
21:24	90
21:25–26	168
21:28–29	168n14
21:29	175
22	48
22:1–22	129
22:2–38	127n2
22:4	92
22:5–23	129
22:5–28	129
22:6	170
22:7–28	130

SCRIPTURE INDEX

22:8	110
22:11	110
22:13–17	112
22:15–23	111
22:17–28	170
22:41–43	92
22:42–43	91
22:43	78, 87, 91n71, 168, 169, 173, 177
22:43–44	92
22:43a	148
22:46	169
111:38	140

2 Kings

1:2–17	127n2
1:3–4	129
2:1–10:31	127n2
2:2–7	170
3:2	169, 175
3:2–3	77, 90
4	129
4:22–25	87
5:18 MT	110
8	138n29
8:9	119
8:15–16	92
8:16–18	91n71, 92
8:18	78n30, 173, 176
8:18–20	74
8:19	1, 9n14, 10, 53, 54, 83, 89, 128, 146, 147, 175
8:26–27	91n71
8:27	78n30, 173
9:1–10	50, 129, 130
9:1–10:28	48, 92
9:1–13	50
9–10	48, 49
9:14–25	169
9:16–28	168
9:24–27	170
9:27–28	125
9:30–37	170
10:1–8	170
10:10	40
10:12–14	170
10:13–14	92
10:14	125
10:20–25	170
10:25–28	169
10:28–31	90
10:29	77, 87n58
10:30	90, 175
10:31	77
11:1	73, 125, 170
11:1–2	92
11:1–4	157
11:1–12:2	170
11:1–12:18	127n2
11:1–20	92n72, 166, 166n11
11:12–16	92
11:12–17	138n29
11:14	170n15
11:14–18	92
11:16	170
11:17	96, 119
11:18	170, 170n15
11:20	92, 170, 170n15
12:1–3	83n46
12:2	91, 91n71, 92, 173
12:2–3	78, 87
12:4–16	166n11
12:18	176
12:20	125
13:2	77
13:4–5	175
13:11	77
13:14–19	130
13:14–21	127n2
14:3	91, 91n71, 92, 170, 173
14:3–4	78, 87
14:8–14	127n2
14:13–14	125
14:19	125
14:24	77
14:25–27	175–176
15:3	91, 91n71, 92, 170, 173
15:3–4	78, 87
15:5	124

SCRIPTURE INDEX

2 Kings (*continued*)

15:9	77
15:18	77
15:24	77
15:28	77, 86n54
15:29	96, 125
15:32–34	91
15:32–38	83n46
15:34	91n71, 92, 170, 173
15:34–35	78, 87
15:35	127n2
16:1–10	173
16:2–3	173
16:2–4	78n30
16:3	173
16:3–4	91n71, 93, 176
16:4	78
16:5	125
16:7–13	173
16:8–16	127n2
16:8–18	172
17	86, 171
17:1–4	172
17:1–6	10, 125, 172
17:1–7	85
17:2	127n2
17:4	84n49
17:6	86n54, 96
17:7–18	70, 78n28, 84, 85, 98, 172
17:7–23	9, 79n31, 85, 91, 93, 99, 127n2
17:7–41	10, 39
17:13–19	85
17:16	87n58
17:19	91, 98
17:19–20	10
17:20–23	77, 78n28, 84, 85, 98, 172
17:21–23	10
17:24–33	99
18:1–6	92
18:1–20:19	127n2
18:1–23:28	78n28
18:3	71, 83n45, 91n71, 173n23, 175
18:3–5	9
18:3–6	9
18:3–7	85
18:3–8	81
18:4	78, 87, 89, 97, 143, 177
18:4–6	95
18:4–12	176
18:5–6	85n51, 173n23, 174n24
18:7b	173
18:8	96
18:9–12	91
18:9–19:30	125
18:9–19:37	68
18:11	96
18:11–12	10
18:13	125
18:13–20:10	8
18:14–16	125, 173, 173n23
18–19	96
18:21	96, 97
18:22	9, 78, 81, 87, 89, 97
18–23	84
19:9	153
19:14–21	88n64
19:15	112
19:20	110, 129
19:20–34	71, 103n9, 157, 172, 177
19:20–37	97, 119
19:34	54
19:36–37	157
20:1–6	129
20:1–11	124–125, 172
20:4–18	177
20:6	54
20:12–19	173n23
20:12–21	68
20:14–19	172
20:16–18	68n2
20:16–20	103n9
20:20	173
20:21–21:3	92
21:1	83
21:1–3	83n46
21:1–15	176

SCRIPTURE INDEX

21:1–22	127n2	23:15–17	79n34
21:2–6	85	23:25	9, 71, 85n51
21:2–11	78n30	23:26	84, 178
21:2–16	9, 10, 177	23:26–27	10, 84
21:3	78, 81, 84, 87, 89, 97	23:29	68, 80n35
21:3–5	78, 176	23:29–24:7	79
21:3–9	77	23:29–30	72, 77, 177, 178
21:3–11	79n31	23:29–35	44
21:10–15	178	23:30–33	80n36
21:12–14	45n35	23:31–24:30	71
21:12–15	84	23:31–25:30	70
21:17–18	83	23:31–33	80n35
21:19–20	84	23:32	71
21:19–22	77	23:33	68, 72, 86n54
21:20–21	176	23:33–34	75
21:20–22	78n30, 81, 177	23:35	68
21:21	78	23:37	71
21:21–22	78	24:1	79n34, 80n35
21:23	68, 72	24:1–25:21	80n36
21–25	82	24:7	79n33, 80n35, 80n36
21:25–26	83	24:9	71, 84n48
22:1–20	129	24:11–12	79n34
22:2	9, 71	24:12	75, 98
22:4–23:27	127n2	24:12–14	75
22:8	77, 171, 172n21, 177	24:12–15	68
22:9–12	124	24:13	127n2
22:10–11	171n20	24:18–25:7	68
22:11–20	91, 128	24:18–25:17	127n2
22:13–20	129	24:18–25:30	8
22:14	110	24:19	71
22:15–23:2	103n9	24–25	10
22:16–17	77, 84	25:1–7	68
22:19	9	25:1–21	10
22:20	177	25:5–7	98
22–25	83	25:6–7	68, 72
23	86n55	25:6–30	128
23:1–3	77, 138n29	25:7–26	71
23:1–9	177	25:17	71n10
23:1–20	77, 81	25:19	71n10
23:2	171, 171n19	25:25–26	45n35
23:3	139	25:27–30	11, 11n17, 40, 46, 47, 60, 68, 68n2, 70, 72, 75, 76, 76n23, 98, 100, 127n2, 178
23:3–25	9		
23:4–16	78		
23:7–8	87		
23:12–13	72	25:28–30	75
23:13	79n33, 106n14	25:30	75, 76
23:13–14	94		

SCRIPTURE INDEX

1 Chronicles

1:1–2:15	7
11:4–8	6
11:13–14	6
13:1–14	6
15:1–24	6
15–16	6
16:4–6	6
16:7–36	149
16–17	160
16:23–33	5
16:37–42	6
17	7n9, 120, 159n1
17:1	110, 111, 112
17:1–14	1
17:1–15	7, 37, 38, 126
17:1–16	9, 34, 154
17:4	6, 60n85, 61, 114, 125
17:4 MT	115
17:6	116
17:9–10a	110
17:10	120n45
17:13	123
21:18–28	6
21–24	160
21:24–22:1	78
22:5–19	146
22:6–19	6
22:8	60n85, 61
22:14–16	6
26	160
28:1–21	146
28:1–29:20	6
28:3	6, 60n85, 114, 125

1 Par (1 Chronicles), 8:34–40 (LXX)

	69

2 Chronicles

1:13	89
3:1	6, 145
6:8–9	114
21:4–6	92n72
22:10	92n72
24:22	91n71
30:1–26	174n25
33:11	97
35:20–24	79n33

Ezra, 1:1–4

	9

Job, 38:4–18

	51

Psalms

1	43n20, 131
2	110, 149, 167
2:1–8	149
2:2–6	110
2:7	5, 123, 175
2:9–10	110
2:12	175
2–41	5
3	5
7	5
17:15–20	5
18	5
20–35	5
21:7	131
23:4	113
24	131, 149
24:7–10	147, 163
30	5
34	5
42–43	82
46	71, 82, 98, 157
46:7	113
46:11	113
47	149
47:2	131
47:7–8	156
48	71, 82, 98, 157
48:1–3	165
48:11–13	165
51	5
51–65	5
52	5

SCRIPTURE INDEX

54	5	93	149
56	5	93:1–2	156
57	5	95	43n20
59	5	95:3	156, 165
60	5	95:11	110, 163
63	5	95–100	149
68–72	5	96:10	156
72	119, 131	97:1–2	156
76	82	99:1–5	156
77	43n20	101	5, 131
78	43n20, 118	103	43n20
78:52–72	4	103–150	5
78:60–69	112	105:1–15	5
78:65–72	5	105;36–44	4
78:68	119	105–107	43n20
78:68–72	1, 147	110	167
78:70–71	139	110:1	110
78:70–72	5	110:1–2	110, 149
80	43n20	110:3	143
83:19	131	110:4	131, 131n12, 143, 160
86	5		
87	82	110:5–6	110, 149
87:1–6	165	114	43n20
87:5–6	131	122	82
89	6n7, 38, 70, 72, 126, 127n1, 157, 167	125	71, 82, 98
		127:1	162
89:1–4	5, 9, 81, 106, 143, 176n27, 178	127–128	162
		132	6, 6n8, 9n14, 12, 81, 82, 95, 98, 103, 113, 126, 139, 142, 143, 146, 163, 178
89:3	74, 140		
89:3–4	1, 5, 37		
89:19–37	5, 9, 34, 37, 81, 106, 128, 140		
		132:1	1, 138n27
89:19–51	70, 178	132:1–2	113
89:19–52	176n27	132:1–5	94
89:20–37	1, 74, 142	132:1–6	16
89:22–23	110, 149	132:1–8	6, 163
89:26–27	5, 175	132:2–5	146
89:26–33	123	132:3–8	115
89:28	140	132:5	119
89:29	122	132:6	89n66, 164
89:30–33	5	132:8	110, 147, 165
89:34–37	122	132:10	1
90:19	121	132:10–11	5
91:1–2	131, 165	132:10–14	147
91:9	131, 165	132:11–12	16, 91, 94, 99, 148, 175
92:1	131, 165		
92:8	165	132:11–13	6

SCRIPTURE INDEX

Psalms (continued)

132:12	55, 95, 140
132:13–14	115, 148
132:14	110, 165
132:17	6
132:17–18	1
132:18	14, 149
135–136	43n20
136	19
136:10–24	4
137	70, 82, 160
142	5

Proverbs, 25:1   95, 96, 145, 177

Isaiah

5:1–7	107
6:1–9:7	68
6:11–13	69
7:1–16	157
7:3–25	130
7:10–14	100
7:13	8
7:13–25	8, 69
9:1–7	69, 100, 160
9:2–7	1
9:6–7	178
9:7	8, 157
10:5–32	96
11:1–9	1, 68, 100, 119, 160, 178
11:1–10	8
11:13	10n15
14:1–3	107
28:16	98
30:1–7	96
31:1–3	96, 97, 153
35	68
36–37	68
36–39	8
37:21–35	130, 157
37:27–36	157
38:3–8	130
39	68
39:3–7	130
39:3–8	68n2
39:4–7	8
40:1–11	68n2
40:9–10	160
40:12–25	51
40–55	9, 68
40–66	69
42:1–4	160
44:24–28	160
45:27–28	160
52:7	156, 160
55:3	8, 13, 107, 178
55:3–5	68, 157
61:8	107
61:8–9	68

Jeremiah

1:9	129
1:9–10	111
1:11–12	129n6
7:1–15	70n9, 77, 79, 79n32
7:4	97, 157
9:23–24	97
11:11–14	76n22
17:25	157
20:7	129
22:1–23:5	8, 157
22:1–30	130
22:10–12	80n35, 80n36
22:13–19	84n48
22:15–16	9, 80n35
22:24–30	68, 75
23:5	1, 8, 69, 100, 178
23:5–6	68
23:16–22	129
23:21–22	129
26:1–6	79n32
26:1–19	124
26:10–19	130
26:17–19	9, 172, 177
26–27	84n48
27:1–28:17	80n35
27–29	80n35
28	111, 129

SCRIPTURE INDEX

28:1–4	70, 70n7, 77n26
28:1–6	79
28:3–4	157
30:9	1, 8, 100, 178
30–35	69
33:14–26	100
33:15–21a	157
33:15–22	160
33:15–26	157
33:17	8
33:20–21	178
34:18–19	132
36	84n48, 130
36:1–26	124
36:21–31	8
37:3–10	130
37:5	80n36
37:15–38:2	80n35
37:17–19	8
38:4–28	130
38:14–18	129
38:14–28	8
42	111
50:1–52:34	128
52	8
52:31–34	68, 68n2

Lamentations

1–4	70
1–5	70n9

Ezekiel

11:16	119
16:1–40	107
17:12–18	8
19:1–4	80n36
19:1–9	8
21:25–27	8
34:1–24	8
34:22–31	68
34:23–24	1, 8, 69, 157, 160, 178
34:24	8
36:12–28	160
37:1–14	160
37:15–24	100, 157
37:15–25	8
37:15–28	10n15, 69
37:24	1, 8, 68, 157, 178
40–48	160

Hosea

3:5	8, 69, 100
4:5	157
5:10	8
14:2–8	69

Amos

2:2:9–3:2	107
2:6–3:2	93
2:9–11	171n19
3:3–8	51
3:7	129
5:13	112n30
6:5	8, 161
7:1	111
7:1–4	76n22
7:4	111
7:7–8	111
7:10–17	130
7:13	78
7:14	114
7:15	117, 139
8:1–2	111, 129n6
9:11	1, 8, 69, 157
9:11–12	8, 178
9:11–14	69
9:11–15	100, 160
9:15	107

Micah

4:7	8
4:8	157
5:1–3	69
5:2	1, 89n66, 100, 157
5:2–5	8

213

SCRIPTURE INDEX

Haggai

1–2	160
1:4	60
2:3	178
2:21–23	178
2:25–28	157

Zechariah

3:6–4:9	178
4:1–10	160
4:5–9	157
9:9–15	160

Qumran fragment, Florilegium (4Q174)   120n45, 159n1

New Testament

Matthew, 1:2	3	Romans, 1:3-6	160

Acts

7:43–49	61
7:44–50	16n26

Hebrews

5:6–11	160
7:1–25	160

Errata:

1. References in the Text and footnotes relating to 2 Samuel 7:1-17 in Chapter V, A literary Critical Analysis (with Commentary) have, for obvious reasons been excluded from the Index of Scriptural References.

2. Verses appearing in the Text or footnotes without book and/or chapter immediately preceding, might be references to the Book or Chapter under discussion and not necessarily, as might appear in the Index, to 2 Samuel 7.